BEHIND THE LINES

To Jon

Happy Christmas 2002.
Please hide this book
in the event of further
employment of staff
from the fatherland.

John

BEHIND THE LINES

The oral history of Special Operations
in World War II

Russell Miller

Secker & Warburg
London

Published by Secker & Warburg 2002

4 6 8 10 9 7 5 3

Copyright © Russell Miller 2002

Russell Miller has asserted his right under the
Copyright, Designs and Patents Act 1988 to be identified
as the author of this work.

First published in Great Britain in 2002 by
Secker & Warburg
Random House, 20 Vauxhall Bridge Road, London SW1V 2SA

Random House Australia (Pty) Limited
20 Alfred Street, Milsons Point, Sydney,
New South Wales 2061, Australia

Random House New Zealand Limited
18 Poland Road, Glenfield,
Auckland 10, New Zealand

Random House South Africa (Pty) Limited
Endulini, 5A Jubilee Road, Parktown 2193, South Africa

The Random House Group Limited Reg. No. 954009
www.randomhouse.co.uk

A CIP catalogue record for this book is available
from the British Library

ISBN 0 436 20534 3

Papers used by The Random House Group are natural,
recyclable products made from wood grown in sustainable forests;
the manufacturing processes conform to the environmental
regulations of the country of origin.

Typeset by Palimpsest Book Production Limited,
Polmont, Stirlingshire

Printed and bound in Great Britain by
Biddles Ltd, Guildford & King's Lynn

Contents

To the brave

Author's Note

This book would not have been possible without the excellent research facilities available at the National Archives in Washington DC and at the Imperial War Museum and the Public Record Office in London. I would like to thank in particular Larry McDonald at the National Archives, whose help in delving through the records was invaluable.

My grateful thanks are due to all those veterans of the Office of Strategic Services and the Special Operations Executive who gave so willingly of their time and gracefully submitted to questions they must have been asked many times before; to Betty McIntosh, who introduced me to many of her former colleagues in OSS; to Lieutenant Colonel John Pitt, secretary of the Special Forces Club in London; to Duncan Stuart, the SOE adviser at the Foreign Office; to Darlow Smithson Productions and Julie Stoner of Carlton Television, who generously made available interview transcripts for *Secret Agent* and *Churchill's Secret War* respectively. No thanks are due to Steve Sierros, secretary of the OSS Society in McLean, Virginia, who neither returned calls nor replied to letters or faxes. Every effort has been made to obtain permission from those who hold the copyright of previously published material, but in some cases too many years have passed and we have drawn a blank.

Finally, I must express my heartfelt gratitude to my wife Renate, who, as always, worked alongside me and is both researcher par excellence and invaluable first-line editor.

Foreword

This is the story of Special Operations in World War Two as it has never been told before – directly by those who took part, the extraordinarily brave men and women who chose to fight, often alone and always in great danger, behind enemy lines. Many of them were barely out of their teens when they strapped on a parachute and jumped into the night, into the unknown. The risks were horrendous. Clandestine wireless operators in occupied France had an average life expectancy of just six weeks. Capture routinely led to torture and execution. Small wonder that agents were equipped with suicide pills and advised to have them to hand at all times.

There were few material rewards. Some were undoubtedly attracted by the excitement, the adrenalin rush that became part of their daily lives. Some joined, paradoxically, to escape military rigmarole, preferring independence and the freedom to fight a highly personal war at close quarters, choosing to be masters of their own destiny rather than pawns in the grand scheme. All, no doubt, were motivated by the certainty that right was on their side and that victory was a prerequisite for any kind of decent future: the Second World War may go down in history as the last unequivocally just war.

Whatever their reasons, they were unquestionably a breed apart. In occupied Europe, equipped with false identities, they played a deadly cat-and-mouse game with the Gestapo while wreaking havoc deep inside enemy ranks. In the Balkans, they had to accommodate the fiery politics of the region and work alongside rival guerrilla gangs as keen on killing each other as on killing Germans. In the impenetrable jungles of Burma and Malaya, they faced primeval hazards quite as dangerous as the Japanese – typhus, malaria, blood-sucking leeches, enraged elephants and drenching monsoons.

Back home, in Britain and the United States, teams of back-room boffins dreamed up an endless stream of ingenious devices – itching powder, exploding rats, invisible ink and the like – to assist agents in the field in causing maximum discomfort to the enemy.

Nearly sixty years after the end of the war, the remarkable men and women who served in Special Operations are now, sadly, few in number. But many of them recorded their adventures contemporaneously, in first-person action reports, letters, diaries and memoranda now lodged in the National Archives in Washington and the Public Record Office in London. It is primarily from this rich, and largely unpublished, resource that I have drawn to ensure that former members of the Office of Strategic Services and the Special Operations Executive are able to tell their stories in their own words.

Undue reverence or excessive caution were not in the nature of those who volunteered for Special Operations, thus it is that many accounts they left behind read like an adventure story for *Boy's Own* rather than a sober military report.

It is as it should be, for they were true adventurers.

I

Set Europe Ablaze!

*B*Y THE *hot summer of 1940, much of mainland Europe had succumbed to the Nazi blitzkrieg. The British Expeditionary Force, cut off by the Germans, had been forced to retreat through France and was miraculously evacuated from Dunkirk. Norway, Denmark, Belgium, Holland, Luxembourg and France had been crushed; Mussolini had committed Italy to the war on the German side. Along the southern shores of the Channel, the Luftwaffe was preparing for the air battle that would precede the invasion of Great Britain in August or September and, most likely, end the war. A German victory seemed assured.*

On the night of 16 July 1940 – the same day that Hitler signed Directive No. 16, plans for Operation Sea Lion, the invasion of Britain – Prime Minister Winston Churchill called Hugh Dalton, the Minister of Economic Warfare, to Downing Street to discuss setting up a secret agency to organise sabotage and subversion in enemy-occupied countries. Dalton had already prepared the ground, as he explained in a memorandum to Lord Halifax, the Foreign Secretary, dated 3 July 1940:

We have got to organise movements in enemy-occupied territory comparable to the Sinn Fein movement in Ireland, to the Chinese guerrillas now operating against Japan, to the Spanish Irregulars who played a notable part in Wellington's campaign or – one might as well as admit it – to the organisations which the Nazis themselves have developed so remarkably in almost every country in the world. This 'democratic international' must use many different methods, including industrial and military sabotage, labour agitation and strikes, continuous propaganda, terrorist acts against traitors and German leaders, boycotts and riots.

It is clear to me that an organisation on this scale and of

this character is not something which can be handled by the ordinary departmental machinery of either the British Civil Service or the British military machine. What is needed is a new organisation to coordinate, inspire, control and assist the nationals of the oppressed countries who must themselves be the direct participants. We need absolute secrecy, a certain fanatical enthusiasm, willingness to work with people of different nationalities, complete political reliability. Some of these qualities are certainly to be found in some military officers and, if such men are available, they should undoubtedly be used. But the organisation should, in my view, be entirely independent of the War Office machine.

Memorandum to the War Cabinet signed by Neville Chamberlain, Lord President of the Council, 19 July 1940:

On the Prime Minister's authority a new organisation shall be established forthwith to coordinate all action, by way of subversion and sabotage, against the enemy overseas . . . This organisation will be known as the Special Operations Executive.

Churchill's directive to Hugh Dalton, 19 July 1940, after he was given responsibility for running the Special Operations Executive (SOE):

And now set Europe ablaze.

Planning began immediately. Initially, Dalton proposed SOE should be a civilian organisation, but it soon became clear that many of the operations it would be called upon to undertake would inevitably be of a paramilitary nature and he realised he would need highly trained soldiers to provide the backbone. He appointed Brigadier Colin Gubbins, an expert in guerrilla warfare, to be SOE's director of operations and training.

Captain Peter Wilkinson, assistant to Brigadier Gubbins:
'Gubbins and I, and his personal assistant, Margaret Jackson, arrived in Baker Street on the 18 November 1940. At that time the headquarters of SOE had moved from a small office next door to St Ermin's Hotel in Caxton Street and was occupying what in peacetime had been the central office of Marks and Spencer at 64 Baker Street. We arrived in Baker Street to find that we had been relegated to a set of apartments opposite Baker Street station called Berkeley Court, where we were allotted two rather grubby family flats to set up our office. Everything

was very improvised, I mean, instead of the nice army trestle tables covered by a blanket which of course we'd all been used to, our offices were furnished with pretty nasty furniture from the cheaper end of the Tottenham Court Road, and instead of the stub-nosed army Humbers which we'd used for transport there was a fleet of sleek black Pontiac limousines, driven by chauffeurs in uniform and peak caps, which really were very inappropriate for future brigands and *condacieri* [bandits].

'At the beginning we only had two floors and one day one of our chaps was coming back from lunch, and getting into the lift, found himself whooshed up to the fifth floor, where he was confronted by a group of grinning Japanese. It was only then we discovered that the floor above our requisitioned flat was occupied by some department of the Japanese embassy. That was obviously highly undesirable and they had to be cleared out.

'Berkeley Court was a very solid-looking building and as we were in the early days of the Blitz this was quite an important consideration, but it had grave disadvantages in many ways because you were separated from the mainstream of Whitehall and you really were not able to indulge in the sort of wartime camaraderie and gossip which in a way was rather an essential part of conducting the sort of activities that we were trying to conduct. I mean, it was too far, for example, to go and lunch at one's club, where one met one's friends and would have maintained relationships on a much easier footing than proved to be the case. Altogether, there was a general feeling, well, to put it quite shortly, that SOE was a racket.

'Relations with Whitehall in the early days were extremely difficult. There were a great many people – and I'm talking not only of regular soldiers but also Foreign Office officials and even politicians – who felt that the sort of work on which SOE was embarked really exceeded the limits of civilised warfare as hitherto understood within the limits of the Geneva Convention, verging on acts of terrorism, as indeed was the case, and they strongly disapproved of that.'[1]

One of those who disapproved was Sir Charles Portal, Chief of the Air Staff:
'I think that the dropping of men dressed in civilian clothes for the purpose of attempting to kill members of the opposing forces is not an operation with which the Royal Air Force should be associated. I think you will agree that there is a vast difference, in ethics, between the time-honoured operation of the dropping of a spy from the air

3

and this entirely new scheme for dropping what one can only call assassins.'

Peter Wilkinson:
'Gubbins suffered, as did we all, from this general disapproval of SOE and all its works. In addition, he had been promoted brigadier rather more rapidly perhaps than some of his envious contemporaries, which did not endear him to them. We also had a claim on scarce materials, things like plastic explosive which was in very short supply, and we could call on facilities, submarines and goodness knows what, in a way which was not available to most people in Whitehall. There was therefore a general sense of jealousy that we were having it all rather too easy and of course we could show no results because we had first of all to drop in the agents, train the radio operators and establish the communications with the various resistance groups before anything could be done. So people said, well, why are we spending all this money and all this manpower and really achieving nothing? So one way and another it was an uphill fight and one that was hard to justify because it was all top secret.

'The only people who could do anything immediately were the Poles [*who had an embryonic resistance movement already in place*], and the first flight to Poland took place on the night of 15 February 1941. This was the first connection with occupied Europe and it was more or less successful: it dropped the agents some sixty miles from their dropping zone in a part of Poland that had already been annexed to Germany but they got through. This was really of enormous importance to SOE. First of all, it was in itself an extraordinary feat, to fly blind, outside the range of any electronic help, across occupied Europe at about 120 miles an hour in the depths of winter, find a dropping zone and to get back. The whole flight took about fourteen hours and it was really a notable feat of navigation and endurance. This in itself was terribly important, to find out that one can do it. But secondly, it was vital really at that time to try to convince very doubting Chiefs of Staff and a very sceptical Whitehall that this sort of thing was feasible at all.

'In those days, in the autumn of 1940 and the winter of 1940/1, everybody was working, almost without exaggeration, right round the clock. As often as not, one slept in one's office in order to get on with the job. One had to face the fact that there wasn't really a single wireless set operating direct to SOE in the whole of occupied Europe. There was no question whatever of any sort of underground warfare, or subversive activities of any kind, until first of all communications had been established with occupied Europe. Then one had to recruit some sort of organisation and deliver arms and equipment and set up the thing.'

Recruiting staff and potential agents was hampered by the absolute necessity to keep the existence of the organisation secret. As often as not, staff had no idea for whom they would be working until they arrived on the job. The 'old boy network' was shamelessly employed to find men and women willing to volunteer as agents. Initially, the only requirements were the ability to speak a foreign language and a willingness to jump out of an aeroplane. Those who 'volunteered' did so for a myriad of reasons – boredom, patriotism, a lust for danger, a desire to 'get on with it' ('it' being the war) or simply to escape the restrictions of conventional military life.

Robert Boiteux-Burdett, aged thirty-four, a Frenchman, was stranded in London when the war broke out:
'One day I was walking down Piccadilly and I met an old friend and we started talking about the war and this and that and he said, "What are you doing these days?" and I said, "Nothing," and he said, "They are looking for silly buggers like you to parachute into France. They've asked me and I'm not mad, but you might be interested." So I went straight to the War Office.

'At first they were very discouraging. I filled in a few forms and said, "I understand that you need French-speaking people to parachute into France." The person who was interviewing me said, "Oh, everybody speaks French," and I thought what a stupid thing to say – everybody doesn't speak French. So I said, "But I speak French like a Frenchman, I know the slang, everything." He just said, "Oh well." It was very discouraging, but it turned out he was just testing me. I said, "All right," and was just walking out of the door when he said, "Just a minute. Here's an address, it's for a Major Gielgud. Go and see him."

'I think he was testing me to see if I was genuine, probably because there could have been spies, possibly the Fifth Column as we called it in France, who were trying to get into the organisation. When I saw Major Gielgud, we had a talk about things and within a couple of weeks, I had a letter asking me to join.

'It was the spirit of adventure that prompted me to volunteer. I have always liked adventure and to me it didn't seem to be so very dangerous. I looked like a Frenchman, I was small and dark, spoke fluent French. I didn't volunteer because I had feelings of hostility for the Germans, although of course I did feel a bit of that, it was mainly because I liked adventure. It seemed very exciting to me to blow up trains and things.'[2]

Lieutenant Oliver Haward Brown, East Kent Regiment, joined SOE in 1941:
'I noticed a little thing on the noticeboard saying volunteers were wanted, preferably who had another language other than English, had a knowledge of demolitions and were willing to undertake any operations for which they were assigned. I thought, well, this sounded interesting. I hadn't got a clue what it was all about. I went to Room 98 at the War Office and was interviewed by two officers, a colonel and a major. I can remember the interview very distinctly. They got all the information they wanted from me but I got absolutely no information from them whatsoever, none. I asked, but got nothing.

'I was not put off by the fact that there was no information, it was still a good interview. I was quite impressed by the people who were conducting it, and in a way, it sort of put me "on" rather than off. I reasoned that if they are telling me nothing, then it must be something that nobody else ought to know. So I was encouraged and it was only about three or four days afterwards that I was told to report to a place in Hertford. I got damn all information there either. I was met at Hertford station. I couldn't see anyone about at all but I saw an expensive car there and a chauffeur who came over to me and said, "Mr Brown?" I said, "Yes," and he said, "I've come to fetch you and another gentleman called Mr Lambert." We were taken off in this car down a magnificent driveway, to a lovely mansion at the end of it. We were greeted at the door by a butler, in full regalia, and were taken inside into the ante-room. Now, remember, there wasn't much drink about in those days, but there was every drink you could think of there – and this was the new unit we had come to!

'When we had been there about a fortnight we obviously began to think there was something peculiar going on, because we did a lot of work with demolitions and our fieldcraft side tended to be more about eluding others than trying to find others and our small arms work was very much on a personal basis. So, at the end of the fortnight we said to Major Clark, who was commandant there, "We would really like to know what this is all about. It must be something very peculiar indeed." He said, "Well, it is funny you should say that, we are having a party tonight and I will give you the details then." So five of us went and were given this pamphlet. We all read the first side of it and more or less all turned it over together and began to get a little bit suspicious about what exactly the job was, and the very first words on the other side of the pamphlet were "You will be expected to parachute jump." That was the first time we had ever heard that this job was anything to do with parachuting, and without more ado, we more or less said, "Not likely! We're not having anything to do with this!" And then came the party that night. I think they were pretty good psychologists at that unit. There were a lot of FANYs in SOE, handpicked and beautiful girls [*FANYs were members of the First-Aid Nursing Yeomanry, an all-women volunteer organisation formed before the First World War to work with the armed services*] – and in the course of the evening, one of the FANYs attached herself to me and said, "I'm sorry, Mr Brown, that you are not going to join us," and I said, "I've never heard of anything so ridiculous. Of course I am going to join you!" Later we discovered that we had all fallen for the same trap.'[3]

Jane Buckland, eighteen-year-old FANY and trainee wireless operator:
'I was terrified of all the senior FANYs. They called us by our surnames – I was Buckland for two years – and I got into terrible trouble because I had red nails and my hair was too long. They took me on as a wireless operator, from square one. My induction was at a lovely Wren house called Fawley Court, Henley-on-Thames. We knew we were in something very hush-hush but didn't know exactly what it was. We came back to London for some leave and I always remember Mummy saying that when a group of FANYs arrived at the station they had what she called a "FANY squeak" – we were all yelling and shouting and we were very excitable and everybody knew we were around.

'The FANYs were described at the time as "Girls of good background, quiet tongues and quick brains" – especially at that stage, the girls actually were. Then, as the war progressed, they took in a slightly different type of girl, but at our stage, I think we were rather from good backgrounds, very nice girls. There was Lavender de Grey, she was Lord Walsingham's daughter, she was absolutely lovely and was in Italy and India with me. There was Elizabeth Cholmondley, Lord Delamere's daughter, Angela Milburn, whose father was a remote Scottish laird, and Elizabeth Batten who was known as "Boo".

'There was square-bashing, marching, washing up, we were real dogsbodies, absolutely, we were lower than low. All these aristocratic girls were doing bashing and washing, we were treated quite toughly. I think I was probably quite a naughty FANY and got into trouble once or twice. Certainly nothing immoral, I was too young. I got into trouble for not wanting to give up my red nail polish and not wanting my hair cut short. They never threw me out or anything. I conceded.

'Our uniform was very nice, it was khaki officer's uniform, nice material and we wore FANY flashes at the top of the sleeves, lovely bronze buttons with the Maltese Cross. We had as the nicest part of our uniform the most beautiful Sam Brownes, lovely wide belts which we had to polish all the time. It was just like the army − we were in the army, but special.

'We would sit round a table for so many hours a day. We had our Morse keys, our training keys. At the end of the table was a Royal Corps of Signals sergeant and he had all us girls lined up on either side and we started very slowly, learning the alphabet in Morse. It was never "dot-dash", it was always "dit-da" and we gradually had to build up our speeds but that came later.

'It was hysterically exciting, I cannot tell you. It was so exciting I didn't even miss my beloved mother. My mother could certainly have stopped me going abroad because I was under age. That she didn't, was wonderful of her, considering I was an only child and all she had.'[4]

Jean Le Harivel, aged twenty-three, trainee wireless operator:
'I was called up in the British Army in Huddersfield, Yorkshire, and joined the Royal Corps of Signals and became a wireless operator; I think I had a B3 certificate or something like that. After that I was transferred to the Middlesex Regiment and became a machine gunner. One day I was called forward and told I had to go to London, to the War Office. There I was interviewed by a certain Major Gielgud, of the Gielgud [*acting*] family. I had not a clue what it was all about. Here I was, in lance corporal uniform, standing at attention before this Major Gielgud, who was very gentle, very kind, had a very soft voice and he explained that there was a plan to create a resistance movement in France and as I was half French − my father being British, my mother being French − was I interested? He appealed to my patriotic sense and asked me if I would volunteer to go to France − volunteer is the key word because you were not forced to join − but of course I said yes, without hesitation and that's how I got involved in what was actually the SOE organisation.

'Why did I react so positively to this request to volunteer? It makes me think back, you know? I'm going to use a word which is a bit fuddy-duddy nowadays: we were patriotic. We really believed in this fight against Nazism, and the fact that France had been invaded hurt terribly. My mother, you can imagine, was very upset, but we were all upset to think of the German army reaching Paris. I mean, it was unheard-of that Paris should be occupied. Do you remember that photo of Hitler dancing in front of the Eiffel Tower? You know, it was something really deplorable and which upset people like me. The British Army had done a good job in making people believe that we were fighting a good cause, so, as I say, we felt patriotic; we felt that we had to fight and that Nazism was something that we had to eradicate.'[5]

Roger Landes, born in Paris of a French mother and English father, came to live and work in London just before the war:
'In December 1939, I was called to register for the British Army and I had my medical and I was accepted good for service and I had to fill up a form asking me where I went to university and did I speak any language and I said yes, I speak French fluently. I didn't hear anything until March '41, when I received my calling-up papers for the Royal Corps of Signals to be trained as a wireless operator.

'When I finished my training as a wireless operator I saw on the noticeboard I have to report to the War Office for an interview. They gave me my fare to go to London from Prestatyn and when I arrived there I saw a British captain, the brother of the actor John Gielgud, asking me questions in French and he said, "Well, we found out that you can speak French and you've been trained as a wireless operator. We want to know if you will go back to France. You'll be dropped by parachute or by fishing boat, you've got a good chance to be arrested, tortured and maybe shot. I'll give you five minutes to say yes or no." I said straight away I will do it. He told me to return to my unit and he would get me transferred within a fortnight. "If they ask any questions why you've been called to see me," he said, "just say we wanted some information about Paris."'[6]

Basil Davidson was a young journalist working on the Star, *an evening newspaper in London:*
'I wanted to get into the war, I thought that's the thing to do. They said, do you want to stay as a journalist, a war correspondent, I said, no, I don't want to do anything like that, I want to go into the army, but it was difficult to get into the army in '39 as the army wasn't yet recruiting, you know. They said, right, you go away and we'll let you know. It seemed a pretty poor thing to do at the time. So I was hanging around and one day my editor called me in and said

the War Office wants to see you. I thought he was joking because I was absolutely nobody, just a young reporter knowing nothing, but I said, that's fine, they've got to win the war, haven't they? You know, joke, ha ha. He said, you've got to go to lunch with a man you'll find waiting for you at Simpsons in the Strand. I said, there could be at least four hundred people waiting for me there, because that was the place where you went to lunch. He said, look here, I haven't got time to swap jokes, you just go there and find him.

'Well, he was hanging around in the bar and I was hanging around in the bar, the way you do, and finally he said, you must be so-and-so, and I said, yes I am. He said, we understand you want to get into the forces, I said, that's right. He said, well now, we may be able to help you but this is a bit different from what you may think it is. It is a secret organisation with the means of doing all sorts of things the army otherwise wouldn't or couldn't have done. The reason they picked up on me is that I travelled around the Balkans a bit as a journalist.

'He asked me lots of questions, you know, what are your obligations, are you married, no, have you any obligations, no, are you prepared to go off to Eastern Europe, yes, and I answered all these questions in a straightforward way and was delighted because I thought, well, here's an answer to my problem, how do I get into the war? I didn't want the war to happen to me, as it were, I thought, let's try and see what one can do, something interesting, and it worked out that way.'[7]

Captain Selwyn Jepson, aged forty-one, SOE recruiting officer:
'I was responsible for recruiting women for the work, in the face of a good deal of opposition, I may say, from the powers that be. In my view, women were very much better than men for the work. Women, as you must know, have a far greater capacity for cool and lonely courage than men. Men usually want a mate with them. Men don't work alone, their lives tend to be always in company with other men. There was opposition from most quarters until it went up to Churchill, whom I had met before the war. He growled at me, "What are you doing?" I told him and he said, "I see you are using women to do this," and I said, "Yes, don't you think it is a very sensible thing to do?" and he said, "Yes, good luck to you!" That was my authority!

'When I was recruiting civilians, or people out of the three services, I would write a letter on paper headed with a simple room number at the War Office saying something simple, such as "Dear Miss/Mrs, I understand you have qualifications that may be of value in the war effort, would you care to get in touch with me, when we might discuss it further . . ." I would then interview them when they came to the War Office and decide whether or not I wanted to go on with them.

'I recruited Odette [*SOE agent Yvonne Baseden*], who subsequently got the George Cross, and that silenced any remaining opposition to what I was doing. Odette was a shrewd cookie who guessed immediately at the interview what it was all about. She said at once, "Yes, I want to do it!" I said, "Wait a minute, what are your domestic circumstances?" I knew she had a husband and a couple of children, but she said her husband could look after himself and an aunt would look after her children and when could she start. I was rather doubtful about her, because although she had perfect French she also had a personality that was so big I couldn't see her passing unnoticed however good a cover story we gave her. I can remember clearly writing on her application form "God help the Germans if we can ever get her near them!"

'All the women were satisfactory in training. They trained in classes with the men and it was noticeable that they were much better than the men in many of the skills that the work required. Funnily enough, they took up pistol shooting with great ability. I don't know what the psychological drive was, but there wasn't one of them who wasn't keen on it – even when the pistol was a .45 automatic with a recoil so shattering they would sometimes fall over. They would just get up and fire again. It was that sort of determination that was so impressive.'[8]

Harry Rée, destined for occupied France:
'I can't say it was simple patriotism that moved most of us – there was very little of that in the last war, it was much closer to simple impatience. You see, after the fall of France most of us in the army in this country had damn all to do. We were pushed off to Exeter or Wales or Scotland, nice safe places where there was very little to do, while wives and families were often in London or Coventry or Plymouth, all places which were being bombed – they were at risk, while we weren't. I think a lot of men resented this. And there was another thing; if we were going to get into a risky situation, we wanted to go somewhere where we would be our own masters. We didn't want a stupid colonel ordering us to advance into a screen of machine-gun bullets when we didn't agree with the order – we weren't the Light Brigade. If we were going to advance into a screen

of machine-gun fire or do something equally suicidal, we wanted it to be our decision. That was something else we shared – and agreed about. But it made us all different. We were all individualists.'[9]

SOE commandeered a number of country estates where fledgling agents could be taught the arcane skills of their craft away from prying eyes. Burglars taught them how to blow safes and pick locks, experts in hand to hand fighting showed them how to kill silently, pretty girls were used to test their discretion. Arisaig, in the Scottish Highlands, was where agents were 'toughened up'; Beaulieu Manor, in the New Forest, the family home of Lord Montagu, was SOE's 'finishing school'.

Leo Manderstam, Russian-born, an early trainee at Arisaig:
'The SOE hopefuls under training when I was at Arisaig were mostly, like myself, well into their thirties and some were overfed City gent types who were almost killed by the mountaineering and survival exercises. We had arrived by train from Glasgow at seven o'clock on a winter's morning, to be met by a trim young lieutenant called Robinson, who announced, "Well, gentlemen, before breakfast we will have a little walk." He then took us for an eight-mile slog through the frozen mountains. Breakfast was an inedible concoction. In fact, all the food was terrible. I preferred K rations, a pack comprising a few raisins, a small bar of chocolate and a tin of self-heating soup. We supplemented our food supplies by throwing hand grenades into the loch to kill trout and roach, which we grilled over wood fires. The officers had a habit of waking us up around 2 a.m. to go for training runs. They also sent a few of us into the frost and snow to spend a night outdoors without any provisions. But we found a snug little croft, where the crofter invited us to be his guests until morning. He gave us a hearty breakfast and refused point blank to accept any payment. I have had a soft spot for Scottish folk ever since.
  'The commanding officer at Arisaig was a Colonel Evans. His training officer was Major Sykes, a marvellous shot, who came to SOE after working with the police in Shanghai. Sykes looked and spoke like a bishop, very quiet and mild. In his lectures he would say the most gruesome things in his soft bishop's voice: "During unarmed combat, if you get the chance, insert a finger into a corner of your opponent's mouth and tear it. You will find the mouth tears very easily." And after describing particularly vicious ways of crippling and disarming an enemy, he would often end with the remark, "and then kick him in the testicles".

'Fortunately, I never had to use the fighting skills I was taught at Arisaig but it did make me more confident, knowing I could pull something out of the hat if I faced an aggressive foe in hand-to-hand combat. The Arisaig CO, in his report, assessed me as "first class", which I did not deserve and which I attributed to the probability that he was drunk when he wrote it. I also collected top marks from the second phase of the training programme, an initiative test carried out in Manchester, in which luck played the most important part. We were each given an assignment during which we had to act precisely as if we were active agents in the field. A War Office telephone number was issued to us, to be divulged only as a last resort, if we were arrested and could not bluff ourselves out of custody. The instructing officer said the local police had been given my description, with the warning that I was a German spy. Then he came to my assignment: to steal the plans of the Manchester Oil Refinery. For anyone else it would have seemed an extremely tough proposition. But when he told me I restrained a hoot of laughter with great difficulty – my firm had built the refinery!

'I walked out of the office, telephoned Francis Kind, a friend of mine who was the refinery manager, and arranged to see him. He sent a Rolls-Royce to meet my train and convey me to the refinery. "I need the plans because we're making contingency preparations in case of bombing," I told Francis, and he gave me all I needed. My instructors were very impressed by the speed and efficiency with which I fulfilled the assignment.'[10]

Ernest van Maurik, explosives and demolition instructor at Arisaig:
'I had never done demolitions before in my life and within about two weeks I was giving lectures on the use of explosives and teaching people how to use them. Why we didn't all get blown up I don't know, but after a bit I got quite competent and enjoyed it. When we attacked the Mallaig train, we put a pressure switch on the line. Of course, we didn't actually use explosives. The train drivers took quite a bit of pleasure in being blown up. If it was a successful attack they would always lean out of their cabs and give us the thumbs up.'[11]

Captain Francis Cammaerts, code name 'Roger', would become one of SOE's most celebrated agents:
'Arisaig was an ideal place to get very fit physically and to learn quite a lot about supporting yourself in very difficult situations. We went deer stalking and fishing for salmon and we continued to use explosives and to learn something about unarmed combat and so on.

'It was very beautiful to look at, very satisfying, a holiday situation, if you like. It was very relaxed, but at the same time it was very energetic and having been brought up in a situation in which training for team games was an important part of your so-called education, clearly this was a well-designed physical course, run by people who were cheerful. For instance, the day we arrived in a boat across the loch, the number two in command, Captain Leech, waved to us and then jumped into the lake in his uniform, which was a gesture to say we were very welcome and it doesn't very much matter if you get your uniform wet.

'Beaulieu was the first point at which you got a very shrewd idea of the kind of thing you might be asked to do. It was where, in a sense, it was most difficult for the teachers to instruct you. They had certain basics you had to learn, like what the German uniforms were like, what the German ranks were, things of this kind. You also had to get some wisdom on following people in the street, or being aware of being followed, but they also set up imaginary situations which might be something you'd face abroad. The ones I went through at Beaulieu were comic and very amusing, such as meeting someone with *The Times* under his arm in a bar in Bournemouth, which was empty except for two young officers who were taking fervent notes. As the man I was supposed to meet happened to be a very old friend we greeted each other as we were, real friends.

'I remember being taught about opening locks and the use of keys and the nature of different kinds of keys and how to get by when you had to break the curfew. For instance, if you needed to move in the streets when there was a curfew, you had to have a story like you were a doctor who had to visit a patient who was dying, that sort of thing. They obviously stressed the importance of not being able to do very much for you if you were caught and therefore you'd got to avoid being caught.'[12]

Captain John Debenham Taylor, assistant instructor at Beaulieu:
'What was taught was basically trade craft – how someone who is living a clandestine existence needs to behave in order to stay alive, i.e. the technique for clandestine meetings, clandestine communications, surveillance, counter-surveillance, the business of providing descriptions of people, and everything that someone who is living an illegal existence, if you like, is required to know.

'The exercises consisted of dividing up into teams. One side would be given instructions to contact a certain person of whom they were given a description. They would be told where he or she could be found and that if the person they had to contact believed he or she was under surveillance they would exhibit a danger signal. Then the arrangements for contact were left to the initiative of the person who was actually making the contact, in other words, whether he or she should approach the chap and say, "Could you tell me the time?" or something of that kind. The actual passwords were pre-arranged, so that one would know whether you'd got the right person.

'Usually it involved going on to clear what we used to call a dead letter box, a place where a message or money or something had been concealed. You had to arrange to go and collect it, making sure that you weren't being followed. In point of fact, you were being followed, although you didn't know it, because another team of instructors or students from another course at Beaulieu would be following you. That was the basis of most of the exercises. Then you would be given descriptions of people that you would have to follow yourself and be able to report on where they went, what they did, whom they contacted, whether they were taking precautions against surveillance and so on.

'Everyone had to have a cover story and after an exercise they would be interrogated by people got up to appear like enemy police, or the Gestapo or whatever, who would try and break them. This was a permanent feature of all the exercises, that they had to have a cover story for whatever they were doing and they had to be able to sustain it subsequently under interrogation. The main reason was that if you were leading a clandestine existence you always had to have some anodyne reason for anything you were doing and anywhere you were likely to be found. Black marketeering was rife at the time and that was very fortunate from the agent's point of view, inasmuch as one could confess to possessing plainly black-market goods in the hope that this would not in fact lead to further interrogation.

'Sometimes the local police were briefed to pick them up and interrogate them as to what they were doing and to treat them as suspects of some criminal activity. Of course, they had no idea that this was going to happen to them. This was a very good means of discovering, firstly, the extent to which the lessons had gone home, but also the general temperament of the student when faced with what he should have realised was real danger. Some proved themselves extremely robust, stuck rigidly to their cover story and never gave in under fairly tough interrogation. I mean, not beating up or anything like that, but designed to make the chap feel fairly intimidated. Others simply fell back on the opportunity that they had to use the telephone number they had been told to phone if something went wrong with the exercise. It was not specified what it would be, but simply as soon as the going got tough they could say, "Look, I'm on an army exercise and if you ring this number my whole activity will be explained to you." That was the easy option obviously, some took it, some did not. It was a good means of discovering just how people were likely to act in real situations of danger.

'We gave them advice on disguise. Peter Follis, the chief instructor, was an actor in peacetime; he gave lectures on simple methods of disguise. Not using greasepaint and false moustaches and so on, because the possession of such things was enough to incriminate you straight away, but how you could change your appearance by parting your hair a different way, by wearing glasses when you normally didn't and generally changing your appearance by simple means – different clothing or walking with a limp – things that were not in themselves incriminating if you were caught doing it, but that did have the effect of changing your appearance.

'We also gave them advice on the conditions in the country they were going to. For example, in some countries it was perfectly all right to go into a café or restaurant, but in other countries it was a considerable risk. I used to tell them an anecdote about a chap who had recently parachuted into France and had gone into a café and had asked for a black coffee, which immediately aroused the waitress's attention, because of course there wasn't any other kind of coffee you could have in France in those days. This immediately drew attention to him as someone who had just arrived or had come from somewhere else and was unaware of the conditions reigning at that time.

'Travel on trains or by any other means was also one of the danger points where you might get picked up in a surprise raid – stopping a train and searching everybody on it, or putting a road block on a certain road or closing the main square of a town, and checking everyone's documentation. We also gave general advice on resisting interrogation, but only in the mildest form, because there was obviously the risk that if you spelled it out in too graphic terms it could have a slightly counter-productive effect.

'I think everybody who was going into occupied Europe knew perfectly well what might happen to them if they were caught, namely torture and beatings up. Well, there was no point in trying to spell that out in great detail. The main thing we would concentrate on was trying to impress upon them the need to stay quiet for as long as they could without giving anything away, for at least forty-eight hours, which would give their colleagues time to learn that they had been arrested and to make themselves scarce, if you follow me. That was one of the principal lessons to drive home.'[13]

Noreen Riols, eighteen-year-old secretary at Beaulieu:
'Beaulieu was the last holding centre which the agents went to before they were parachuted. They'd gone through all the other horrendous things they had to do and Beaulieu was, in a way, a bit of a rest cure, because there was no crawling under barbed wire at three in the morning in the pouring rain. But it was the final testing ground and if they failed Beaulieu, all the rest was useless, they didn't go. I think they were trying to find out if they would stand up, not necessarily against terrible interrogations, but against the ordinary little things which made up everyday life and which quite often tripped them up.

'They would bang on the doors of the students at 3 a.m. – you know, just at the worst time – saying, "Open up, Gestapo!" I remember one woman student said, "Come in," and that put her back for several months because when you're wakened up like that you don't always answer in the language you're supposed to be using. If they said the wrong thing, they were dragged in their nightclothes, possibly without their slippers, and made to stand on a cold floor to be questioned with bright lights shining at them. The questions would be shot at them from every angle to see how they reacted because I suppose you react in a very different way at midday from what you would at 3 o'clock in the morning when they were cold, half asleep and frustrated, I imagine, too.

'Being in the field was a very lonely life for a lot of them. It sounds terribly glamorous but it was lonely; they lived cut off from their families, from their country, with a false identity, they couldn't really have friends to confide in and I think they wanted to make sure that they wouldn't break down and let on what they were doing.

'Colonel Wooldridge was the head at Beaulieu and basically we were working for him. I was very much in awe of him, but the others called him Woollybags. He organised everything in this rather large house called The Rings. We used to go over to the office every day and do office work, typing, answering telephones, running around doing what anybody wanted, but there was also another side to it because we were used in mock operations.

'About two or three times we were decanted by car in civilian clothes in Bournemouth or in Southampton to do exercises. The students, as we called them, were also decanted in another part of town and were told either to discover a woman who would be a certain height and follow her, see where she was going, or to pass a message to a woman sitting on a certain bench in the park or in the cinema café. If they were trying to follow us without being seen, it was very useful to be a woman because a man in civilian clothes was more noticeable, but a woman with a shopping basket could stand or just walk around. A very good thing was to look in a shop window because then you could see who was coming behind and work out more or less who it was who was following you. Men didn't have that advantage.

'When I was the one who was being trailed, trying to find out who was trailing me, I would be terribly naughty. There was a big department store called Plummers and I used to go into the ladies' underwear department because it was embarrassing for a man to be in there and therefore any man who came in and lingered you could more or less work out that this was the one you were trying to get rid of. From there onwards there were steps leading up to the lifts, so I would then nonchalantly walk up to the lift and press the button and he would think I was going in, but when it arrived I would zoom down the stairs on the other side and take off my hat and coat on the way, so that I would look like a completely different person going out through the door. The poor man would be looking for somebody wearing a hat and a coat and maybe carrying a shopping bag – well, all that was clutched in front of me, so I completely lost him.

'If we met somebody on a park bench, we'd be told that there would be a man sitting on the bench who would pass a message and so one would go and sit on a bench near the man you thought would be the one. He might be reading a newspaper, which was quite normal in the middle of the afternoon, and then he would discard it on the bench and leave and I would nonchalantly pick up the newspaper, which is another quite normal thing to do, glance through it and take the message. We also did this in telephone booths. You had to queue up quite a lot to get into telephone booths in those days. You'd see the man in a booth and so you would go and wait and when he came out he would have left a message in the directory. As he passed he would say a name, indicating to you what page the message was on. We got awfully clever at speaking without using our mouths. So you'd go in and open the telephone book, which was quite normal, see the message, pick up the phone and make a fictitious call and then leave and nobody noticed. It's extraordinary, nobody in Bournemouth knew what was going on under their very eyes.

'We also had to try and get the students to talk. There were two hotels in Bournemouth, the Norfolk and the Royal Bath, and those were our meeting points. They would be sitting there in the early evening with one of the instructors and I, or somebody else who'd been assigned, would walk in, whereupon the instructor would say, "Oh, how lovely to see you, I haven't seen you for ages, come and have a drink," and so you'd say yes and you'd have a drink and he'd say, "Well, you know, if you're not doing anything, why don't you join us for dinner?" whereupon a telephone call would come for the instructor and he would come back and say, "I'm most awfully sorry, but I have to leave you. Why don't you two go ahead and have dinner and I'll join you as soon as I can," and so we would trot into the dining room and have dinner and my job was to get him to talk. Mostly they didn't, they were terribly phlegmatic, terribly good, but sometimes they cracked, although not often.

'One evening the student said, "Look, it's rather a warm evening, let's go out on the terrace and look at the sea," terribly romantic, so off we trotted onto the terrace to look at the sea and then after a bit of hand-holding – we were all, you know, terribly virtuous – he cracked. I said something like "What are you up to? Are you going to be here for long?" and he said, "Well, no, I'm leaving next week," and I said, "Oh, where you going?" and he said, "I'm being parachuted back into Denmark." I don't remember whether he said parachuted or whether he was being infiltrated by submarine, he may not even have told me, but then I went all goggle-eyed and said, "What are you going to do?" and he said, "Well, you may not know about it but a lot of people are parachuted now into enemy-occupied territory to act as agents, spies," and I said, terribly excited, "What will you do when you get there?" and he said, "I'm organising resistance groups so that when the invasion comes there are people ready there to stand up and rebel against the Germans." I don't think I pressed him very much more than that because I knew that there was no point, he was already in it up to his neck. He was finished by telling me what he was doing. I suppose he was a young man and I suppose at eighteen I was a pretty face and I was sympathetic and I was ready to listen. I think that's what was the important thing, I listened and gave him my full attention and it was too much. I don't think he would have said anything if I hadn't let him hold my hand and get a bit sentimental. We made an arrangement to meet the next Sunday, which I knew I would not be able to keep. It was awful to have to deceive him.

'Next day we had a confrontation because always the next afternoon Colonel Wooldridge would have us in and say what happened and how did you get on? I said, "Well, I'm afraid he cracked," at which point the door opened and this unfortunate man came in. Colonel Wooldridge said, "Do you know this woman?" and he just looked at me and said, "You bitch!" People didn't use strong language in those days, not in front of women, and it did upset me rather because it was a horrible thing I'd done, but Colonel Wooldridge was very nice to me and said, "Look, if he can't resist talking to a pretty face here, he's not going to resist when he goes out in the field and it won't be only his life but it'll be many others which are put in jeopardy." So of course he couldn't go. It was dreadful, he'd gone through all this training and just for the moonlight on a warm summer evening he'd cracked.'[14]

Henri Diacono, aged twenty, trainee wireless operator:
'My first training school was at a place called Wanborough Manor. There were between fifteen and eighteen in each course, including a couple of young women. We were trained to do all sorts of things, wireless operating, demolition, shooting, making explosives. They also tried some tricks on us, to teach us, for instance, not to be caught by booby traps. One day we were going down the demolition pit along a small path and I saw a branch of a tree had fallen across the middle of the path. The first thing I did was to give it a big kick and there was a terrible explosion just near me. That taught me to be more careful. Another day they put a group of about ten or twelve of us at the edge of a road and told us that three men were going to cross the road twenty yards away from us and we wouldn't see them. We thought that was impossible, so we sat there and watched carefully. Suddenly there was a big explosion behind us and of course we all turned to see what was happening and when we turned back again they told us the three men had crossed the road.

'They also taught us how we could hide, how it was more easy to hide at night when the moon was shining than when it was completely dark. When the moon was bright you could hide in the shadows and when it was completely dark there wasn't shade at all and you were much more conspicuous. Sometimes they took us for a walk in a forest with revolvers in our hands and targets came up suddenly and we had to shoot very fast. I remember there was a conducting officer there who was captain – his real rank was sergeant, I think in the Intelligence Corps, but he was dressed as a captain – and his job was to get very friendly with us and he used to take us out in town and have us drink a little bit more than we should have drunk and after that judge our comportment, if we talked too much. It was all very interesting but it was like a game for us, you know.'

Harry Marcel Despaigne, Anglo-French officer, trainee wireless operator:
'I went to the various SOE training schools, the first one to find out if I had the capability of leading that kind of life, then I went to other schools to learn what an agent is supposed to be doing. At the time, I didn't realise what it was, but they tried to get you drunk, they listened to whether you dreamed in French or English, how you managed a knife and fork. They did not succeed in getting me drunk as I have a very good liver. I don't know why they wanted to know how I used a knife and fork.

'At Beaulieu it seemed to me that we learned silly things, things that we could never use in the field at all – like how to pass messages. I believe the instructor was an actor and he was very good at disguise but not very good on security. Passing a message in a café or on bits of paper in newspapers was so obviously wrong, we never did it in real life. It was the sort of thing you see on TV nowadays but in real life it didn't work that way. It was my feeling that you should never write anything down. At the time, it was all a bit of a laugh, I just couldn't take it seriously.'[15]

Robert Boiteux-Burdett:
'The training on the whole was satisfactory but there was a lot of stuff which I thought was rubbish. They taught us how to bury a parachute, for example. Now, you jump into France by moonlight. Either the Germans or the French police have seen this jump. You are not going to spend half an hour burying a parachute. At least I didn't, I just folded mine up and threw it in the bushes. Also, another thing I thought was rather stupid was that every night, the wireless operator was in contact with London. We sent a message. Next day they would send an answer. We would meet the WO in a café and have an aperitif and he would offer a cigarette – I don't smoke – and then he would give me a matchbox with matches to light my cigarette. Inside was a message. I would open the matchbox and take out the message. That seemed a bit stupid to me, all he had to do was whisper, or even just talk. I mean, nobody was going to hear that. Passing messages in a matchbox, well, really.

'But otherwise, the practical side, the explosives training I thought that was very, very good. We had things to do to test us. For example, I was told to go to the Severn Tunnel and spend a night there to study what damage I could do – and I could have done a lot of damage there if I had been an enemy agent. And then I was sent to Portsmouth, on a second exercise, to get a job in a factory that built aeroplanes, where I worked for a week, to find out all I could about where different parts came from.'

George Langelaan, former correspondent for the New York Times *and future SOE agent:*
'At the end of my training I knew that I could fight more intelligently and efficiently than the majority of men and that, single-handed, I was capable of blowing up a bridge, of sinking a ship, of putting a railway engine out of action in a matter of seconds with a mere spanner, or of derailing an express train with my overcoat. I had been taught to drive a locomotive, how to kill an enraged dog with my bare hands, jump from a fast-moving train, throw a horse, decode a message, make invisible ink, receive and transmit Morse.'[16]

Address by Lieutenant Colonel S.H.C. Woolrych to new students at Beaulieu:

'First of all, let me bid you welcome. I hope you will enjoy your course here and will find it helpful.

Now, let's get to work. The purpose of the organisation to which you and I belong is subversion. Subversion, properly applied, is one of the most potent weapons one can use. It is the fourth arm in modern warfare. What are its objects? They are fourfold.

In the first place, the objective is to damage the enemy's material to the maximum extent, and also his means of communication and production. The second objective is to strain the enemy's resources of manpower . . . the third objective is to undermine the morale of the enemy . . . and finally there is the converse of this, to raise the morale of the populations of the occupied countries in order that they may give us vital assistance when the right moment comes.

During the next few weeks you will have the task of studying the underground life in every aspect – starting with the moment at which you arrive on the ground and disengage yourself from your parachute. You will have to learn to bury it safely, and to start your new life in your new surroundings. We shall be discussing with you every kind of measure to take for your own safety – the importance of having the right story to tell, the right kind of job to do, and how to lead your life best in accordance with those facts. We shall teach you how to build your organisation from zero.

There is only one word of warning I wish to make here. If you follow conscientiously in the field all that we teach you here, we cannot guarantee your safety, but we think your chance of being picked up is very small. Remember, the best agents are never caught. But some agents when they get out into the field find it apparently much easier than they expected, and they are inclined to relax their precautions. That is the moment to beware of. Never relax your precautions, and never fool yourself by thinking the enemy are asleep. They may be watching you all the time, so watch your step.'

2

First Forays

*U*NABLE, IN *the early days, to obtain either aircraft or ships to transport agents into occupied Europe, SOE set up its own 'private navy', largely comprising converted Breton fishing vessels, under the command of Lieutenant Commander Gerald Holdsworth, RNVR. Based on the Helford River in Cornwall, the so-called Helford Flotilla would make fifteen night-time sorties across the Channel, negotiating vicious tides and a rocky coastline to deliver agents into occupied France and supplies to the embryonic resistance movement.*

Lieutenant Francis Brooks Richards, second in command of the Helford Flotilla:
'In 1940 I was captain of a minesweeper, a very nice little whale catcher from South Georgia, which sank on an acoustic mine on the approach to Falmouth. I got a broken leg out of that and while I was in hospital a pre-war friend of mine, a retired naval officer called Bill Lord, told me he was sure there were comings and goings already with Brittany. We're talking now about November 1940. Bill knew Brittany quite well, because he'd built a yacht over there and he'd written about the place a good deal. He said there was a little group of Breton fishing boats in a creek off Falmouth harbour and they couldn't possibly be there for fishing because there was no ice and no fuel. They had French crews and he concluded that they must be there to try and establish contact with Brittany.

'So Bill Lord and I wrote a paper saying, slightly tongue-in-cheek, that if one knew one's way round the Brittany coast, using a Breton fishing fleet was a way of making contact with the other side. Once my leg was mended I went back to sea minesweeping, but eventually was sent for in August 1941 and interviewed in London. They asked me what I knew about Brittany and why I had written the paper and if I was willing to get involved. Of course I said yes. They said, right, you're in SOE. Your boss will be a chap called Gerry Holdsworth, down at Helford in Cornwall.

'Almost immediately I went down to Cornwall, where Gerry Holdsworth was assembling a small flotilla of ships on the Helford River. At that time SOE really was in a real jam about how to get people into France. There'd really only been one successful operation – by a high-speed craft across the channel – since the fall of France and that was thirteen months back.

'The first operation I was involved with was in fact an intelligence operation for people from a Polish network. We had to meet a boat off the coast close to where my friend Bill Lord had built his yacht before the war. I did the navigation and fortunately I got the boat there at exactly the right moment, about ten minutes before the tide turned. This chap we were to meet – an old man with a beard accompanied by his grandson – had come about six miles downriver in a very small boat. He couldn't start an engine because the Germans would hear and he couldn't hoist a sail because that would be too visible, so he had sculled down with the ebb tide. We came alongside and he had the right password and he chucked across to us a full bundle, mail from this Polish organisation, and we took it back to the Helford River.'[1]

Signalman Len Macey, crew member on the Mutan, *a French yawl used as the Helford Flotilla's flagship:*
'When the *Mutan* was fitted out, we did a lot of tests and whatnot and then eventually we sailed her down to Helford with a crew of five or six. I was told I would be staying aboard as a member of the crew. The Helford was a beautiful river. There was the Ferry Boat Inn on one side and the Shipwright's Arms on the other, so I thought, well, this is jolly nice, but what are we going to do? I plainly thought it was Special Forces of some kind, but I'd never heard of SOE or any of these other names, so I really didn't know.

'I think the first trip we did to France we picked up six or seven chaps all wearing suits, overcoats and Homburg hats. I remember they were sitting in a big rubber dinghy waiting for us. We just picked them up and took them away. I realised we were doing something extraordinary, but I didn't know anything about it, like who they were or where they were going. You'd come back, get in your bunk and sleep for a couple of hours, and then you'd carry on with work just as it was before. You'd think about the chaps you'd brought, where they had gone, but as far as we were concerned they just vanished. We on board never knew where on earth they went.

'The dangers were part of the excitement. Directly we got over there, there was a feeling of tension that went all through the boat. Everything was so quiet and when people spoke it was only to relay an order that was to be carried out. Then you heard them coming and you took them aboard and just got out of it. Then you were all right, so it was only ten minutes or a quarter of an hour of anxiety. We didn't have much to be frightened about, or it didn't seem so at the time. Perhaps we should have been, but we weren't.

'I think on a small boat you get used to being out there in the elements and you can cope with them well. You see things that other people perhaps don't see. When you are looking for something and then it suddenly appears there's always great excitement. I remember one pretty rough night we met this chap in a boat. He was sculling in the French way, with one hand, and he'd got a little boy with him who he was telling what to do as they came alongside. I think he was very pleased that we had been able to find him in such rough weather. He gave us a parcel which we brought back to London. I couldn't think of how they'd get back ashore, I mean it was so rough, but they did. And we came home to London and I had to take the parcel up to Baker Street. I never did know what was in it.'[2]

Tom Long, a quartermaster on a Royal Navy destroyer, was recruited into the Helford Flotilla when it became known that he had served in the merchant navy before the war, crossing back and forth to the northern coast of France:

'I was told to go to this office in Baker Street where I was interviewed by Admiral Holbrook [*head of SOE's naval section*]. He said I'd been selected for Special Service, was I prepared to do it? So I said, what have I got to do? He said, well, we can't tell you, but if you don't want to do it, you don't have to. So I said, well, I don't know what you want me to do, but I'll do it. So he said, we knew you would. Go and see Miss Maidment at the desk. She's got the railway warrant made out. You're going to Falmouth.

'So I went to Falmouth. I reported to the Imperial Hotel and about a half hour later I was picked up by Lieutenant Van, a Belgium officer. He drove me down to the top of Helford and when I saw this beautiful river – it was a lovely May or June day – I thought, God, I'm going to be happy here. But when we went alongside the *Mutan* there was shipwrights digging out shrapnel from all over the vessel and patching it up and there was a heap of sails with blood all over them. I thought, Jesus Christ, what the hell have I let myself in for now?

'The next morning, Lieutenant Van said to me we're going over the other side tonight, would you like to come? So I said, yes please. We picked up two French chaps and we pushed off that afternoon. It was dark when we got over to the other side. These two French chaps assembled a three-seater foldable canoe, got in, shook hands, pushed off and went ashore. So when we got back the next morning, Lieutenant Van said we're going to make you fully operational. I didn't know what that meant but anyway I was pleased.

'We done several more jobs landing agents with a canoe. There was a ruined church, right near the edge of the coast, and they slid the boat right tight inside the wall where it was covered with brambles and foliage. One day someone decided to clear up the old churchyard and uncovered the canoe. Just as he uncovered it, the Germans come along and they smelled a rat. So the next thing we knew they said there's going to be no more canoe work – you've got to land the agents and supply them with stores and all the rest of it and pick them up from the beaches by boat. So then we ran into our first snag. You rowed ashore, done your job and when you came back again, you had a hell of a job to find the mother craft.

'Well, we tried all kinds of things. First of all, we had balls of twine all joined together and you rowed ashore towing that, but there was always a weak place and that broke. So that was out. Then someone thought a good idea would be to get a grass rope with loads of corks on and let it stream out from the stern of the mother craft, and then if you saw that, you knew which way she was. But the best thing we had were these luminous balls, smaller than a golf ball. They was the most wonderful things we had. You'd go ashore and do whatever it was you had to do and then you'd just come down to the water's edge and hold up your luminous ball so the mother craft could see it.

'Normally, they stopped between two and three mile out and that's what you had to row ashore. It all depended on the wind and tide how long it took us to row in. First, you wouldn't be able see a hand in front of your face, but as you was in the dark and you got more used to it you was able to pick things up slightly, but it was still awkward. When we'd land on a beach, we didn't know whether it was mined, and we didn't know whether there was a party there of Germans waiting to welcome us. We had an "Operational Box" and when you was briefed you took whatever you wanted. I mean, you would load yourself right up or you could travel light. In the Operational Box there was rubber truncheons, a tommy gun, a Smith and Wesson automatic, all kinds of fighting knives and knuckledusters. I was personally given a machete and I was told if I got near a German and gave a swipe, it would take his head clean off. I carried that several times, hoping to meet a German, but never saw one.

'I think about the third time we went to take stores ashore, there was three or four new chaps and I said, well, I'll show you what to do, you'll be all right. So we were down below having a last smoke. At that time I was smoking a pipe. When it was time for us to go up on deck and get our eyes used to the dark, I took an extra swig at my pipe and swallowed a lot of nicotine and gave myself hiccups. Well, we launched the boat for going ashore and I was hiccuping like mad and I thought, well, they'll hear this bugger in Paris! We loaded up the boat and the hiccups was getting louder and louder all the time, there was everyone laughing like hell. Gor blimey, I didn't half feel a bloody fool!

'One time we was ashore working on the beach when suddenly a lighthouse lit up and of course it showed us all up. We nipped quickly behind the rocks and thought, what's on? We heard our boat start up its engines and she was away. Later on, we saw a German battleship, a cruiser and several escort vessels going past. The lighthouse swung around and lit them up. After they went past, the boat came in and picked us up. Another time, we couldn't find the mother craft, because she'd dragged her anchor and was miles away. So we decided to row for Dartmouth and we was pulling for Dartmouth when it come daylight and they came and picked us up.'[3]

While the Helford Flotilla was delivering agents and supplies by water, SOE was preparing agents to be parachuted into occupied France. The first four recruits were ready for dispatch in the spring of 1941, but the house in which they were lodging in Knightsbridge suffered a direct hit during a German air raid. Two potential agents were killed and a third severely injured. The fourth, Georges Bégué survived unscathed as he was out of the house at the time of the raid. Bégué, also known as George Noble, was the first SOE agent to be dropped into France on 5 May 1941. He parachuted 'blind' – without a reception committee – near Châteauroux and within two days had radioed his safe arrival and given the address of a 'letter box' where he could be contacted.

The next agent to go, Pierre de Vomécourt, was almost arrested within hours of his arrival:

'I landed on 11 May, in the same area as George Noble. As the blackout was in force throughout France, it isn't surprising that I should have been dropped about eight kilometres from the intended spot. But I eventually found a road and signposts showing place names that I recognised, and at last I reached a little station on the line to Châteauroux.

'Noticing a few people entering a café opposite the station, I went in too, being absolutely frozen; it was five thirty in the morning and I had had no sleep. I asked for a cup of coffee laced with cognac. "It's our day without," snarled the café owner. Seeing that I didn't understand, he said it again. I didn't want to cause a fuss, so I just mumbled: "Oh, I see." But I'd been spotted already. As a precaution, I left the train one station before Châteauroux and went the rest of the way on foot. Just as well! I heard later that at Châteauroux station the police had been scrutinising everyone who arrived by train. The man at the café had telephoned them to say he had heard an aircraft circling that night – and that this clown, who didn't know what "day without" meant, had just caught the train.'[4]

Autonomous networks, each known by a code name, provided the basic structure of SOE operations in the field. Jean Le Harivel, wireless operator with the 'Corsican' network, parachuted with three other agents on the night of 10 September 1941:

'The objectives in the early days were extremely simple. The main work was information, information on everything that could be useful to the Allies. If there was a specific factory they wanted to know about – it might be making some secret weapons or something like that – then we were told to find out. Information, information, information, that was the key thing. The other part came a bit later: in the early days sabotage was not encouraged because it was too early and dangerous to start blowing things up.

'The other part of the work was setting up networks, called in French *réseaux*. The idea was to gradually find people you could trust and enrol them. That was the difficult thing, to know who you could trust. The concept under which we were operating was a bit idealistic in the minds of the early organisers because one didn't really know the state of mind of French people. This was basically a terrible problem because you weren't sure with whom you were talking, with whom you were dealing and whether they could really be trusted. I think that was a key factor which made the work extremely difficult and which led to some disasters, you know, the Germans penetrating into a *réseau*.

'The period just before one left for the mission was an extremely difficult one because people were a bit tense, a bit nervous, and the atmosphere was a bit unreal. Luckily there were some very nice FANY girls who were very kind and who understood that we were in a nervous situation and who looked after us very nicely, so it was made as pleasant as possible.

'What happened in the very last stages was that we were checked for all sorts of details. We had a French tailor who made our suits in the French style. We even went to a dentist who checked our fillings, because the French fillings were not like the British fillings, and of course in the very last hours they checked that we didn't have anything on us that could be detected as being foreign. We were given a watch that was non-British, maybe Swiss, I can't remember, and we had of course to get rid of any English money that we may have had and so on and so forth. A very meticulous check was made in these very final stages.

'When we left the Nissen hut, walking from there to the Whitley bomber, we were not very comfortable because the parachute was heavy and we felt rather tight in this stuff. Our emotions were a bit mixed, glad to get off at long last, but thinking what the devil is going to happen to us once we get there.

'The plane was a Whitley bomber stripped of everything inside. I remember feeling very cold, but the RAF escort officer was very kind and he had a Thermos of hot coffee which helped. The flight was not very long. The Whitley was a slow twin-engine bomber with a very wide wing which helped it to slow down just before you jumped.

'The period just before the jump is of course crucial. The pilot warned the dispatcher that we were coming near the dropping area, but unfortunately the people on the ground hadn't given a recognisable code. They had torches and they had to signal two letters in Morse but we didn't receive the correct signal so the dispatcher wasn't satisfied and we went round, oh, I think two or three times, before we were given the all-clear. The all-clear was a light which turned from red to green and when it was green you had to jump. The Whitley was the old type: there was a hole in the floor and you dropped two at a time, one, two, very quickly. The curious thing about jumping is that the sensation as you leave the plane is fantastic, you're on a current of air, you don't drop suddenly, you drop gently for about three seconds and then the chute opens and you drop slowly. I can still remember the drop as if it were yesterday. It was a full moon, beautiful scenery, there was a large field and trees all round. The countryside was absolutely wonderful and I remember for a few seconds just admiring the countryside, not thinking about the actual jump.

'After that, it was not so funny because my chute decided to go slowly towards some trees. Luckily I remembered the sergeant at Ringway saying if ever you have to jump into trees keep your blooming legs together – actually, he didn't say blooming – but luckily I remembered that and I kept my blooming legs together and jumped into a tree and then had to get down to the ground – not too difficult but not very pleasant!

'Having managed to struggle down to the ground from this wretched tree, the first thing I did was to pull out my little revolver and say "*Qui va là?*", because I heard some steps nearby. One of the members of the reception committee answered and we realised we were with friends but what was sad was that we found out that there were only three of us instead of four. The fourth person had been dropped miles away and the containers, including my wireless, were not there. What was I going to do without my wireless set? However, the friends who received us, there were three or four of them, helped us to bury the parachutes. Then we were taken to a car which belonged to a doctor – doctors were allowed to drive at night – and driven to a barn and there we hid because everyone in the area knew something had happened, the plane having turned round so often, and the police were on the alert.

'We stayed in the barn five or six days, something like that, and we were forbidden to go out. We had to sleep in the hay which smelled rather strong, not unpleasant, but it was a strong smell. We were bored because we had nothing to do. The farmer and his wife brought us food regularly throughout the day, but it was a very dull, uninteresting and difficult period. We stayed there until we went to the town and took a bus to a train station and a train to Marseilles, where I was to work. We had been given an address in Marseilles, the Villa du Bois, where we were supposed to meet up with Mr X or Mrs X. It was to be a safe house which was a point of contact from which we were going to set up our *réseau*. The fact was we knew nobody there.

'We travelled separately by train to Marseilles because it wasn't wise for the three of us to travel together. The train journey was our first contact with the French population and we felt a bit odd sitting in the train, British among French. However, nothing happened, except at Marseilles station the police were on the alert all the time and there I was with a little suitcase with practically nothing in it except clothes and a toilet bag and there was a plain-clothes man there who asked me to open the case. I felt terrible because if I had been with my big wireless case how would I ever explain that? However, there was nothing in the case so he couldn't stop me and then I went to a hotel near the station.

'The first days in Marseilles were rather long with nothing to do. For some reason or another I was told not to go immediately to the Villa du Bois, so I had three or four days in Marseilles doing nothing except going to restaurants. Funnily enough, I went to see Fernandel, the French comedian, who had a show on at Marseilles at that time. But generally I had nothing to do all day. When I eventually went to the safe house, I rang the bell and a rather attractive lady answered and said, "Oh I'm terribly sorry, my husband isn't here, we'll have to make another appointment for you." She gave me the name of a café on the Canabière where he would meet me the next day.

'The next day, as agreed, I went to the café on the Canabière and as I approached I saw on the terrace the lady I'd met the night before and a man whom I supposed was her husband. Pleased, I walked up to them, sat down and chatted for a little while but then two plain-clothes policemen came up and arrested me. There was no fuss, no handcuffing or anything like that, but I couldn't understand what had gone wrong. It was a shock to be arrested, I can remember my stomach churning, I was so surprised and shocked and upset. The police took me to my hotel, which was about five hundred yards away and went up to my room and I was asked to pack my things, my few clothes and toilet bag in my suitcase. Fortunately, the inspector who had arrested me was rather kind and he turned his back on me for a minute or two during which I was able to swallow my little card with all my wireless codes and so on, so that he didn't find that at least. Then from there we went down to the police car and to the prison in Marseilles, where my second shock of the day was to find my two friends, Jumeau and Hayes [the agents with whom he had been dropped] already there. They had been caught like me and we discovered there were twelve others, all in the same prison, all caught in the same *souricière*, mousetrap. You can imagine my stupefaction. Everything had gone wrong, it was a catastrophe.

'We very quickly realised that the safe address had not been safe at all. But we were still in a fog. What typified the early days was the fact that we were fumbling. We were really entering into a new kind of war, it was a strange, peculiar type of war and we hadn't any experience of managing that kind of war at all.'

Le Harivel later escaped from a prison camp, made his way across the Pyrenees into Spain and eventually returned to Britain via Gibraltar. By the end of 1941, SOE officers in Baker Street were becoming increasingly concerned by the number of agents, like Le Harivel, who had simply disappeared from the moment they were dropped into France. At that time they did not know that the Villa du Bois in Marseilles had been compromised, that the Gestapo had discovered the address and set it up as a souricière to ensnare every agent who visited it. Another SOE agent, George Abbott, was sent out to try and discover what was going on:

'I was in fact ready to go over at the end of October 1941. When I say I was ready to go, I went as far as boarding a plane. At the last minute we were disembarked – we didn't know why at the time – and taken back and more or less told, "Well, you'd better go and have some leave in London." To cut a long story short, from the end of October '41 to February '42 I was more or less hanging around. Afterwards, we learned that something rather unfortunate had happened on the other side and a lot of chaps had been arrested. Anyhow, at the end of January I was called and told that I would be landing in France by a Lysander light aircraft somewhere north of Paris. Then I was to proceed to Paris and one of the things I had to do was contact some people to see if their line of communication to London had been blown. Obviously, if their line was blown, the chances were that they were blown too.

'To put it quite bluntly, I was going there as a guinea pig. I mean, if something happened to me they would know that the line was blown. If I made my own judgement that the line was blown, I had to communicate that to them and make myself scarce and more or less warn the other chaps to make themselves scarce too. Then I had to come back to England some way or another. I had been given a contact which, fortunately, I never went to because I discovered later that that contact was blown also.

'Although I was given all these instructions, a few days later they called me back and they said, "Well, it's all cancelled. You're not going that way. You're going to be dropped blind near Le Mans and you're going to make your way to Paris and you're going to a certain bar near the Champs Elysées and you're going to see the barman there. You're going to ask him about Roger. And then you will try to contact so-and-so" – he showed me a photograph of the chap I was going to contact – "and you're going to tell him that we have doubts that his line of communication . . ." and so on and so on. Anyhow, that was also cancelled.

'Then in early February I was told all this had changed and I was going to be landed by motor gunboat on the coast of Brittany. I was still going to go to Paris to see this chap but another bloke was going to meet me when I landed on the beach. They didn't give me any more details than that.

'I finally went either on the 12th or 13th of February 1942. The whole thing was a catastrophe from start to finish. When we landed the sea was very bad. We were supposed to land some equipment. That finished up in the sea. We finished up in the sea. Anyhow, when we finally got ashore we were informed that the Germans were observing the whole operation.

'The chaps on the beach were in a panic. They told us, "Nobody lands. You have to re-embark immediately." But nobody was able to re-embark because the sea was very rough: the dinghies collapsed, they lost the oars. So the two of us that were supposed to have been landed in France found ourselves on the beach with a naval lieutenant, RNVR [*Royal Naval Volunteer Reserve*], in uniform. And there we were. We didn't know too much what to do. The chaps on the beach said, "Well, if the sea is not so rough, probably the MTB [*motor torpedo boat*] is going to come back tomorrow." There'd been a lot of signalling between the naval officer and MTB by lamp, Morse and all kinds of things. They said, "They'll come tomorrow night. You'd better hide." There was a hut there, somewhere on the beach, and they said, "You'd better hide in there and see how things go. We're going to go on our way."

'We didn't understand very well how they would be able to go through the German lines, although we found out later. There was a woman with them, an infamous woman called Mathilde Carré, known as the Cat. She was a kind of Mata Hari: she played more than a double game, she played a treble game. Anyhow, she was there on the beach with two other blokes and we hid in this little hut. We were in pretty poor shape, all of us. I mean, the three of us had been in the sea, we were soaking wet, it was pretty cold and we were shivering and feverish.

'At around eight in the morning, the naval officer, who was an Australian, said, "I can't stick it any more. I'm in uniform, I don't have to fear anything, I'm going to give myself up." Well, there was nothing much we could do: either bump him off or let him go. As we had no possibility of bumping him off – we lost our arms during the landing – and no inclination to do this anyhow, he said, "I'm going. I won't do anything, I haven't seen you." I said, "Good luck to you. Goodbye."

'So he went off and we stayed in our little hut. During the morning we could observe lots of commotion on the beach. Germans in uniform with Alsatian dogs were looking at a lot of things that were on the beach. I assume the wireless sets and ammunition and explosives we had brought had been washed up. We were at the time rather intrigued because at one stage a German and his dog approached the hut and got to within about a hundred yards of us but turned round. We were surprised that nothing happened, but I think as we were soaked by sea water the dogs couldn't pick up our scent.

'Anyhow, we stayed there until the evening. We saw that the sea was still very rough. And we said, well, there is no chance whatever of the operation taking place again. We said, we'll have to try and do something, somehow. We had some money, but we were not in the best of shape, having been soaked. At the time I was fairly young, twenty-six I think. The other bloke was the wireless operator. He didn't know anything about our suspicions that the lines had been blown. He was completely in the dark. He was about forty-six or forty-seven, a little bit shaken up and not in very good physical shape. Anyhow, we made our way out of the hut, we climbed the cliff until we found a road and started walking in the night, hoping to find a town and perhaps a train.

'We were very tired and hungry when we came across a farm. We knocked at the door. To cut a long story short, it was the wrong farm. We had been told the Bretons, absolutely all of them, were pro-English, but this particular one wasn't. He was a Breton nationalist. After having given us something to eat and put us up in the barn he called the Germans and we were caught.

'We were arrested by the military police, I would say probably very much to the annoyance of German intelligence, because they were hoping we would go back to Paris and they would be able to link us up with other people and they would arrest us with the rest. There is no doubt that they had penetrated this particular network but they were hoping we might be able to lead them somewhere else. We were transferred to a prison outside Paris where we stayed for the best part of twenty-two months, eleven of which were in solitary confinement.'[5]

Despite setbacks like the debacle at the Villa du Bois, more and more agents were being sent to France ever more frequently. Squadron Leader Lewis Hodges, aged twenty-six, commanded a flight of Halifax bombers, part of 161 Squadron at Tempsford, specifically designated to drop agents in occupied territory:

'The base was a fairly new one but extremely primitive. We lived in Nissen huts and the airfield itself was pretty rough-and-ready. I remember in the winter it was not a very congenial place, but it served the purpose. On arrival, as a brand new chap, the flying side of it was fairly straightforward because I'd been doing it from the beginning of the war, but the special duties side of it, that is to say the parachuting, one had to learn. We had to drop the agents from about six hundred to eight hundred feet above the ground, so a certain amount of practice and training was needed on that.

'The procedure was that every morning we appeared in the operations room. The orders would have come down from London telling us what had been laid on for that particular night. The maps were in the operations room and we were briefed on which areas we were to drop in and I, as the flight commander, would allocate the crews to the particular jobs and then the crews would go off to the navigation sections and crew rooms to start planning the routes ready for the final briefing, which consisted of the weather forecasts and preparations for the take-off that evening. We usually took off for operations between late afternoon and early evening, depending on the time of the year, because we aimed to cross the coast in the dark. These operations required good weather conditions and moonlight, and we only flew during the moon period for parachuting.

'Containers were hung on the bomb racks to carry the weapons and explosives which we were going to parachute into the occupied countries for use by the agents. These containers were prepared during the day and then transported out to the aircraft on bomb carriers and loaded on ready for the actual flight. The agents were held at special holding centres within ten miles of the airfield and they were brought down to the airfield about an hour before take-off, to a special area where they were fitted with their parachutes and their clothing searched for any incriminating evidence like bus tickets or underground railway tickets, or photographs, so that if they were caught, there would be no indication as to where they'd come from.

'We didn't personally have direct contact with the agents. Naturally we saw them when they arrived at the aircraft, but the crew of the aeroplane, myself and the rest, we were already on board and

I'd be sitting in the cockpit so I never actually had an opportunity to speak to them directly.

'When we crossed the Channel to go to France or the North Sea to go to Denmark or Norway or Holland, we normally came down to a low altitude over the sea to avoid detection, as far as possible, by enemy radar. Arriving at the coastline, we would normally climb to about one thousand, one thousand five hundred feet to be able to get a clear indication on the coast as to our exact position. One needed to be sure of the point that you were crossing the coast from the navigation point of view. Having crossed the coast, we would descend down to low level again, perhaps eight hundred or a thousand feet, depending on the terrain and depending on the weather, of course, and then we would fly at low level all the way to the dropping zone, again trying to pick up landmarks such as rivers and railways as we went along. When we finally arrived at the dropping zone the agents on the ground would flash a recognition signal and then we would know we were in the right place. The navigation was quite difficult and one did have to have good weather and moonlight to see where you were going and what you were doing.

'One was always on the lookout for night fighters and making sure as far as you possibly could that you avoided any areas where there was likely to be anti-aircraft fire. We of course studied the routes very carefully and routed the aeroplanes to avoid known places like airfields where there would be opposition. One had obviously a certain amount of anxiety, one always did on these occasions, but one was so busy, there was plenty going on all the time that one didn't have too much time to think about it.

'There were two lights over the dropping hole in the rear of the fuselage, a red light and a green light. As you approached the dropping zone and you saw the signal, the red light would be switched on to indicate to the dispatcher and to the agents that we were near. They would then hook up their parachutes on to the static line, so that when the agent jumped out, the parachute was pulled open automatically. They then sat with their feet on the edge of the hole ready to jump and then when the navigator indicated that we were in the correct position over the DZ for dropping, the pilot would switch on the green light and the agent would be told to jump.'[6]

Gilbert Turck, a Paris architect, escaped to London after the defeat of France and was dropped back into France near Montluçon on the night of 6 August 1941:
'Sitting in the plane waiting to jump, I was not afraid; I simply did not

think about being afraid. I had an extraordinary feeling that my whole life was a preparation for that moment. My parents had instilled in me a great sense of duty and devotion to France and it seemed to me to be perfectly natural to do what I was doing. So when the signal came to jump, I pushed myself out of the plane with such vigour and enthusiasm that I hit the underside of the wing, knocked myself out and dropped to the ground completely unconscious.

'When I came to, I was in a police station, surrounded by policemen. Apparently, two peasants had found me lying on the ground and had taken me there. I was groggy for a couple of days and can't remember very clearly what happened, but I know I was taken to a military prison in Clermont-Ferrand for interrogation.

'Somewhat to my own surprise, I was able to talk my way out of trouble by convincing my captors that I hated the English so much I had bribed the RAF to drop me back into France.'[7]

For radio operator Jean Holley, getting into France was quite as nightmarish as anything he experienced once he finally arrived:
'We went three times to the South of France before we were actually able to jump. The first time, the pilot could not find the landing ground, or if he found it, there was no marker, which indicated there was no reception committee and no one wanted to jump. There were three of us to parachute and eight parachutes with containers. So we returned to England. The second trip was even more dramatic. We were fired on by German planes as we flew south of the Channel, but the gunners in the Halifax soon put paid to them and we flew on over Tours. Unfortunately, we were caught in the searchlights which defended Tours which lit us up like it was daylight, so the anti-aircraft guns began firing on us. With each explosion, the plane seemed to suffer, but we carried on nevertheless. The pilot was extremely hard-nosed and stepped up the speed of the plane in order to try to dodge the fire but the plane was, unfortunately, hit. Minutes later, the co-pilot came in and told us we had been hit, but the controls were unaffected by the hit and we would continue. Therefore we continued flying, but it was more or less flying blind and we were out of contact with everyone. Soon afterwards, we were completely lost but the Halifax bomber carried reserve fuel which allowed us to carry on flying for another twelve hours.

'At the end of twelve hours, the co-pilot again came in and told us we were lost and were above the clouds, south of Norway. The pilots, had they jumped, would have been taken prisoner of war, but we were in civilian clothes, plainly spies, and we ran the risk of being shot, had we jumped. As I recall it, we took out our pistols, loaded them and prepared to jump anyway. While we were waiting, the co-pilot came back and said, "Don't jump, barrage balloon in sight." We were over England! We landed, I don't know where, but it was possible to make contact by radio and someone came and picked us up and took us back to base. We were given a break until the following full moon.

'Finally, on the third attempt, there were no problems, except a small brush with a German plane but this was of no consequence. We landed about twelve kilometres north of Mauriceaux in the worst possible kind of terrain, full of boulders, but we had no problems with the reception.'[8]

Captain Oliver Haward Brown:
'The first thing that happened when you were alerted that your mission was coming up was that you were bundled into a lorry and off you went to London. The briefing was extremely good, very long to start with since you had all the Morse and wireless side to deal with, the recognition signals and so on, your cover stories. So it was a two-day briefing really. Then at the end of the briefing, you had to repeat the briefing back to them because you had to carry it in your head. Then you just waited.

'One of the most amusing things that happened was that by that time I had grown my beard and I was going down Upper Regent Street and I suddenly saw my father-in-law coming up the other way. I went "Oh my God!" but he walked straight past me without recognising me. It gave me great confidence. So we just hung about London, although we had to have a conducting officer with us all the time in case we did anything stupid.

'The first night we went over, we couldn't find the DZ anywhere. We had a hell of a trip; we went first slap over Cherbourg and they threw everything at us and we followed that by going over Lorient and they threw everything they had at us. We then flew straight down the Loire to Orléans and got tagged by a German fighter. We didn't realise until we got back to England that he had actually hit us.

'The second night something went wrong with the aircraft. We dropped René and then Smithy [*the two agents who were going in with him*], but then the pilot said something had gone wrong and he couldn't decelerate the plane. He said he was going to have to take me home as he couldn't risk dropping me out under full power. I said, "I'm not going home. You've dropped my two mates, you've got to put me out!" So I had a hell of a bad drop and banged myself badly and had only just come out of the spiral when I hit the ground. Luckily a Frenchman was running towards me from the reception committee and I actually landed on him. He was a good, fat rotund Frenchman and I think this just about saved me but I damaged my leg very badly and was unconscious for forty-eight hours.'[9]

Roger Landes, wireless operator, made four fruitless trips across to France before he actually got on the ground:
'On the first trip the pilot could not find the landing ground and so he came back. The night after that, we went again to Bordeaux and the signals on the ground were not well directed and the pilot refused to let me go. We went back to England again. Then we waited another three nights, during the moon period, and as we crossed the Channel, the ack-ack from the Germans started and the pilot said, "I've got difficulty controlling the plane, we must have been hit. We have got to return." When we were back above England, he told the crew and me to get ready to jump because he was having more and more difficulty. But the crew had never jumped by parachute before and they said, "Can't we do a forced landing?" I said, "I would prefer to jump!" but he did a forced landing and I didn't feel anything, it was so good. In the morning, they found out we had not been hit by the ack-ack at all; a bird had gone through the wing and made a hole in it and that was why he had difficulty controlling the plane.

'By then, of course, the moon period was finished and so they decided to fly me to Gibraltar in a flying boat, with three women agents. They made me a passport in my real name, as a civil servant working in Gibraltar. We were waiting on the flying boat ready to take off when they came and told us we had to get out, because the fishing boat which was to take us from Gibraltar to the South of France had not arrived.

'They decided then that I should wait for the October moon period. This time the weather was so bad over the dropping zone the plane had to descend to 250 feet. The pilot said, "Well, do you want to jump or are we going back to England?" I said, "I'm fed up with going back, I'm going to jump!" The plane was going at two hundred miles an hour and when I jumped I was a mile away from the reception committee.

'When I landed, the first thing I did was to bury my parachute, which we had been trained to do, using a little spade strapped to my leg. While I was doing this, I heard voices and because I didn't know who it was – it could have been Germans who saw the parachute coming down – I hid under some bushes. Then I heard someone calling, "Robert, Robert," which was my code name. It was the reception committee who had seen the parachute and taken forty-five minutes to find me. I was never frightened while I was waiting to go, I was excited. I was twenty-five after all, I had been trained to do this and the training we had, I think, made you a man.'[10]

Single-engine Lysander light aircraft, able to land or take off in a distance of only two hundred yards, were increasingly used to pick up agents in occupied countries who needed to be brought back to London.

Squadron Leader Hugh Verity, Special Duties Lysander Flight Commander:

'I was in charge of the operations room in Fighter Command which controlled long-range night fighters operating over *Luftwaffe* bases on the Continent. One night I saw a plot on the radar screen of a single aircraft leaving England and then later on coming back from the French coast. I didn't know what these so-called "specials" were, but somebody explained to me that they were Lysanders landing in occupied Europe by moonlight and picking up SOE and SIS agents. I thought that this would be rather more fun than what I was doing. I talked a bit of French and I'd done quite a lot of night flying, so I thought I'd try to get into the act. I asked if I could join the squadron that was doing these jobs and luckily for me the squadron leader who was running the Lysander flight at that time was just about to become tour-expired and so they gave me the flight to run in his place. That's how it happened.

'It was quite a small flight actually. I think there were only about five pickup pilots at that time and we operated from Tangmere, near the South Coast, every moon period. The main base was Tempsford, in Bedfordshire. That's where the bomber-type aircraft doing parachute operations flew from, but the pickup flights always went from Tangmere. We had a little cottage just opposite the main gate of Tangmere airfield. The agents had to be anonymous and unrecognised and they could come in through the back door and nobody could see them. We'd have a drink with them and take them to show them the aeroplane, if they didn't know it already, and later when we picked them up and brought them back to the cottage for a night-flying breakfast, we would hear the most amazing stories about their adventures.

'The cottage was a fairly primitive sort of holiday house. There were two rooms on the ground floor, one for an operations room with a green scrambler telephone and big maps and everything and across the hall there was the dining room. Upstairs we had a few bedrooms where as many beds as possible were squeezed on to the floor space, rather like a cheap Turkish hotel. The kitchen was like a guard room. We were well away from all the administrative controls of a proper RAF station, so we were free to have a little party every time we had a new decoration to celebrate. It was a very friendly, relaxed unit, but, my goodness, we were jolly keen to get all the operational details right.

'We got an air-transport form for every pickup and this gave the location of the field and the Morse signals that would be flashed from the ground and from the air, so that you had mutual recognition before landing. We had air photographs specially flown from the Photographic Reconnaissance Unit at Benson, which had been annotated by interpreters to show where there were cart tracks and shrubs and anything which could be any sort of an obstacle. They even told us how high every tree was; they were an amazing bit of work, so we could really spend about two hours mugging up each operation, devising a route. The first leg was from Bognor across to Normandy, that's about an hour flying over the sea, then on to the Loire, where we had a favourite crossing place, which you couldn't mistake, near Blois. Even on quite a dirty night you could always tell the difference between water and land, where the coastline or a river or a lake gives you a fix and you know where you are. Then the last little leg would be quite short, just two or three minutes from some recognisable village, railway junction or whatever, and then at the end of that little short leg you'd see your friend on the ground flashing the Morse letter that you were expecting, so it was marvellous.

'You'd probably be only on the ground for about three minutes if everything went smoothly. While we were there, as often as not someone climbed up on the port undercarriage to shake one's hand and say hello and give one either a bottle of champagne or brandy, or scent for one's wife, and one would give him some coffee and cigarettes in exchange. It was all very amiable, totally unofficial. It rather shook me, some time later, when a senior officer said to me, "You know, Hugh, what you were doing there was really smuggling, wasn't it?"

'It was the duty of the *chef de terrain* to make sure that the field was safe, and of course sometimes it wasn't all that safe. On one occasion I landed on a field where the agent in charge was horrified to find that most of it had been ploughed up since his last visit. Luckily there was just a narrow band of grass left for one to land on. That worked out all right, but it could have been embarrassing. The main trouble we had with fields was mud. We had two occasions when Hudsons [*light bombers also used for SOE operations*] got stuck in the mud and it took hours to extract them and there were several Lysanders which couldn't be extracted at all and had to be set on fire. Then the pilot would go and hide up with the Resistance until he could be picked up, possibly in the next moon period.

'One had to do all the navigation as well as the flying and trying to work out what was happening to the weather. If you had a spell of flying over fog, you'd stick to your compass heading and speed and then hope that when you could see the ground again, it would be more or less where you were planning to be. But if it wasn't, you had quite a job to find yourself on the map on the ground, and so one didn't have enough time to get really alarmed by what was, after all, quite a dangerous operation. If, because of bad weather or whatever, our pilots got lost and they stumbled over a *Luftwaffe* base by accident, they were really quite likely to get shot at and were in some cases shot down. My most dangerous incidents were landing in fog at Tangmere, where I broke a Lysander rather badly, and another occasion when I nearly flew into a wireless mast near Lyons because I was looking at a map in my cockpit just a minute too long.'[11]

A private house near Tangmere was also used by agents departing on missions to France. The owner was Barbara Bertram:
'The party would arrive from London at about three thirty. We would have a cup of tea and then each of them going out would have to search themselves to make sure they had nothing on them that would show they had been in England – no bus or cinema ticket, or letter. This searching was very necessary and more and more care was taken over it, but even so slips were occasionally made. One Frenchman was in the Metro in Paris one morning, standing in the usual squash of passengers, when he found that a copy of the day before's *Daily Telegraph* was sticking out of his overcoat pocket. He waited till he was nearly at his station then he slipped it out of his own pocket and into the pocket of a German officer standing next to him and quickly got out.

'After they had searched themselves, they gave up any English money they had on them. If there was a lot it was kept for their return, but small change they generally put into a Red Cross collecting box we kept handy, or, if they had been with us for a day or so and met Tim and Nicky [*the Bertram children*], they often gave it to them.

It was even thought dangerous for men to go out with hairs from our dog on their trousers, so a clothes brush always had to be handy for them to use at the last minute.

'Then they were given a fake French identity card and a fake ration card and lots of French money – fake, too, for all I know. They were also given, if they wanted them, a revolver, a kind of cosh they could conceal up their sleeve and a thing that looked like a fountain pen but squirted tear gas if you pressed a knob. They were always rather sceptical about these, so one day someone let one off in the bathroom and shut the door, and then, without telling me what they had done, asked me to fetch something from the bathroom cupboard. My state when I rejoined them in a fury was enough to convince them that it was *very* effective.

'They were also given imitation French cigarettes, and matches and soap and a toothbrush, pocket comb and razor blades not marked "Made in England". At first, I had to find these things, which was not easy. I did find unmarked toothbrushes once and bought twenty-four, but it was too chancy and soon they were specially made for us. At first, I also kept cakes of soap once the name on them had worn off, but this was found to be dangerous. If used in a public lavatory, it was noticeable that it lathered too well. So soap was especially made almost as gritty and bad as wartime French soap. There was also a difficulty about the imitation Gauloise: the gum used on the packet was too good, so that it didn't disintegrate as soon as it was opened as the real ones did. This, too, was remedied.

'While this searching was going on, the drivers and I went through their luggage looking at everything they had bought while in England to see if it was marked "Made in England". If they had bought a new suit, the buckle on the back of the waistcoat had to be cut off and the straps sewn together. Hats were confiscated – they were stamped on the leather band inside and you can't remove that without making the hat too big. We had nine hats at the end of the war! Gloves had the buttons wrenched off. Shirts were easy. We rubbed the mark very hard with Milton [*sterilising liquid*] and it either rubbed out the word or it rubbed a hole in the shirt. Once, I seized a pair of beautiful pink silk pyjamas and was just starting on the Milton when their owner snatched them from me: he had bought them in Paris before the war and refused to risk them being spoiled.

'During this time of packing and repacking I was often asked for all kinds of probable and improbable things. I had to be careful these were not marked too. I was asked for string, nails, boxes, bags and tins, for safety pins, hairpins, scissors. I got into the habit of hoarding everything in case someone should ask me for just that. They were also given tiny compasses, knives, pencils, magnifying glasses and cards printed in microscopic letters and maps printed on fine silk.

'Then I had to do a horrible thing. They were going out to occupied France and were going to be in great danger of being arrested and they knew that if they were, they would be tortured. Some of them felt they wouldn't be able to withstand torture so, to prevent themselves giving away their friends, they asked me to sew their poison pills into their cuffs. I hated doing that.'[12]

SOE report, dated 22 January 1942, classified 'Most Secret', confirming that two agents had been dispatched by parachute to Czechoslovakia with orders to assassinate SS General Reinhard Heydrich, Heinrich Himmler's deputy and one of the architects of the Nazi's 'Final Solution' – the mass extermination of the Jews. The operation was code-named 'Anthropoid'.

The operation ANTHROPOID, consisting of two agents, was dispatched by parachute on the night of 28/29th December 1941. They carried with them a package containing two metal boxes, the contents of which are shown in the attached schedule.

'The object of the operation is the assassination of Herr HEYDRICH, the German Protector in Czechoslovakia, and the small box contains equipment for an attack on him in his car on his way from the Castle in Prague to his office. The larger box contains assorted equipment for alternative attacks by:

(a) Getting into the castle.
(b) Getting into his office.
(c) Placing a bomb in his car or in his armoured railway train.
(d) Blowing up his railway train.
(e) Mining a road along which he is going to travel.
(f) Shooting him when he is appearing at some ceremony.

The time and place of this operation will be decided on the spot but the two agents concerned have been trained in all methods of assassination known to us. They intend to carry out this operation whether or not there is any opportunity of subsequent escape.

This project is not known to the Czech organisation within the Protectorate.'

Report, dated 30 May 1942, three days after the attack: Heydrich was seriously injured when his car was ambushed outside Prague on 27 May 1942.

As it was known that HEYDRICH lived at the castle in Prague, it was agreed that the attack should take place when he was travelling in his car from the castle to his office or to any known appointment.

47

Practical experiments proved that such an anti-personnel attack on a car must be carried out at a corner where it is forced to slow down. The two men were therefore told to obtain as much information as possible about HEYDRICH's movements in the first place, and then to get jobs as road sweepers. On the day chosen for the operation they were to begin sweeping the road at a selected corner. Their explosives and arms were to be concealed in their dustman's barrow and were to consist of three one-pound contact fused bombs, one four-second Mills bomb, one Colt Super 38 automatic pistol, to be carried by No. 1, and one one-pound contact fused bomb, one Colt Super 38 automatic pistol and one Sten gun (optional) to be carried by No. 2.

The first bomb was to be thrown by No. 1 at the front of the car when it came within 15 yards in order to kill the driver and so force the car to stop. The second bomb was then to be thrown broadside to hit the rear window, the panel just behind it or the rear door. Simultaneously No. 2 would open up with the Sten gun (or with his pistol if he had not been able to conceal the Sten under his coat). The Mills bomb was to be thrown into the car by No. 1 if HEYDRICH was not already dead, as contact bombs cannot be relied upon to explode if they hit soft surfaces. The last contact bomb was to be retained by No. 2 as a reserve in case of failure of the primary attack. If a hit was not scored, the party was to kill HEYDRICH at close quarters with their Colt Super 38 automatic pistols, which they would carry in shoulder holsters.

In the event of the operation being successful the Colt pistols and spare bombs were to be used during the withdrawal, which was to be made separately.

A suitcase containing 30-lbs of Plastic Explosive was also to be concealed in the dustman's barrow. This suitcase would be fitted with a five-second delay fuse and could be thrown bodily at the car or, as a last resort, No. 1 was to rush the car with the suitcase in his hand while No. 2 threw his last bomb at the front axle.

At the request of the party themselves the operation was planned so that no attempt at withdrawal should be made or considered until HEYDRICH had been successfully liquidated, and they made it quite clear that, unless the initial action were entirely successful, both members of the party would share HEYDRICH's death.[13]

Heydrich died from his injuries five days later. In retaliation, the Germans destroyed the nearby Czech village of Lidice. All two hundred male inhabitants were shot, the women were sent to concentration camps and the children to German institutions. Many disappeared without trace.

3

Washington Weighs In

THE OFFICE of Strategic Services (OSS) was set up on 13 June 1942 – six months after the Japanese attack on Pearl Harbor catapulted the United States into the war – under the inspired leadership of William 'Wild Bill' Donovan, one of America's most highly decorated American soldiers and a prominent Republican lawyer. Brilliant, mercurial, short-tempered, a man of great energy and courage, he would be responsible, more than any other individual, for the ultimate success of OSS. The organisation's original brief was to prepare intelligence studies, plan and execute subversive activities, and collect information through espionage. This was later extended to include 'psychological warfare', economic warfare, sabotage, guerrilla warfare and counter-espionage in support of military operations. At its peak, the OSS employed more than 13,000 men and women and established more than forty overseas offices, in cities ranging from Casablanca to Shanghai.

Memo dated 25 June 1942, containing a philosophical 'Primary Blueprint' for the creation and functioning of an OSS Secret Intelligence (SI) section in Eastern Europe:

Following the orders of Colonel Donovan we submit herewith the preliminary plans based on which initial actions operating an American Secret Intelligence System in Eastern Europe are proposed.

APOLOGETIC
Espionage is not a nice thing, nor are the methods employed exemplary. Neither are demolition bombs nor poison gas, but our country is a nice thing and our independence is indispensable. We face an enemy who believes one of his

51

chief weapons is that none but he will employ terror. But we will turn terror against him – or we will cease to exist.

Espionage is mentioned in the Bible and was employed by the Greeks and Romans. In 1870 thirty thousand German spies operated in France and the machinations of the *espion* in the World War are well known. But the League of Nations hoped to diminish secret intelligence by the simple expedient of publishing the military and naval strength of the forces of all nations so that all people would know about each other. Here we fell into the traps by which the honest man usually is trapped. The League knew the strength and intentions of the decent powers; the others kept theirs hidden.

Today our unpreparedness, born of the evangelical idealist's desire to see things the way he wishes them to be, and encouraged by clever secret foreign agents, also abridged our secret gathering of essential intelligence. We are, then, faced with the almost impossible task in time of war of creating a system of secret intelligence that could only have been efficiently established by painstaking preparation over long years of peace. The task would be hopeless except that we have scores of thousands of willing helpers, who, not deceived, maintained their intelligence services.

The Eastern European theatre is at once one of the most promising of all the scenes of future military action but also is a disjointed empire peopled by 100,000,000 aggressive willing friends and corruptible Axis dupes. By employment of the one and the seduction of the other, by cross-checking with the professional operators of our Allies, we can and must make up for lost time, speedily obtain the fullest intelligence and encourage the 'silent peoples' whose courage gained for us time while losing their own freedom and their lives.

On the one hand we must freely use stratagem and on the other, we must be frugal in civilized scruple. We are in a nasty business, facing a nastier enemy.

PROPOSALS FOR CREATING AN INDEPENDENT
AMERICAN SECRET INTELLIGENCE SYSTEM TO
OPERATE IN THE EASTERN EUROPEAN THEATRE
Our agents will describe all conditions in their areas; the number and sort of organized irregulars actively engaged against occupation troops, describing the nature and extent of their activity. Advice will be sent informing us of the attitude of the

public towards occupation authorities and troops, as well as a description of the 'puppet governments' and their relationship to peoples and conqueror. Names will be given of those who should be willing to collaborate or who are collaborating with occupation authorities.

(Note: Fighting an enemy as ruthless as ours, it will be necessary to develop a technique with no holds barred. It will be found that the elimination of dangerous persons frequently can be taken care of by the actual framing and betrayal of these traitors . . . neither scruple nor moral should deter our loyal agents in the prosecution of their duties, else they will neither produce, nor long exist.)

FURTHER DETAILS

Each area is divided naturally into districts or compartments in which agents' activities will be separated. It is advisable that each District have a central agent working on his own initiative, so far as possible communicating directly with the outside. Where this is not possible an elaborate chain with frequent 'cut-outs' will be necessary. District agents will select subagents on their responsibility from among the local population, again protecting themselves with such 'cut-outs' as are possible.

EQUIPMENT

Clothing – The item of clothing is important. Especially in Eastern Europe there are marked differences in dress in geographically near areas. In some areas peasants have rather extensive liberty of movement. Peasant dress is difficult – almost impossible to obtain out of the areas involved. Pioneer agents will have to secure such clothing for their colleagues who will follow. Exaggerations will have to be avoided. The sharp eyes of the primitive native are quick to detect the slightest incongruity in areas.

Middle-class garments are easier to procure in the Levant where many middle-class refugees have fled to neutral countries. Turkey is a fruitful field for the procurement of middle- and upper-middle-class clothes of Balkan origin. Clothes, however, cannot be in too sound condition. There is an acute shortage of clothing. Since greatest liberty of movement exists among the Vlachs and Kutso-Vlachs, the Nomadic tribes who have crossed frontiers from the beginning of time, garments of the upper-class Vlachs are of prime importance. However, this Section is examining and recruiting true Vlachs who, themselves, are the best authority on the costuming of their fellows.

Radio – Certain agents will be equipped with suitcase radios.

Weapons – In the wilder reaches of the Balkans, the common man is frequently armed. In some cases agents should carry modern small arms, but in others they should be provided only with the type of weapon common to the district in which he operates. Short knives are admissable and, on occasion, very useful.

Emergency Ration – Due to acute food shortage it is advisable to provide agents with concentrated foods and vitamins.

Money – Money is a powerful weapon of defense and offense, especially in the Balkans. Judiciously used, money will win the round in much of the in-fighting which the agent may face. Especially in the most eastern countries of this Section, the dollar is the most important coin. The Greek drachma, the Yugoslav dinar and the Bulgarian leva are vastly debased. Italian occupation lire and German occupation marks are unpopular and accepted only under protest. The circulation of United States dollars is not legal but dollars are in great demand and through age-old tradition the Eastern European welcomes black-bourse trading in 'better' currencies. Today a dollar brings from 1,500 to 2,000 drachmai, or more than two times the officially established rate. 'Loans' are privately negotiated between persons of mutual trust. A sum of debased currency is paid the 'borrower' against his pledged word to have deposited in the United States the agreed equivalent in dollars to the credit of the 'lender'.

Agents should be armed with both dollars and drachmai, and after establishing their bona fides will be able to negotiate the above described 'loans'.[1]

At the beginning, OSS was beset by bureaucratic problems. Lieutenant William Casey, US Navy (later to be director of the CIA), was an early recruit:

'It is no exaggeration to say that Donovan created the OSS against the fiercest kind of opposition from everybody – the army, navy and State Departments, Joint Chiefs of Staff, regular army brass, the whole Pentagon bureaucracy and, perhaps most devastatingly, the White House staff. When I came aboard, the OSS still had not won a final government charter setting out its functions and authority. Donovan [with his lieutenents] was spending an inordinate amount of time fighting a legal and bureaucratic battle for survival. They drafted paper after paper setting forth why the OSS needed complete organizational independence and the broadest possible turf for intelligence activities. At the same time they were on a tiresome merry-go-round handling countless requests and debates over OSS authority. Donovan would submit a request for manpower slots to the Joint Psychological Warfare Committee. The committee was made up of representatives of the army, navy, State Department, Board of Economic Warfare, Office of War Information, and OSS. Donovan was Chairman but such deliberations bored him and he rarely attended. So after hearings his request would be passed on to the Joint Staff Planners who would pass it on to the Joint Chiefs of Staff where it would go back to the Joint Psychological Warfare Board for further hearing. It was the kind of grinding opposition calculated to wear down anyone with the kind of imagination and lust for action that Donovan had. But nothing could alter Donovan's vision of the role intelligence had to play in a successful American war effort.'[2]

Although there would inevitably be rivalry between the two organisations, OSS and SOE agreed from the start that they would do their best to cooperate, as Sir Charles Hambro, executive director of SOE, confirmed in a letter to Colonel Donovan, dated 9 September 1942:

My dear Colonel,

On your last visit to London in early June this year, we both agreed and initialled a record of discussions between our officers which resulted in an agreement for the co-operation of O.S.S. and S.O.E. throughout the world, on the understanding that this agreement would not come formally into force until it had been submitted to and approved by United States Joint Chiefs of Staff and the State Department on the one hand, and the British Chiefs of Staff and the Foreign Office on the other.

I am happy to be able to advise you that I have received formal confirmation from both our Chiefs of Staff and the Foreign Office that they are agreeable to the arrangement reached in June coming into force as a binding agreement with no amendments of any sort. I understand your authorities have taken up a similar attitude.

I, therefore, suggest that by an exchange of letters (such as this one of mine to you and a confirmatory reply from you if you are in agreement) the June agreement should be formally ratified between us and come into full operation immediately.

Yours sincerely,

Charles Hambro[3]

Despite this agreement, SOE was privately concerned by the operational and bureaucratic chaos within OSS. This secret assessment was written by a senior SOE officer after a visit to Washington in October 1942:

OSS itself seems still extremely embryonic and not yet capable of any serious work. Donovan however does seem to be getting down to problems of organisation and certainly has a good man to help him in Magruder [*General John Magruder, deputy director*].

At present they are concentrating more on the Planning and Services side than on the operational side of their organisation. They are collecting a strong batch of experts who will form a Planning Committee and be capable of preparing what Donovan refers to as a 'plan' but which is really a cross between an appreciation and an outline of their projects . . .

They do not seem to realise, however, that they will never begin to get anywhere until they have developed their operational organisation, consisting of Country Sections (which they call Geographical Desks) at Headquarters and missions abroad. Their S.I. [*Secret Intelligence*] side has got a certain way along that road, but the S.O. [*Special Operations*] side has unfortunately scarcely begun. As yet, there are no S.O. Geographical Desks, except where the S.I. man is acting in a dual capacity, and there are, of course, no real organised missions abroad.

Unfortunately, Huntington [*Colonel Ellery Huntington*], who should be concentrating on the recruitment and training of these personnel, has to waste most of his time in waffling conferences with Donovan, Magruder and other senior officers, which are of no use to him whatever.

Neither Donovan nor Magruder really has the S.O. idea yet. They like to produce papers on the general strategy of the war and projects on broad general lines for the Psychological Warfare Committee and Chiefs of Staff without much regard as to who will carry them out or how . . .

Nevertheless, however much of a mess OSS might be in at the moment and however useless they are likely to be for the next six months or so, they will eventually get themselves straightened out and then will be a very important factor indeed in our sphere.

American resentment at England's still playing the leading part in this war is going to cause difficulties in all spheres. SOE's best insurance against trouble of this sort is the development of close collaboration with OSS. It will be easy now, when we can be of great help to them while they are still floundering in their initial difficulties, to get them more or less on the right track. It might be very difficult indeed, later on, when they have got the bit between their teeth, particularly if they are given the impression in these early months, that we have gone ahead without bothering about them.[4]

OSS was organised on similar lines to SOE, as was the recruiting and training. Everyone who volunteered was first asked a single, blunt question: 'Would you be willing to jump out of a plane behind enemy lines if you knew in advance that, if caught, you would be tortured to death?'

Anonymous OSS recruiter:
'Recruits might be picked out by talent-spotters as they passed through Bermuda en route from Europe to the United States, or identified as activists in American trade unions. A batch of Peruvian airmen, in New York on their way home from Italian flying schools, provided one recruit. Another was a Yugoslav-born American official of the United Mine, Mill and Smelter Workers Union. What seemed like faults to rigid disciplinarians of the regular services often appealed to us as evidence of strong will power and an independent cast of mind.'

Henry Murray, OSS agent:
'The whole nature of the functions of OSS was particularly inviting to psychopathic characters; it involved sensation, intrigue and the idea of being a mysterious man with secret knowledge.'

Antonio Martinelli, OSS agent:
'I remember there was a complaint from Washington that we had recruited too many "Mafia types" to fight in Italy. They were largely

Italian Americans, tough little guys from New York and Chicago, with a few live hoods mixed in, who couldn't wait to get back to the old country and start throwing knives.'

Lieutenant Elmer Kitchen, OSS:
'Besides going through basic infantry training, we were taught how to pick locks and blow safes, how to make booby traps, how to handle dynamite and plastic explosive, how to use knives, chloroform and poison and how to kill, silently, with our bare hands. I thought the worst part was jumping from a balloon in the dark. It is not at all like jumping from a plane. When you jump from a plane the wind takes you so fast horizontally that your chute opens almost before you have started to fall. But when you jump from a balloon, you drop about 250 feet before anything happens. It takes about five seconds for the chute to open. Everything is quiet; there is no horizontal wind, no roar from the plane's engine, just this terrifying sense of the increasing velocity of your descent from the sound of air rushing through your uniform. And since you can't see how close you are to the ground you start to think that your chute won't open in time.'[5]

Elizabeth McIntosh, a twenty-six-year-old journalist working for Scripps Howard Newspapers, was recruited into OSS while assigned to Washington to cover the White House:
'I hadn't heard of OSS at that time, I don't think anybody had at that particular point. It was a very hush–hush group that nobody talked about. I was following up a story and arranged to lunch with a man in Georgetown who later turned out to be one of Donovan's assistants, very high up in fact. I told him I wanted to get involved, especially after Pearl Harbor, perhaps as a newspaper correspondent overseas, as some of my buddies were doing. I was stuck in Washington with Mrs Roosevelt and I just wanted to get out and I felt that anything overseas would be serving my country. He suggested that I might be able to get a job working for the "government".

'I went back to the office after lunch and started thinking about it and mentioned it to my editor and he said, "You don't want to go and get in the government – we can send you overseas." But about a week later I got called for an interview in an office complex at 23rd and E Street. It was the administration building of OSS, although there was nothing outside it to say what it was, it just looked like a great big government building. There were about fifteen of us, men and women both, in a big room, sitting there, wondering what in the world we were doing, as they explained to us what it was all about, that the Strategic Services were designed to support the armed forces and this would involve not only behind-the-lines activities but also morale operations, disinformation that would work away at the enemy's will to fight. We were warned that if we were accepted we would have to swear not to mention, ever, where we worked and never to write a diary.

'It took about three weeks for the security checks, I guess, before I was told I was in. When I finally told my boss that I was leaving, he was a little mad at me. First of all, we were given a lot of stuff to read about what was being done in this particular field, in England especially, and then the training started. Men and women were mixed up. We were a very strange batch, because each one of us was going to do something different. I remember one was a doctor, he was always shaking his head at the things we had to do. There was a place where they would try to psychoanalyse you to figure out what you were capable of. One of the things they did was put you in a room and tell you someone lived there and we were supposed to figure out from the traces left behind who the person was, what did he do, what did he look like? It was a kind of a fun thing and everybody had a different idea. Another time we were told to go outside to where a group of men were building something or other and make them do it in a different way. I failed that completely, I couldn't persuade them. I was told later I should have picked up the pistol lying in the room where I was briefed and used it to make the men do what I wanted.

'We learned how to handle weapons and throw hand grenades out on the golf course at the Congressional Country Club in Maryland. The members were furious because we ruined the greens. I don't remember the training being particularly rigorous. There was a lot of writing stuff and sometimes we had to trail people, so that we would not lose track of them when we were in cars. A lot of speakers would come down and talk to us. Margaret Mead, the anthropologist, came to talk to us about the pattern of life of people of the South Pacific and how we should approach them – a lot of it had to do with the Japanese, Indonesians and Burmese, the people we were going to be dealing with, and the Japanese mentality.

'The training lasted about a month, it wasn't too long because they were shooting us over to Europe as quickly as they could. It was very enjoyable, especially the parties. There were a lot of drinking parties which I think were deliberate, to see how we acted in social situations and how we behaved after drinking alcohol. We figured this out, because we were plied with liquor.

You had to be pretty smart, on your toes and know what you were doing.'[6]

Major Frank Mills, US Army gunnery instructor:
'I had volunteered for overseas service, but when I was told that I had been selected for OSS, I didn't even know what the initials stood for. Someone told me it was the Overseas Supply Service. I think I may have been selected because I had studied French, but the truth was I couldn't really speak it. I was like every young college student – you study French for a couple of years, but you don't have any chance to practice it. So I reported to OSS headquarters in Washington and was rather surprised when I discovered what it was all about. There was never any discussion about whether or not I wanted to be a part of it. We all wanted to fight overseas, whether it was the Germans or the Japanese.'[7]

Major Franklin Lindsay volunteered to join OSS while he was serving with the US Army in Cairo. After parachute school he was sent to a British school for special operations on Mount Carmel, south of Haifa:
'My mornings at Mount Carmel consisted of training with German and Italian weapons, and demolition exercises using plastic explosives and various types of timers and detonators. Afternoons were spent on codes and ciphers, on arranging clandestine meetings, and on resisting interrogation.

'Evening mess at the school was a formal occasion with full uniform required. The commandant of the school, a lieutenant colonel, was addicted to liar's dice. He would assemble eight or ten of us after dinner each evening to play. Each time someone lost he was required to buy a round of drinks. I was the only American student and the commandant, on starting the game, always called out: "Where's my American major?" The game lasted until after midnight, through quite a few rounds of drinks. The commandant was rumoured to base our grades entirely on how we played his game. It was probably true since we never saw him at any other time.

'Thanks to the commandant's addiction, the mornings were sheer hell. I was roused out of too short a sleep at six with a cup of "sergeant major's tea" – very strong, very sweet, and lots of canned milk. The mornings were spent setting off explosive charges, or running through an obstacle course with sudden pop-out targets that I was expected to hit accurately with a sub-machine gun – all with a raging headache.

'But one afternoon made up for it all. It was the fulfillment of a lifelong fantasy. I was taken down to the Haifa railroad yards and taught to drive a steam locomotive. My instructor and I spent three glorious hours running the engine up and down the tracks blowing the whistle as we went – boyhood's ultimate dream becomes reality. The school's theory was that if one were being chased by the enemy and suddenly came upon a locomotive sitting on a track with steam up, a well-prepared person should be able to jump aboard and drive the locomotive off. While it was great fun and, I thought, would make a great movie escape scene, I figured the odds were heavily against ever being able to use that particular skill. I was wrong. A group of Yugoslav partisans, including Tito himself, escaped German capture by driving off on just such a fortuitously parked steam engine.'[8]

Major William Fairbairn, a former officer in the Shanghai police, was in charge of teaching recruits the black art of silent killing. Fairbairn had devised various techniques for dispatching the enemy using a double-edged commando knife of his own design and became notorious in SOE and OSS for his no-holds-barred attitude towards hand-to-hand fighting.

Lieutenant Aaron Bank, OSS, training at Milton Hall near Peterborough to parachute into France:
'He waited for a really dark, moonless night and had us called out for sentry-elimination training. We had been taught how to approach a sentry from the rear, snap an arm around his neck in a choke hold, and thrust a stiletto of Fairbairn design between his upper ribs while bending him backward. When it came to my turn, I approached the dummy, grasped it, and bent it back as I plunged my knife into, of all things, a knapsack instead of the ribs. Had this been for keeps, the sentry would not have been eliminated. All our previous practice had been on dummies without a knapsack. Fairbairn drove his point home. We never forgot. You had to determine before the attack whether a knapsack was being worn. A two-man elimination team was the safest and quietest, since one man effected the assault while the other grasped the sentry's rifle before it dropped, clattering, to the ground.'[9]

Fairbairn also served in Camp X, an SOE training school for OSS recruits on the northern shore of Lake Ontario in Canada. Lieutenant Geoffrey Jones, twenty-two-year-old OSS volunteer:
'You had to use the Fairbairn knife more like an épée than a dagger.

After some instruction, Fairbairn himself would stand in front of the class and say, "Today I am going to test you in the use of the Fairbairn knife," and then he would invite members of the class to try and attack him. On one occasion there was a big guy in front of me, he must have been about six feet four and 210 pounds, and Fairbairn said, "Come on, go for me," but he wouldn't do it. I suppose he was afraid of hurting the instructor. So Fairbairn got mad and yelled at me, "OK, Jones, you do it!" So I went out and circled him for a moment or two, then struck out with the knife and to my horror I managed to slash him down the side of his face. I thought, Jesus Christ, I've done it now, he's going to kill me. But he was delighted. All he said was, "Good boy, well done!"

'OSS was never just another military outfit, it was unique. People in Washington didn't even know it existed. We weren't supposed to tell anybody what we were doing or where we were. My family never knew where I was, whether I was at home or overseas. There wasn't even much social life, there wasn't the time. When we were training, it was up at six, work until nine, study until ten, then lights out and up again at six.

'The agent training was done at bases in northern Maryland, one of which is now Camp David. That's where we were given "sabotage" missions to test homeland security. Three of us were given a mission to blow up the boiler plant of a steel war-effort factory in Baltimore. We could use anything we liked to disguise ourselves, so we bought appropriate clothes in a hock shop, then got jobs in the plant. The idea was that we should put a note in the boiler saying "This is a bomb" and then call the FBI, which we did. The FBI got as sore as hell because we were successful. We were also given a telephone number to call if we were caught, but I heard when I got back to the camp that some of the guys, when they called the number, the FBI didn't believe them.

'My second mission was even better, because I got a bonus. I was told I had to get the plans of a steel plant in Philadelphia. I had a few friends in Hollywood, so I got a letterhead from Twentieth Century Fox and using my middle names – Montgomery Talbot – I wrote to the managing director and told him I was considering making a film about his plant's contribution to the war effort. OSS told us we could spend whatever we liked on a mission so I checked into a big suite of rooms in a hotel in the middle of Philadelphia and invited him and his wife over to dinner.

'After I had wined and dined them – I eventually ran up a bill of about $3,000 – he was delighted to show me round and I was able to note all weak spots where potential "saboteurs" could effect an entry. Then he took me out to lunch and I made several more visits, during which I was able to construct detailed plans of the plant. One morning when I was waiting in his secretary's office, I noticed she was working at a big typewriter, using carbon papers which she discarded in a wastepaper basket. I asked her what she was doing and she said she was typing out orders for raw materials. While she wasn't looking, I grabbed the carbon papers and was able to include in my report not only the plans of the plant but an itemised list of what was being ordered and what was being produced.

'When I got back to the camp my instructors were delighted but they were less pleased when they saw my hotel bill. After a bit of a row, they made me pay most of it myself. I was furious.'[10]

Robert Kehoe, aged twenty-one, was serving in the Army Signal Corps when he volunteered to join OSS:
'On arrival in Washington, we were escorted to the OSS offices in the old Navy Hospital buildings, where we had another medical examination and filled in more forms. Before coming to Washington, we had each completed a Personal History Statement that was used as the information basis for a quick investigation by the credit-rating firm, Dun and Bradstreet. There was, among us, little to investigate, but the inquiries by the investigators evoked curiosity among family and friends. I believe we all enjoyed the implied prestige.

'We then travelled to 'Area F', our temporary base in the grounds of the Congressional Country Club just outside Washington. It was a beautiful spot, and the tents scattered about added a note of romantic intensity to the lovely fall weather. We lived in the tents, but activities and meals were centered in the former clubhouse. It was here that I became acquainted with the men who were to be my close comrades for many months. They were a fascinating collection, possessing a wide range of language and specialized skills. There were, for example, members of the operational groups, whose training emphasized weapons and demolitions. They impressed us as being fierce people ready to throw the Germans out of occupied Europe on their own. They were not quite so forbidding on closer acquaintance; like most of us, they were big on talk but more cautious in action.

'We remained for a short time at Area F. This included a weekend leave (a quick trip home to New Jersey for me), more testing (mostly psychological), and the beginning of our training, with emphasis on physical conditioning. We spent the next six weeks at our main domestic training base, Area B-2. This base, in the Catoctin Mountains of northern Maryland, had been a private hunting lodge in pre-war days. OSS had taken over the base for specialized training of groups such as ours. With winter approaching, we were happy to be housed in cabins rather than tents.

'We were young and enthusiastic. At twenty-one, I was among the younger but by no means the youngest; some radio operators were twenty, and one was barely nineteen. The officers were not much older. One senior officer, John Olmstead, was affectionately called Pappy in recognition of his mature thirty-two years. All of us were eager to plunge into the training. Officers and men all received instruction in small arms – contemporary American weapons and a vast potpourri of foreign arms we might encounter in enemy-held areas, plus range firing, compass and map work, French language, a broad range of physical conditioning, and, finally, some orientation on conditions in occupied Europe and our possible role. We were to receive much more of this later in England. We practiced hand-to-hand combat using the famous Fairbairn knife under the guidance of the designer, British Colonel Fairbairn; at the least, this helped us develop a spirit of daring.

'Considerable attention was paid to conditioning for parachute jumping, which seemed pretty dangerous to most of us. A few officers had qualified as parachutists but only one of the radio operators had done so. These men laced their experiences with tales of adventure and horror. It was great cabin talk, with the listener's ability to absorb tales of gore regarded as a sign of toughness. The experience at Area B-2 was a great morale builder, and, when we departed in mid-December, we were in top physical condition.'[11]

Lieutenant Al Materazzi, aged twenty-six, Corps of Engineers:
'Donovan had convinced the Joint Chiefs of Staff and President Roosevelt that first-generation Americans of ethnic European descent should be recruited and sent back to their countries of origin to help organize resistance, so one fine day, shortly after I had graduated from Engineer Officer Candidate School, I got an order to report to Washington. At the time I had no idea there was such a thing as OSS.

'I was interviewed by a Major Russell Livermore, who later became the CO of all the operational groups in the Mediterranean, and Max Corvo, head of Secret Intelligence, who was there to test my Italian. Well, my Italian is from birth, I never spoke English until I was four or five years old, so I passed that all right.

Eventually they got round to asking me if I would be willing to volunteer to go back to Italy to work behind the lines. I don't remember volunteering, I think I said I would consider it, but, the next thing I knew was I got a set of orders to report to the Adjutant General, which was the cover for OSS, some temporary World War One buildings that had been erected along Constitution Avenue.

'Actually, I was happy at the thought of returning to Italy because I had a sister there with three children and the thought of seeing them was one of the things that spurred me. I did have some reservations about the possibility of firing on some cousins who might be fighting on the other side, but I put that to one side. I don't think I paid too much attention to the possible dangers, quite frankly. We were told we would always be in uniform [*OSS operational groups went into action in uniform, unlike agents working independently*] and we had the Geneva Convention explained to us, of course – all that was part of the orientation.

'We were supposed to get some preliminary training at a place called Area C, near the marine base at Quantico, but it was obvious whoever was sending down the training exercises didn't know anything. One of them was ridiculous. They put us in a truck on a very dark moonless night and dropped us on a road adjoining a dense wood, two at a time, about a hundred feet apart. They said the camp was on the other side of the wood and told us to go find it. Without a compass on a pitch dark night we would never have found our way. We were too smart to try that, so we hitched a ride into a town near the camp, found a bar, shot pool for a couple of hours, then called a cab to take us to the camp. The cab dropped us a couple of hundred yards from the camp gate and we just walked in. We never caught hell for it.

'The training at Area C lasted about three weeks, by which time OSS had taken over the Congressional Country Club, where a good part of the training concentrated on dirty tricks. There were pyramid tents on the parking lot out front, where we lived, and a lot of the lectures took place on the eighteenth green, as I remember. After that, they must have run out of ideas because they sent us to Fort Benning, Georgia, for an infantry course in jungle warfare. My God, where were the jungles in Italy? But we did get some preliminary parachute training and a lot of exercise and we came back from there real healthy.'[12]

Aline Griffith, a graduate from Mount St Vincent College, was recruited into OSS after complaining at a dinner party in New York that she was too young to serve overseas in the military:

'I was unaware that the work would be intelligence, despite the mysterious attitude of the man who informed me that tests for overseas work with the War Department would necessitate my using a false name and address when reporting in Washington DC. I also did not know then that my background and affiliations, as well as those of my parents and grandparents, would be investigated.

'The training at "The Farm", a country estate about twenty miles outside of Washington, was the same for men and women. During my weeks there, one other woman and about thirty men of different ages and nationalities were being prepared for intelligence work. Although students were predominantly American, there were Yugoslavs, a Belgian, several Frenchmen and a German or two. Frequently, someone would come back from Europe and give us a lecture on working "out in the field", but for the most part our training covered handling weapons, self-defense, detailed European geography, Morse code, coding, memory tricks, surveillance, organizing networks, recruiting agents, and anything else that our instructors had ever read in a spy story or seen in a movie. We were even taught how to roll a newspaper into a fine point to serve as a stabbing knife.

'When I was informed I would be going to Spain, I was advised to study that country and two other countries as well, so my companions at the school would not know which was to be my destination. We used code names to protect the secrecy of our identities, and we were constantly reminded that intelligence was a secret business and that we were not to trust anyone. Students were transferred to other schools if they could not put up with the grueling regime or if they divulged their identities.

'When being readied to fly to Spain, I was told there had been a triple agent working for our group who had blown the covers of many of our people and that I would be sent with a number-one priority because help was needed urgently. I left at night on a Pan American clipper from Long Island Sound, the only woman among about thirty-two men.

'In Madrid, the offices of the Secret Intelligence department of the OSS were on the second floor of a low apartment building on the Calle Alcala Galiano, number 4. Later, we moved for greater security to the attic of the American ambassador's residence on the Calle Eduardo Dato, which had been rented from the Duke of Montellano. We were made to realize from the start that the OSS's remaining in Spain depended on not irritating the ambassador, who was striving to get us out of the country. But despite our efforts not to, most of us got into trouble now and then.

'Most of us organized chains, as we had been taught, as soon after arrival as possible. We had been trained to keep all our activities secret from one another. For the head of my chain, I used a Spanish communist who had been a private secretary to one of the ministers in the Republican government. She was supposed to select one woman in whom she would have total confidence, since her life depended on this, and that woman would select another, and so on, until fifteen women had been recruited. That way I knew only one other member of the chain, the last woman only knew one; the others knew two, but no more, so that if we were to be caught the chain would not be uncovered in its entirety. These women were chosen to be located inside suspects' offices as charwomen, secretaries or maids.'[13]

Czechoslovakian-born Barbara Lauwers Podoski was pulled out of Women's Army Corps (WAC) officer training school and ordered to report to Washington when her language skills – she spoke French and German in addition to Czech and English – came to the attention of OSS:
'Neither I nor two other girls with me knew why we were pulled out of officer training. We were simply put on a train and sent to Washington, where we were given a bunk in the WAC barracks on C Street, before reporting to an OSS temporary office near the Lincoln Memorial. They told us nothing about OSS, not a damned thing. We knew it was the Office of Strategic Services, but what it meant nobody explained to us, although all of us had enough intelligence to realize it was something out of the ordinary. We were just given a very brief pep talk. We were told we were working for an elite group, that we mustn't talk about our work to anybody and if anybody asks us what we were doing, we were to say we were file clerks. The only thing we were told was: "Mind your own business, don't ask any questions, be available twenty-four hours a day, seven days a week."

'One of the things I had learned by then was that you don't ask questions. If you were told to do something you did it. My job was to sort out reports in various languages, identify the language – whether it was Slovene, Croatian, Serbian or Bulgarian, et cetera – and then file it. I'd work on these piles of various documents from eight o'clock in the morning with maybe a half an hour lunch break and finish in the evening when a truck came to pick us up. There was no time for small talk. I didn't even have the time to think about what was going on, but it seemed to me that most of the people in OSS were either from Harvard, Yale, Princeton or Wall Street and in between there were a few people with foreign accents, knowledge of foreign languages and a mentality that was not American.'[14]

Lieutenant William Casey was posted to London to run the OSS office under David Bruce, commander of OSS operations in Europe, and within two years was promoted to Chief of Secret Intelligence for the European theatre of operations. He was put on 'inactive duty' so he could wear civilian clothes and hold his own with much more senior officers. The London office worked closely with SOE and became the model for other OSS offices around the world:

'I had arrived in London toward the end of October 1943, and presented myself to Bruce. In this, my first visit to London, I surely contributed to the impression that moved Malcolm Muggeridge to comment, "Ah, those first OSS arrivals in London! How well I remember them, arriving like *jeunes filles en fleur* straight from a finishing school, all fresh and innocent, to start work in our frowsy old intelligence brothel; all too soon they were ravished and corrupted, becoming indistinguishable from seasoned pros who had been in the game for quarter of a century or more." The British traitor, Philby, then a high official in British intelligence, was no less unkind, characterizing us as "a notably bewildered group" whose arrival was "a pain in the neck". Yet only a year later that "bewildered group", working entirely on its own, was preparing, outfitting, documenting and dispatching 150 agents into Germany itself. And 95 per cent of them returned safely.

'Bruce gave me an office in his command suite at 70 Grosvenor Street, which housed the OSS European headquarters. The five-story brick building was smack in the middle of the wartime American compound in London. It was halfway down the street from the US Embassy. On the opposite side of the square, soon to be known as Eisenhower Platz, were US military headquarters. Our headquarters were bland, grey, nondescript. It had elevators, for which we were thankful, and was heavily guarded inside the front door.

'The atmosphere was informal. I recall an occasion when we gathered for a meeting in Junius Morgan's office. Raymond Guest, a lieutenant commander in the Navy, fresh from the polo fields of Long Island and Virginia, was in attendance. He was the chief of our maritime unit – three fast motor boats that the Royal Navy would not let out of their harbor. Guest barked at me: "Lieutenant Casey, get that chair!" Having somehow skipped basic military training, I said, "Get it yourself." That moment of tension passed. Later that afternoon Captain Morgan called me in. "Raymond has been here to say that I ought to call you before the mast. I don't know how to do that. But do try to be nicer to Raymond." I must have succeeded, because when Raymond Guest went back to Washington in October of 1944, he rented me his family's townhouse on Alford Street, off Park Lane.

'The London in which we lived and worked had the feeling of a city under siege. The beleaguered atmosphere enveloping the city came from the buildings, drab and unpainted, the preponderance of uniforms of all sorts and varieties, the scarcity of motor vehicles, and the strangely mingled sense of shabbiness, devastation and commitment. After long days at 70 Grosvenor Street we would feel our way home in the blackout, hoping not to tumble down a flight of stairs into someone's air-raid shelter in the basement. Later on, in those days of the little Blitz, we would expect the air-raid sirens to send us down for a while to the basement for shelter. But after we discovered how long the odds were on a bomb picking you out of the millions in London, we would go to the roof where we learned to tell whether the sound of the anti-aircraft came from Hyde Park or Regent's Park or St James's Park so we could put the chimney between us and any falling shrapnel.

'As we settled into our new life, the mission of our tiny headquarters group came into clearer focus. We had to sell ourselves and our organization to the various constituencies that made up the strata of wartime London. Our most indefatigable salesman proved to be Donovan himself, who came often to London.

'Whenever he could find time between visits to British and American headquarters, and discussions with Allied leaders, usually including Churchill himself, he would always hold court in a large suite at Claridge's. These sessions would always go on well into the morning hours. His barber and the overnight cables would be on hand at 6 a.m. to clear the way for an early breakfast.

'The thing that sticks most powerfully in my mind is my amazement at how and when he found time in four or five hours of privacy to get enough sleep and still go through the half-dozen or more books which I or Bob Alcorn or John Wilson would pick up for him. One of us would go to the Bumpus bookshop on Oxford Street and get any new books about military, political, legal or diplomatic events, whatever we thought he'd want to know about. Waiting in the General's suite, I would turn pages in these books and find them filled with underlinings and marginal comments. The drive and vigor with which, in the next few days, he would press headquarters generals and army commanders to make fuller use of OSS capabilities proved he got all the sleep he needed.

'Those capabilities, however, proved as hard to sell in London as they had been in Washington. Grudgingly, the British conceded that American wealth and power required a US intelligence capability, but they preferred to engage the OSS in new projects and to do so under British tutelage. Much to his later chagrin, Donovan agreed to British supervision. That meant we could not mount a single operation on our own without the approval of our hosts. Understanding the panoply of British clandestine operations – from intelligence and subversions to sabotage and resistance activities – became a necessity of survival.'[15]

Anne Mary Cairns, a twenty-year-old driver in the OSS motor pool in London:
'I knew I was working for a rather secret organization. I was briefed to keep my mouth shut, keep my eyes on the road and to ignore whoever was in the back seat. Once I picked up two civilians from Paddington Station and when they were settled in the back, they started to speak in French. Not wanting to compromise either them or me by eavesdropping, I thought I ought to tell them that I could speak French. One of them grunted a thank you and they switched to German. Increasingly embarrassed, I told them I could speak German too. At this, they started speaking Russian and I kept quiet for the rest of the journey.

'For each trip I had to sign a ticket with the name of the passenger on it and one night my ticket was General Donovan. I was supposed to pick him up outside the US Embassy and drive him to Claridge's. I was terrified. I said to the dispatcher, "Jesus Christ, please not me!" But it was no use. I remember polishing the big black Buick, unfurling the flag with two stars and praying that we wouldn't get stuck in an air raid or that I wouldn't run off the road. I needn't have worried. He saluted as I opened the door and gave me a big friendly smile. On the way to the hotel he chatted to me, asking me where I was from and what my plans were after the war. It was difficult talking and driving, but we made it safely and when we arrived he wished me good luck.'[16]

Operation orders for Lieutenant Marcel Clech, OSS wireless operator to INVENTOR network, dated 11 May 1943:

Operation: GROOM
Christian name in the field: BASTIEN
Name on papers: Yves LE BRAS

MISSION
You are going into the field to work as W/T [wireless transmitter] operator for two organizers, PAUL and ELIE. You will be under the command of Elie, whom you have met here and who will be traveling with you. Besides his job as organizer, he is to act as our liaison officer with Paul, who has an organization already established in the district bounded by Troyes, Nancy and Besançon.

APPROACH
You will go into the field by Lysander with Elie and his courier, Simone, to a reception committee at a point
  14 km. E.S.E. of Tours
  11 km. W.S.W. of Amboise
As soon as possible after your arrival, you will make your way to Paris to a safe address which you already know and stay there until you receive further instructions from Elie. This address is
  Monsieur Conie
  22 bis rue de Chartres
  Neuilly s/Seine
If, by any mischance, you should lose contact with Elie the following address is given you to enable you to get in touch with Paul
  Mme. Buisson
  203 ave. du Roule
  Neuilly
  Password: Amour, amour.
There you should ask to be put in touch with Monsieur Frager or leave a letter for him. Frager is the name by which Paul is known at this address. It is stressed that you should contact him ONLY if you lose contact with Paul.

METHOD

1. You have been given a cover story and papers in the name of Yves le Bras, which you will use for your normal life in the field. To cover your personality as an agent, you will use the name BASTIEN.

2. You will receive and send messages for Elie's circuit. You will send only those messages which are passed to you by Elie or which are approved by him. Although you are under his command and will take your instructions from him, you are the ultimate judge as regards the technicalities of W/T and W/T security. We should like to point out here that you must be extremely careful with the filing of your messages.

The circuit password of Elie and Paul is
'Je viens de la part de Celestin.'
'Ah, oui, le marchand de vin.'

FINANCE

You will be taking with you Frs. 151,335 for your own use. You will endeavour to keep an account of what you spend and will apply to Elie when you require further funds.

COMMUNICATIONS

1. You will sever your contact with the people who receive you as soon as possible and, after that, will refrain from contacting members of any circuit apart from your own.

2. As regards your wireless communication with us, we would stress that you should only be on the air when necessary and that your transmissions should be as short as possible. You will encode the messages yourself.

3. You will send us as soon as possible the address of a post-box through which we can contact you personally should the wireless communication break down.

4. You will also send us the address of a 'cachette'. Should you be in difficulties you will go to your cachette and advise us of the circumstances by coded letter or card to this address:

Snr. Leonel Martins,
20 Travessa Enviado Inglaterra,
Lisbonne.

We will then contact you at the cachette with a view to getting you out.

5. For communicating with us by other means than W/T, you will use your personal code.

CONCLUSION

You have had our general training, our W/T training and a W/T refresher course during your visit to this country. You have had our general briefing and with regard to the briefing herewith you have had an opportunity of raising any questions on matters that have not been clear. You have also had a trial viva voce of the methods outlined. You understand that you are to receive your instructions from Elie and that you are to carry them out to the best of your ability. If through any unforeseen circumstances, Elie should disappear, you will advise us and receive further instructions direct from us.[17]

4

La Vie Clandestine

*A*GENTS WORKING *in occupied France lived a lonely and dangerous existence. Cut off from friends and family, never able to trust strangers, constantly at risk from random searches, moving about with sometimes less than perfect false papers, they needed a modicum of luck, and considerable ingenuity, to stay alive, or at least out of the clutches of the Gestapo. The first problem was to blend unobtrusively into the community, the second was to maintain communications with headquarters and the third was to carry out their mission without being arrested. Communication was always the weak link − the only way they could stay in contact with London was by radio transmitter and as the war progressed German techniques for tracking down clandestine transmissions became ever more sophisticated.*

Henri Diacono, twenty-year-old wireless operator with the Spiritualist mission in Paris:
'When I left England they told me they were not expecting news from me for at least a fortnight. But as soon as I had recovered my wireless set I found that in the farm where we had been received there was a barn which was just right for my aerial so I thought I'll make a message straight away, telling them we have arrived safely. I put my aerial in place, connected my set and tuned on the right wavelength. Without searching I heard London calling me, but they couldn't hear me. I called them again and again but they couldn't hear me, so I said that's a real pity. You know what happened? I had forgotten to put my crystal in the set, so what I was transmitting was going all over the place and not in the direction of London. That was the first mistake.

'I stayed about ten days in that farm and after that I was introduced to the brother-in-law of René, who was a young student exactly the same age as me and he was the fellow who would be my guardian angel. When we left the farm to go to Paris by train, he was carrying the set. When we got on that train and I saw a German soldier for the first time, it was a little bit of a shock. I looked at him, and thought now I'm in an occupied country. But he looked at me as if I was just another Frenchman and so I soon relaxed.

'I lived for a little while in my friend's apartment but then I found a room of my own and everything went smoothly after that and I settled in my role of wireless operator. There was quite a lot of work to do, coding and decoding the messages. I enrolled at the University of Paris with my new false papers and settled into my role as a student, but working all the time as a wireless operator. I was a little bit isolated, you know. I didn't have much contact with the others and I didn't want to know what they were doing, so that if one day I was caught I would have less to say. It was difficult, stressful, to be on your own all the time. And I also had to take all sorts of security measures: never go out of the house without thinking of where I was going and what my cover story was, never cross a street without looking on the right and the left, but mostly behind to see if you weren't followed, to stop in front of a shop window to look if there was somebody following you, all sorts of things like this every day.

'One of the precautions I used to take was never to connect to mains electricity because when the Germans were trying to find a clandestine operator they used to cut the power to different parts of the town, and when they cut the power and at the same time the transmission stopped they knew that the operator was in that small sector. I used to connect my wireless set to a car battery which worked quite nicely. The other precaution was not to stay too long on the air. I also asked London to parachute me a few more wireless sets. I think in the end I had six or seven hidden with people around Paris.

'Most of the time I was relaxed but I remember one instance, at about one o'clock in the morning, I heard people coming up the service stairs of my apartment. Only Germans would be out after the midnight curfew and I listened and heard they were talking German. So I said, that's it, they are coming for me. I had time to swallow a piece of paper with some incriminating notes, but there was nothing else I could do. I was unarmed. I thought if they came to my front door the only thing I could do was to push them over the balcony outside my flat and try to escape. In the end they stopped at the flat underneath mine and arrested whoever it was who lived there. They were Gestapo. I heard them shouting at a woman, "Your husband's a spy!" or something like that. Either they went to the wrong flat or it was a fellow who really was something in the Resistance. Anyway, the next day I moved.

'Another day I was cycling with a friend to a point where I was going to transmit a message. We had the coded messages hidden in the tubes of the bicycles. I hated transmitting inside a house; I didn't like the idea of being in a room and suddenly having somebody who could open the door and arrest me. I liked to be outside in open space, where I could see things coming. It was a very hot day and we were very thirsty when we came to a small village with a peach tree outside one of the houses. We stopped and each picked a peach when suddenly the owner of the house, an old man, came out and started shouting at us. On the other side of the road there was a small café with German soldiers in it and they heard that fellow shouting at us and they came out and started arguing with him and us. That was very embarrassing because we couldn't do a thing but excuse ourselves, give him back his peaches and say we were very sorry· and we went on our way.

'Once, I was in a restaurant with a companion and suddenly I saw two fellows coming in, talking to the waitress and looking in our direction. After that they went out again and another one came in and again talked to the waitress, looking in our direction. I told my companion, don't move, don't do anything, but I think there's something queer going on. After that all three fellows came in, turned in our direction as if they were coming for us. One of them was taking handcuffs out of his pocket but he put them on the fellow who was at the table in front of us. It was apparently some black-market affair.

'I never carried a gun because I considered that it was useless. Once, I was getting out of the Metro and there were Germans stopping one person out of twenty or thirty. When you're in the crowd and you see people being stopped you wonder if you'll be one. I was. I was stopped and searched and if I had had a gun I would have been lost.'

Lieutenant Arthur Stagg, aged thirty, wireless operator with the 'Farmer' network in Lille, parachuted 18 November 1942:
'My first encounter with officialdom was while travelling on a train with my radio transmitter. I was going from Lille to St Erme Laon, near Amiens, to get in touch with a radio technician as I was having trouble with the set I had brought from England. We stopped at Douai, a station which was reckoned to be a checking point. This soon became apparent from the presence of two plain-clothes officers. They were very thorough. I had put the case containing the radio on

the luggage rack and left to go to the toilets hoping that somehow they might overlook me. But no, there was a loud knock on the toilet door ordering me out. Angrily, I answered, "Is one not allowed to go to the toilet?" I emerged from the toilet and returned to the compartment where the second officer was waiting.

'They asked what the case was, to which I replied that it was equipment for synchronising talkie films. The *douaniers* were not convinced. As there were other people in the compartment, I requested that we discuss the matter elsewhere. We proceeded to the end of the corridor. By this time I was getting nowhere, so the last resort was to hope that they were patriotic. I came straight out with it. "You are Frenchmen, aren't you? So am I. How about a thousand francs each?" They looked at each other and accepted this offer. By this time the train was approaching the next stop, so I said to them that I was getting off. I showed the officers the butt of my revolver tucked into my belt and threatened them I would shoot if they followed me.

'I left the train with my transmitter and, not surprisingly, no one followed. I deposited my set at the left-luggage office after asking that it be put out of harm's way on the top shelf as it contained medical glass vials. On leaving the station, I made enquiries about bus services to St Erme. After ascertaining times and place of departures, I found I had plenty of time, so I proceeded to an *estaminet* for a coffee and rum (this being obtainable off the rations). When the time drew near for the bus departure, I cautiously returned to the station but fortunately the case was exactly in the same position as it had been in the first place. So I went ahead and retrieved it and then went to the bus station. Suddenly a voice from behind me said "Is that the bus for St Erme?" I turned round and looked straight at a German officer. I replied, "No, it is this one." He said he was told it was the bus in the next departure bay from mine. My answer to this was that I should know which one, as I was going in the St Erme direction and that my bus was the right one. With this, the German officer was most grateful and offered me a cigarette. I then thought that as long as I kept in conversation with him, the better it would be for me. So this I did. We boarded the bus together and sat side by side talking about the weather in Germany.'[1]

Blanche Charlet, the courier for wireless operator Brian Stonehouse, code name 'Celestin', was arrested in Lyons while Stonehouse was transmitting from the house of a friend, Jourdan:
'Celestin was either receiving or broadcasting and I was encoding an

urgent message when the light went out. Celestin said that this meant danger. In fact, Jourdan, who was in the garden and had seen the police arrive, had cut the current. Celestin knew of a good hiding place in the cellar. As there was no time to burn the papers on which we had been working, we packed them all in the set and took it downstairs by way of a back staircase and buried the set in the sand behind a lift shaft.

'By this time, the house had been surrounded and we could hear men talking above us. We decided to go out and sit as innocently as possible in the garden, Celestin in his dressing gown. We sat outside on the steps talking. After a while, we saw a German coming towards us, he shouted and said something to us, pointed a gun at us and pushed us towards the front of the house.

'Meanwhile, the Germans were searching the house and found the set. I think that in our hurry we had probably not buried it properly. In the meantime, I had managed to give Mme Jourdan my personal address and my keys, and asked her to go and burn some compromising papers which I had hidden there. I was put into a car with a German and a French police inspector. I had in my bag a small notebook containing all the compromising names which I had managed to hide underneath a pot in the garden while the house was being searched; I slipped it underneath the cushions of the car during the drive to the police station.

'When we arrived at the police station, Celestin and I were left alone long enough to arrange what we would say. Celestin was interrogated first, and when I came into the room after his interrogation, I was asked for my address. I answered that I could not give it for sentimental reasons, explaining that I was the mistress of a married man, and that his wife was probably back by now, and I did not want to compromise the married life of my friend. Also, I said that as I had been arrested with Celestin, I did not want my lover to think that I was his girlfriend. At that time I did not know whether Mme Jourdan had been arrested or not and it was therefore imperative for me not to give away my personal address. Obviously, the fact that I had failed to disclose this gave the police grounds for suspicion. When they asked me whether I knew that Celestin was a W/T operator, I replied that I did not even know what a W/T operator was.

'I was then put in prison and interrogated every day on small details. The men were on a different floor from the women, but the women were allowed out into the courtyard for a walk every day and as the men's cells were on the ground floor, I was able to communicate with Celestin and we were able to find out what each had said. The main preoccupation of the police during these interrogations was to find out my address. It was therefore vital that I found out whether the papers in my flat had been destroyed. I managed to pass out a letter by the canteen manageress, warning Aaron [*another member of the network*] that I had been arrested, and asking him to tell me if my flat had been emptied of all compromising material.

'On 1 November, I was fetched from my cell by two policemen who took me to the office of the Commissaire, who greeted me by saying, "*Bonjour, Christiane*," my code name. At first, I thought I had been betrayed by the canteen manageress who had passed on my message. As Aaron did not know me by any other name, I had had to sign my note "Christiane". I was, however, told by the Inspector that they had found, among the papers which had been hidden with the set, a coded message giving the address and the password of Aaron's office. They had visited it and had found my prison note. Aaron was arrested a few days later.

'In the office where I was taken were several Germans and a French police Inspector. I was asked if I was really Christiane. I pretended to faint, and when I recovered, pretended to play the part of a stupid woman who wanted to play her glorious part in the Resistance but knew nothing about it. I said that I had only worked with Celestin for eight days and therefore knew very little about what he did. They asked me if the Jourdans knew anything about the activities of Celestin and myself, to which I replied that they knew nothing about it, and that my greatest remorse was the fact that I had taken advantage of their hospitality by using their house for transmitting.

'I, Celestin and another wireless operator who had been arrested in Lyons, were taken to Castres prison on 13 November 1942. While in Castres, I made friends with a Yugoslav who cleaned the prison. They were not supposed to talk to us prisoners, but the discipline was fairly lax. We were not locked in our cells, and the door of each floor was the only one locked. I had a long talk with the Yugoslav and asked him if he could not help us to escape. He replied that this was quite impossible, that everything was guarded and that such an attempt would be bound to fail. Two days later, I heard footsteps at about nine o'clock at night, outside my door. The door opened and the Yugoslav appeared, telling us that the prisoners had free run of the prison for two hours. The warders were all locked in the cells, except for one or two who were in the plot. We met downstairs ten minutes later and were put in the charge of a young Frenchman, who knew the way to the pre-arranged rendezvous.'[2]

Charlet took refuge in a Benedictine monastery and after a failed attempt to cross the Pyrenees into Spain she was taken out of France by sea in April 1944.

Roger Landes, wireless operator with the 'Scientist' network:
'The whole time I was in France I only twice forgot myself and spoke in English. The first time was on the day after I arrived. I slept the first night in the mayor's house and next morning when he knocked on my door I said, "Come in." The second time was in Bordeaux. I went to the hairdresser and he was cutting my hair and asking me questions and at one point I said "Yes" to him. But he didn't take any notice, you know.

'I used to transmit from a house on the outskirts of Bordeaux. There was a garage which looked as if it belonged to the house next door and I always used to go in through the garage. I kept my set under the bed in the main bedroom. One day I arrived at the house to transmit and as I opened the garage door, the woman's daughter, a girl of about sixteen, said, "Mama has been arrested this morning and they are looking for a British officer who is transmitting to London." Luckily they hadn't found my set. I tried to get rid of it by dumping it in the septic tank, but it was too big. Then the girl told me there was someone from the Gestapo keeping watch on the house. She said that he'd been there for about three days and that from time to time he would go into a café opposite for a drink. The girl asked what she should do with the set and I said, "We'll fix it on the back of my bicycle. When you see the fellow from the Gestapo going into the café, tell me and I will leave at that time." And so I waited in the garage until she said, "Now you can go!" I went out into the street and got on my bicycle but right in front of the café the suitcase with my transmitter inside fell off. Just at that moment the man from the Gestapo came out of the café. When he saw my suitcase on the floor he helped me to put it back on the bicycle. He had been told to look out for a British officer but I was small and was wearing a big Basque beret and didn't look in the least like a British officer. I just said, "Thank you very much," and cycled away. He never knew I was ready to shoot him.'[3]

Yvonne Cormeau, wireless operator with the 'Wheelwright' network in the Gironde, volunteered for SOE after her husband had been killed during an air raid in London. She dropped into France on 22 August 1943:
'My boss was Lieutenant Colonel George Starr. His code name was Hilaire and he had been in France since November 1942, organising

his circuit, setting it up and finding the people. When he asked for a radio operator, he made it a condition, owing to the recruiting by the enemy of young men for obligatory labour in Germany, for someone over the age of thirty-five to be sent out. London's answer was to send him a woman. He must have cursed!

'It was a completely different kind of life to what I had lived before and I must admit to butterflies floating in my tummy all the time. You had to be very careful, with eyes in the back of your head as well as in front. We didn't want people to know much about what I was doing but those who offered me a roof and offered me food always knew that I'd come from England and that I had a wireless set. They were asked beforehand, "Would you take a radio operator?" because that, more than anything, doubled the danger for them. And I'll give it to these people, not once was I refused accommodation. As the area was quite big, I would stay three nights, at the most, in one house.

'In a way, I was left to my own devices in whatever house I was in. I tried to help with the housework, it was about all I could do. First of all, I took the cover of looking after the children or something like that to enable the women to go to work in the fields when their husbands had gone. But moving around so much, that became too difficult and then I tried to be a district nurse with my bike, going about the countryside on a bike. That worked very well. At other times, there had to be another cover, because I was going to spend about five days in one place, simply because I had toothache and therefore two visits to the dentist had to be covered.

'On that occasion I was asked to look after the cows, take them out in the morning and bring them back at sunset. It was a very hot day, September, but still hot, and I went out into the field, closed the gate so they could not get out and sat down in the shade of the trees in the corner of the field. I was given two tomatoes, a chunk of bread and a teeny bottle of wine for my lunch and when the sun seemed to be getting at its hottest, I had my little meal and gave up looking at my cows. I turned my back to them and half slept, I think. Before going out, the farmer's wife had told me not to wear a watch, because no woman who looked after cows would be able to afford one, so I had no idea of the time. When I woke up I noticed the cows were moving towards the gate and I wondered if it was time for them to go back. The rays of the sun were getting pretty long, so I opened the gate and we went back, through the courtyard, to where the cows lived and then I found I had one animal too many and this created a great hullabaloo. I went to the farmer's wife to ask her where to put the sixth cow and she said, "There are only five." We discovered then that one had come through a hole in the wire and at the same time a very irate neighbour rushed into the courtyard claiming that I had stolen his cow. This cost me my job looking after cows.

'After the war I discovered that the Gestapo knew there was an Englishwoman in the region with a clandestine radio transmitting in five-letter groups. They knew it was a woman's fist on the key. They found someone who was willing to talk, a Spaniard, a communist running away from Franco, who told them that I was transmitting from a village called Castelnau. But in that one department alone there were eight Castelnaus and they never happened to come to the one where I was because it was such a small hamlet it had no electricity or running water and in their methodical way they'd decided no Englishwoman would live in such primitive conditions.'[4]

Once the Germans became aware of the extent of the radio traffic between occupied France and London, they set up special direction-finding units to track down the operators. Captain Hubertus Freyer was in command of one such unit in northern France:

'At the beginning we had no experience at all. All we knew was that there were radio agents working with England, and it was our job somehow to find them and catch them. At first, there were only three or four transmitters in the whole area, but later there were much more than a hundred and with every month the war was continuing, we became better and better at our job. We exchanged all our military vehicles for civilian vehicles of wooden construction that would not disturb our direction-finding equipment and we made them look like tradesmen's vehicles, with removable signboards for a laundry and baker and local registration plates.

'As we became more experienced we could identify a triangle in which the agent was transmitting and then we would send in the near-field direction finders, the *Nahfeldpeiler*, to take bearings nearer. He would be a man with a wire running through his sleeve into his ear, probably hidden under a beret, and he would stroll through the triangle rotating his equipment. When you got close you had to look for the antenna and see where it went inside. Most French houses have their fuse boxes outside, so if you screwed out a fuse and the transmitter stopped you knew you had him.

'As you closed in, you had a lot of adrenalin running in your blood, but I didn't like much having to seize and arrest men. I didn't think it was suitable work for a soldier. The captives reacted in totally different ways. Some were calm and superior, some of them knew what would happen to them and accepted it. In one case we found a ticket from the London underground railway in a pocket of an agent who had just been dropped, and in another case we found he was wearing a coat which had been made in England, which was not very helpful to him.

'When we captured an agent, first it was important to find his security check, or to force him to give it to us. Mostly they didn't want that, but in most of the cases we found it. It was important because we wanted to use the transmitter to send false messages to England and without the security check they would know that it was in enemy hands. When we captured a man we explained to him how unpleasant it would be when he was handed over to the executive – normally he would be shot according to martial law. When he would come into the hands of the Gestapo, they would have finer methods to kill him off, and this would not be very pleasant. If he wanted to save his head, he would have to help us and play a part. And some said "Yes" and joined in. They were scared because they knew for them it was the end of the song – not very pleasant!

'When we wanted to start a "game", sending messages to England, we had to get authorisation from OKW Berlin [*German high command*]. We sent our proposals to Berlin but might wait weeks for authorisation and meanwhile our "head office" in England was becoming impatient. So we would send them messages in which we didn't say anything important and which we used to ask for supplies, like tea or coffee or things like that, to be sent by parachute. We got a lot of good things like that. When an agent with a transmitter was willing to work with us, he was observed very closely. There was always a specialist sitting next to him, who inspected every key-pressure and who paid attention that he didn't give them something wrong. And normally they didn't try that. That worked actually well.

'We called it a game because that's what it was – we were playing with England. When they didn't recognise that a transmitter was in our hands, they gave us a lot of instructions for the organisations and we came to know the members; sometimes they even gave us the names. It was through one of these games that we found out a leading agent was to meet someone at a café in Paris and so we went to arrest him. We caught him and were taking him to our car when he hit the officer with me in the chest and ran away. I followed him as he ran down into the Metro and tried three times to shoot him, but there were crowds everywhere and he got away. Then we got a message from England that he was in this certain hospital. We went to the hospital at three o'clock in the night, but they told us they didn't have anybody with a gunshot wound. So I asked "Well, do you have anybody who maybe has a fracture at the arm or leg?" They said they did, so we went upstairs to his room and it was the man we wanted. When he saw me, he said, "My compliments, you are a good shot." I had hit him in the arm three times with my three shots. I found that fantastic!'[5]

Jean Holley, a wireless operator in Lyons, was picked up by a direction-finding team:
'Everyone has their own style of transmission. For example, if the operator is nervous, this can be detected in the sound quality. If someone is experienced and confident, then the transmission is fast and expert and the sound quality is regular and peaceful. Every operator, in this way, has his own signature even if they are all transmitting the same thing. This is how the Germans were able to identify each radio operator. When I was captured, the Germans showed me a whole filing cabinet of messages that I had transmitted but which had not been decoded and which they were guarding zealously.

'When I was arrested, the Germans themselves told me how they pinpointed wireless operators. Apparently, there was a listening centre in Berlin which controlled all radio output operations and which was able to identify the direction from which the transmissions came. If they came from France, then the Germans alerted their people in Paris and so it was narrowed down. In my case, I was operating in the Lyons area and they tracked me down there. In Lyons, there was a sort of direction-finder van in operation, a *radiogoniometre* vehicle, which picked up the messages and concentrated on detecting me and the exact position I was in. This was exactly how it happened on the day I was arrested.

'On this particular day, I was transmitting in Annecy, at the house of the wife of an officer of the Free French Army. There were children in the house, so, as a precaution, I had unloaded my pistol and put it in my suitcase. I was working away at the wireless, when the lookout said to me, "The direction-finder van has just arrived." So immediately I stopped the transmission and folded up the equipment. There were three of us, the lookout, myself and another radio operator who was going to replace me. So we waited several hours, without moving, to see what would happen. After these hours had passed, we were told the danger was over and so the three of us departed from the house. And that was our mistake: the three of us left together to go to the hotel where

I had rented rooms. The Germans had left someone behind, who followed us to the hotel, and the next morning they followed us to the station at Annecy, and on to the train.

'We were sitting on the train at the Annecy station and suddenly, we saw a large number of people on the platform. From the way they walked it was easy to recognise them as Germans and it was obvious they had come to arrest us. Now, I didn't have my gun, because it was in my suitcase and the only thing I could do was run for it. So, I just jumped right into the middle of them and tried to lose myself among the crowds who were waiting for trains. But a large, well-built German, much bigger than I was, ran after me, tackled me to the floor and whacked me in the face with his fist, crying, "You bastard, I've been after you for four months."

'In a weird sort of way, I was quite pleased to realise that I had been leading them by the nose for as long as four months. They put me in handcuffs and loaded me on to a lorry, accompanied by French policemen who seemed to be very annoyed, and took me off to the barracks at Annecy. During my brief flight, I had been able to empty my pockets of all my keys – nine altogether, including for the postbox and for the flat I was living in.

'We were put into the cells in Annecy. Once there, as I did not have my cyanide pill on my person, I tried to hang myself. I am still suffering back pains as a result of it. I strung myself up, but the material I used was not strong enough and it snapped, so I fell to the floor, making a great deal of noise. The Italian sentry who was guarding me heard the noise, opened the door and beat me with his rifle butt. It wasn't particularly serious, he simply thought I was trying to escape.

'My decision to try and commit suicide was completely normal and rational. I knew I would have to face an interrogator and I couldn't swear that I wouldn't talk. It is simply not possible to say if a person will yield to torture or not. One never knew. So there remained nothing for me to do but kill myself. That was the reason we were given cyanide pills, to prevent anyone from talking under torture. I realised this, but as I had no pill I had to find another way.

'They left me there for a few hours, I don't know how many, and then the Germans returned, picked us up with our hands cuffed behind our backs, and put us in vehicles and took us to Lyons. In Lyons, the Hôtel Terminus had been selected as their particular base. So, we arrived at the Hôtel Terminus, where the Germans occupied the top two floors and the hotel's normal clients used the rest. The three of us were separated and interrogated individually. This was a nuisance, since no one knew what the others were saying.

'I stuck to the story I had rehearsed in England. The method of interrogation used by the Germans was to ask a question and if they didn't like the response, they called in a couple of men to beat you with a cosh until you gave them an answer they liked. Then they asked a second question and it began all over again. I think, though I am not sure, that the whole procedure lasted two to three days. I was forced to lie on my stomach while they beat me, so I was unable to see anyone. I think there were at least four Germans working on me.

'The advantage of being beaten with a cosh was that they beat you only on the buttocks and the calves of my legs, they never got near my head. That would have been dangerous because damage to my head would have meant that I would lose control. In this way, I was in control of myself. The mad thing was that when they beat me, I screamed with the pain, and eventually, one of the Germans asked me not to scream so loudly, because the hotel guests on the lower floors would be disturbed. And so I did scream less loudly! I could see that they were swallowing my story whole so I continued with it and never once changed my original answers to their questions. Eventually, they must have believed that I was telling the truth.

'They told me that I was going to be transported to Paris and made to do radio transmissions for the Germans. In the end, this never happened, as I was deported to Turin, since Annecy, for some reason, fell under the jurisdiction of the Italians.'[6]

Captain Oliver Haward Brown, SOE agent in occupied France:
'You never knew how you were going to react if you were caught. One day I was just wandering about, not doing anything at all, when I was picked up. Germans would randomly pick up a whole bunch of people and take them for interrogation and I was picked up in one of those raids. The only thing I had got on me that was incriminating was a book with a coded message in it that I was going to get Smithy [*his wireless operator*] to send to London later that day.

'So we were herded into this room, and as I got in, I just put the book on a desk. My papers passed, everything passed, no trouble at all and I was told I could leave. I went outside and then turned and went back inside and said to the German guard, "Oh, I left my book behind. Can I get it?" He said it was fine, so I picked up the book and left. Now I would never have thought of doing that if it had not been for the training at Beaulieu: I would have automatically picked up the book when I went out and he would have said, "I'll take a look at

87

that." But as I gave the impression the book was so unimportant that I almost forgot it, he never thought of examining it.

'The unexpected was always the great danger. We nearly bought it in the very early stages when we arranged to meet Raoul in a certain farm. Smithy was there, for some reason or other, even though he didn't speak French, and I said to him, "Smithy, what's the matter? You seem curiously on edge today." "Yes," he said, "I don't know but something doesn't smell right to me." Anyway, we finished the meeting and Smithy wandered out into the garden and came back and said, "Oi, there are some bloody Krauts out there." We hadn't been warned that there were Germans in the area but they had somehow found out that we were there. Fortunately, there was an outside loo, as there was in most places in those days, and we started off down there as if we were going to it. I said to Smithy – we could see the Germans by then – "Walk, Smithy, walk as slowly as you can and when I say run, run and break the record for the one hundred metres." We had got to the other side of this loo before the Germans woke up to the fact of who we were. I said, "Run!" and we were out of there. And that was that. We never even got fired at, not once. But they burned the farm down and in the farm were all our uniforms and everything else, all our clothes. So, in the end, I went back in the clothes that I had started out in. I never changed the whole time I was there. When I got back to London, I went to my mother-in-law's and she opened the door to the conquering hero and immediately said, "Go and have a bath. You stink!"'[7]

Francine Agazarian, wife of Jack Agazarian, the radio operator in the 'Prosper' network, landed by Lysander on 17 March 1943 and joined the group in Paris:
'Although we were in the same network, my husband and I were not working together. As a radio operator, he worked alone and transmitted from different locations every day. I was only responsible to Prosper [*SOE agent Francis Suttill*], whom we called François. He liked to use me for special errands because, France being my native land, I could get away from difficulties easily enough, particularly when dealing with officialdom. For instance, calling at town halls in various districts of Paris to exchange the network's expired ration cards (manufactured in London) for genuine new ones.

'From time to time I was also delivering demolition material received from England. Once, with hand grenades in my shopping bag, I travelled in a train so full that I had to stand pressed against a German NCO. This odd situation was not new to me. I had experienced it on the day of my arrival on French soil, when I had to travel by train from Poitiers to Paris. A very full train also. I sat on my small suitcase in the corridor, a uniformed German standing close against me. But, that first time, tied to my waist, under my clothes, was a wide black cloth belt containing banknotes for Prosper, a number of blank identity cards and a number of ration cards, while tucked into the sleeves of my coat were crystals for Prosper's radio transmitters. My .32 revolver and ammunition were in my suitcase. The ludicrousness of the situation somehow eliminated any thought of danger. In any case, I believe none of us in the field ever gave one thought to danger. Germans were everywhere, especially in Paris; one absorbed the sight of them and went on with the job of living as ordinarily as possible and applying oneself to one's work.'[8]

Jean-Marie Regnier, head of the 'Mason' network based in Lyons, took the train when he needed to deliver a radio transmitter to Toulouse:
'At Toulouse station, there was only one way for passengers to get out and this involved passing between two lines of police, customs men and officials checking our cards. They picked people out at random to look at their identity cards and examine the contents of their luggage. My suitcase containing the transmitter weighed eighteen kilos, which obviously made me walk rather heavily and so there was a good chance that I might attract unwanted attention.

'Suddenly an idea came to me. Crowds of passengers were starting to file through the two lines of officials, and on my immediate left stood a very smart-looking captain in the Armistice Army. Just as we reached this human funnel I knocked my suitcase quite hard against the captain's right leg. He staggered and gave me a thunderous look. I apologised profusely and went on talking to him, all about the problems of making a journey nowadays and how exhausting it was – and I continued talking all the way down the inspection line. Admittedly, I got no response whatever from the captain, and he must have thought me a terrible windbag. But the police and other officials, seeing me talking to this army officer, did not dare pull me out for a spot check.'[9]

Dorothea 'Coco' McLeod, twenty-one years old, fluent in French, Dutch and Flemish, was sent on a mission to northern France in June 1941. She had grown up in Belgium and knew the area well:
'I used to go on a bicycle from village to village. I always kept on the village roads, or on a dirt track road – the whole of Flanders was criss-crossed with dirt track roads. I knew them very well from

when I was a child and was familiar also with the dunes because we had spent summers up there as children. We did a lot of movement after curfew. We knew what time soldiers were on duty, more or less, from watching them, what time they would go into the pub for drinks, when they would go off duty. The soldiers in the coastal villages did not like to go out into the country roads on their own, or even in twos. They were often frightened, as many disappeared.

'I didn't carry a gun but I had a knife and I did use it on one occasion against a German. It wasn't very nice. I was at a railway station in the country, trying to plant some Semtex on one of the railway signal boxes, when I came face to face with a sentry. I was going round the signal box to tell the chap inside that I was going to start planting the explosive and he came round from the other direction. I think he was more shocked than I was, so I was quicker to react. I knifed him and he died – immediately. I was quite good at that sort of thing. After I did it, I had to get the chap from the signal box to help me with him. We dragged him further down the track and left him lying across the lines so the first train would run over him. I hoped no one would notice he had been knifed. I felt numb afterwards; it did upset me for quite a while. I began to grow up after that incident and ask myself, what am I doing? It all became less of an adventure after that. The thing I had hoped never to have to do – to kill someone – had come at me, sheer out of the blue. If I hadn't had the quicker reaction, I wouldn't be here today.

'I was eventually betrayed by a girl from my own village, I think a little bit out of sour grapes. She had always been envious of my family, her mother had been one of the cleaners at our home in Belgium. Anyway, she had got very involved with an SS chap and they were on holiday in one of these places where I was operating and she spotted me. That's how I was caught. I was staying in what was supposed to be a safe house near Le Touquet and they just walked straight in and took me. I was taken immediately to Paris, to St Denis, a former women's prison. After I had been in the prison a few weeks I was interrogated. It was pretty brutal – they knocked some of my teeth out. They wanted to know who I was working with, things like that. I agreed with all the information they had about me – where I came from, who my father and mother were, et cetera – but I never gave them any real or significant information.

'I was very fortunate in that, although I was kept in solitary confinement, a lot of the people who looked after the women's prison – cleaners and laundry people – were in the Resistance. They eventually got me out. I didn't know what was happening or who was taking me. They just came into my cell one night, blindfolded and gagged me and put me in a laundry box. Next thing I knew, I was in the laundry box, in a field, no idea where I was at all. Soon afterwards I was shoved into a plane and went back to England.'[10]

Robert Boiteux-Burdett, code name 'Nicholas', a member of the 'Heckler' network in Lyons:
'After six months in the Lyons area I had a fair number friends, teams of agents and men trained for sabotage operations. As I had three flats in different suburbs of Lyons, there was always some safe place for me to go. This particular night, we'd had the curfew at six o'clock and I spent the evening in my flat reading and making plans. It wasn't until nearly nine o'clock that I realised the police were in the middle of searching the district. Too late to move: in the street I would be picked up straight away. The streets were being combed by lorries full of German troops and French police. In my flat I had about fifty kilograms of explosives and a transmitter set. But the die was cast; there was nothing I could do but wait and see what happened. As well as the explosives and the radio set, a courier had arrived from Avignon with messages to tap out on my transmitter. The courier, a young woman, had been worn out after travelling all day standing on a bus, and she was now sleeping in the room next door.

'I tried to read, but was far too worried to concentrate on whatever the book was. It was not until two in the morning that I heard someone knocking on the doors of the flats below mine. My heart was beating at twice the normal speed, my mind was racing with thoughts of what sort of sentence I would get . . .

'My explosives were hidden in a little cupboard under the window, a place where one normally kept coal and logs for the fire. The explosives were covered with bits of kindling and if these were moved it would be impossible to miss the explosives; they would never escape even a simple search. And my transmitter was in a big drawer in my bureau, so I had no hopes of avoiding trouble. Shortly after I'd heard the first noise in the building, someone knocked at my door. I opened it and found myself facing two plain-clothes French policemen and a third man in uniform holding a revolver which was pointed at me. "We've come to search your flat," one of them said, and while the plain-clothes men started searching, the one in uniform kept me under guard, his revolver covering me all the time. I did my best to look calm but my nerves were in a terrible state. I felt the search would never end. They looked everywhere, and I still don't know how I stood the shock when they opened the log cupboard. They were, I think, very wary about soiling their white hands, for they didn't deign to touch any of the logs. They slammed the cupboard door shut without noticing anything unusual. They went on searching and came now to the bureau. They opened one drawer after another – and then the one where the transmitter was. I couldn't watch, it was too much to bear. When I heard the drawer being closed again, and realised they hadn't found anything, I could hardly believe my luck.

'In France, as in England, everyone had to observe the blackout. My flat was very dark, the transmitter was only small, and it was hidden right at the bottom of a very deep drawer. It was undoubtedly this that saved my skin.'[11]

Gilbert Turck, code name 'Christophe', ended up in Buchenwald after being betrayed while working in Paris:
'I had been meeting with other Resistants in the back room of a small shop called France Parfums on the Boulevard St Germain and I stopped at a *pissoir* on my way home. When I looked up, I suddenly saw three men in civilian clothes, with guns drawn, advancing towards me from different directions. There was no possibility of escape from that situation; I was handcuffed and taken away.

'The questioning was very thorough and went on for a long time, but I did not give them any information. My main worry at the time was that my fiancée would be compromised. I had borrowed her bicycle permit and, seeing that, they went off to search her apartment, where I had stacked a lot of explosives in an old armchair on one of the landings on the staircase. I learned later that they turned the apartment over, but never took a second glance at the armchair on the stairs.'[12]

Frederick Forest ('Tommy') Yeo-Thomas, a bilingual Englishman who had lived most of his life in France, was leader of the Marie-Claire mission in Paris:
'On four occasions I was trailed but threw off my followers. The first time was on the occasion of an appointment with Oyster [*code name for fellow agent Georges Pichard*] in front of the Madeleine. Neither of us was followed prior to meeting and as we walked off together we noticed a man who had been standing nearby, seemingly with nothing to do, fall in about twenty yards behind us. We ascertained that he was really following us by making a few detours, and having made sure that he was definitely interested, we made tracks back to the Madeleine Metro station arranging to part very suddenly; Oyster

was to dive into the Metro and I was to cross rapidly over to the rue Royale, thus forcing our follower to choose between us. Our manoeuvre was carried out and the follower tacked on to me.

'As I had an hour to kill, I took him for a fast, long walk – he was wearing a heavy grey overcoat and I am sure he must have lost some weight. Having given him a good run for his money, I dashed in the Printemps and I went down to the basement while he was being slightly held up by a group of shoppers, and having gained a lead, took one of the service passages reserved for employees, thus getting rid of my persistent follower.

'On two other occasions I was picked up after contacts, but both times threw off my men very quickly, one by using the old trick of taking the Underground, getting out at a station, walking along the platform and suddenly jumping back into the train at the last minute. On another occasion Brossolette [*fellow agent Pierre Brossolette*] and I had an appointment on the Boulevard Haussman with Necker [*code name for agent Jacques Bingen*]. We met him and noticed that he was being tailed by no less than three men. He had not realised it and would not believe us so we proved it by walking fast, turning down the rue d'Argenson and again into the rue de la Boetie and waiting just round the corner in a big arched doorway; one by one our three followers came tearing round the corner and left us in no doubt as to their intentions. We then doubled on our tracks and made rapid plans to dodge our unwelcome friends.

'We sent Necker off on his own into the rue Laborde before the three sleuths could come back on us. Brossolette and I then walked briskly towards Place St Augustin and agreed to separate and meet an hour later at the corner of Avenue de Villiers and Boulevard de Courcelles. As we arrived at Place St Augustin, we saw two velo-taxis and each jumped into one, thus leaving our followers with no means of catching us up.'[13]

André Lebreton, aged twenty-two, telephone worker in Bayeux, and SOE contact:
'I used to sleep with the rifle I got from a night drop. The oil got all over the bedclothes, but it didn't bother me. I loved that rifle and longed for the day when I would be able to use it. In my resistance group we thought of nothing but the Liberation, we talked of nothing but the Liberation, dreamed of nothing but the Liberation.

'Because I was a telephone engineer, I was often called in to repair the telephone equipment in offices used by the Germans. The telephones were always going wrong because none of us ever repaired them properly. We would leave the connections loose so that they would work for a little while, but it was only a question of time before the connections started breaking.

'I would always keep my eyes and ears open whenever I was in the local German headquarters and if I found anything that was remotely interesting I passed it on to my chief, who could get it back to England. I was always very polite and friendly with the Germans so that they would get to know me and trust me and sometimes I would be left alone in an office. Occasionally I swiped papers from desktops – always taking them from the bottom of the pile in the hope that they would not be immediately missed – and stuffed them under a false bottom I had made in my tool kit. I didn't dare do it too often because it was so dangerous.'[14]

Captain Francis Cammaerts, head of the 'Jockey' network in south-east France:
'I didn't really find it a strain maintaining a false identity. Of course, you had to have a cover story covered by suitable papers that were able to explain why you were travelling in the way you were, so that if you were travelling in a car at night you had to be a doctor or an engineer or something like that.

'You had to be certain that the people you were working with had the same understanding of security as you had yourself. You had to work through trusted leaders, that is to say every cell had to have someone whom you knew was loved and trusted by the people he was working with and you had to work through him or her and they had to accept your basic principles of security, which meant a whole lot of things including not using the telephone, not going into black cafés and eating huge black-market meals and that kind of thing. You had to make quite sure that the people you were working with understood those things which were dangerous to do.

'I don't remember the pressure being something that I felt acutely except just occasionally when you were doing something which you knew you oughtn't to be doing, such as travelling by car with weapons and explosives in the back of the car. I had a close shave transferring some weapons and explosives from Avignon to the north of Marseilles, to a group who had got some work prescribed to do and they had no equipment and nothing to do it with. We were stopped at Senas, which was about halfway on the trip, by some SS troops. This worried us a lot because usually you were stopped and checked by the German version of the military police. Obviously there was a scare on. Pierre and myself were told to get out of the car and then they started to cut the seat material in the back of the car. Pierre, who spoke very good German, said, "What on earth are you doing?" They said an American bomber had been shot down and they were looking for the crew. Pierre said, "You don't think we've sewn them into the back seat, do you?" at which the Germans laughed. They didn't open the boot which was not locked and which was full of weapons. They just told us to get in the car and drive away.

'Another way out of a problem was to spit blood and pretend you had TB. The Germans were very frightened of TB, and if you spat blood they tended to tell you to go on your way. Once, I got out of a train at Avignon station and there was a rather heavy control and they were spending a lot of time looking at my papers and I coughed and spluttered, bit my lip and spat blood on the platform, where it could be seen on the hard surface. My papers were returned very quickly and I was sent on my way.'[15]

Claude de Baissac, aged thirty-five, organiser of the 'Scientist' network in the Bordeaux area:
'I used the cover story provided for me by HQ, that of publicity agent. Provided that I lived extremely quietly and did not attract any particular attention, this rather vague profession was extremely useful, and at that time aroused no suspicion either with the French, or German police. I also gave several people to understand that I was engaged on minor black-market activities, as I was of the opinion that this would help me considerably as an alibi, should I be questioned in a snap control. The papers with which I been provided in London did not, however, pass police investigation, and I had a very lucky escape. I was brought before a *commissaire de police*, who examined my papers with great thoroughness, and then asked me: "And how long have you been here? You should tell London to be more careful." The man was pro-Ally, and did not take any further action on the matter, but I naturally set about immediately to find better papers.'[16]

Guido Zembsch-Schrève and his wireless operator, Jacques, were dropped blind, close to a small farm south of Paris, in July 1943. Fortunately, the farmer, Robert, was a member of the local resistance. He advised them that the best way to get to Paris was to hitch-hike:
'Robert advised us not to take the tram to Barbizon because it was frequently stopped and searched as it entered Paris. Our best bet, he said, was to disguise ourselves as campers, hike through the forest and hitch a ride on the Route Nationale. We put on old clothes and put our city clothes into rucksacks, also knife, fork, cheese, bread and a

bottle of water. Fortunately, I knew the forest quite well, having camped there before the war, so finding the Route Nationale was not in the least a problem.

'It was now six in the morning and Jacques and I were stretched out along the edge of the road, ready to thumb rides from any car going north. But there was not a single car to be seen. Finally, I decided I would stop the very next vehicle. Suddenly, there was a car, silhouetted against the horizon, an open-topped car favoured by the German military. Since I was already standing in the middle of the road, it was better to carry on with my plan. The car stopped, the driver and passenger were two non-coms of the *Luftwaffe*, returning to barracks at Orly. I started speaking to them in German, explaining that we had been camping in the forest and we had failed to find the car that was going to take us back to Paris where we were working. We didn't have any money to take the tram into town and that was why we looked the way we did, having camped out under the stars, rumpled clothes and embryonic beards. They laughed at our adventures and agreed to take us to Orly.

'The two Germans had noticeable Bavarian accents and were really quite jovial. They had clearly had a good night. I told them how, in 1939 I had been to Munich. I extolled the charms of that city, the Hofbrauhaus and the museums.

'Confidence reigned, cigarettes and chocolate were offered. Jacques stayed completely silent as he spoke not a single word of German. En route, we passed through three control points and we were not questioned. Our non-coms dropped us at a bus station near their barracks with a cordial "*Auf Wiedersehen*" and "*Heil Hitler*". If only they had known that twelve hours earlier we had been in London!'[17]

Charles Birch, a twenty-three-year-old driver with the 33rd Field Regiment, Royal Artillery, was accepted by SOE for a sabotage operation in France even though he could not speak a word of French. It was a one-off action and it was thought he would be able to avoid contact with the French. He parachuted in with a team led by Captain Hugh Dormer in August 1943. Their orders were to destroy the Shell fuel refinery at Les Telots:
'We went down and blew the factory up about three days after we landed. We were two or three fields away when the first charge went up. We ran back to our hideout for the rest of the night. All that day we were sitting down, sort of taking things steady, and about eight o'clock at night, we picked up our belongings and went off in twos. I went with Dormer. We walked all that night and were just going

to walk into a village when we heard the village dogs, so we knew there were people about. We stepped off the road and three French gendarmes went by on bicycles.

'We walked up to the top of the hill, lay down for a rest and when we woke up, we could see Germans in the village below us, which was about half a mile away, so we just ran like ruddy hell. That evening, we took a chance and asked a Frenchman if there were any troops in the next village, Château-Chinon. He said no and said that a bus leaves next morning to the nearest big town, which was Nevers. So we laid low that night in Château-Chinon. Got up next morning, washed and shaved and dumped everything we didn't want – revolvers and whatnot, walked into the village, got the bus to Nevers, went into an *estaminet* for a drink and asked for a cognac. I was pretending to be deaf and dumb because I couldn't speak French. They said we couldn't have cognac because it was not the right day of the week, but we could have beer! So we had a beer and went up for another beer and then she said we could have a cognac now.

'Dormer said, "But you said it wasn't the right day for cognac," and she said, "I know you're English." She sent her boy to the station to find out the times of trains to Paris and we walked out and got a train to Paris. She was friendly, thank God. "I know you're English"; that's all she said to us. Maybe she thought we looked English. But everything we had on was French, even our suits were made-to-measure French.

'When we got to Paris, we stayed the first night in a hotel Dormer knew from before the war. Next day, we went to a black-market restaurant and had a meal. Dormer borrowed my shoes, because the only shoes he had were black army plimsolls, and went out and made contact with a safe house. The only place I was frightened was in Narbonne, when we were going down to the Pyrenees by train. We had to cross a demarcation line between Vichy France and the occupied zone and that is where they checked my identification card. The German said something – I don't know what – but I just shrugged my shoulders. I knew that if I opened my mouth I would have had it.'[18]

Hugh Dormer had a plan for extricating Birch if there was a problem during the train journey:
'I kept my eyes on the corridor to make certain Birch was all right and no one was speaking to him. I had arranged to say that he had had a bad accident and a paralytic shock and was struck dumb if someone

tried to speak to him. Suddenly, while the train was still running, a German Gestapo official in uniform entered the carriage, turned on the lights and demanded to see all our papers. He wore glasses and had a square torch clipped to his tunic, and imparted a great atmosphere of fear and malevolence. I showed him my card, and after one look at me, he handed it back. But to my horror, when he reached Birch in the corridor, he examined the back of his card closely for several seconds (it was of course forged) and then I heard him ask Birch something in French. As he could not speak a single word, my heart nearly stopped beating, and I was on the point of getting up out of my seat and intervening, as I had promised. Meanwhile, Birch, like the farmer's son he was, just shrugged his shoulders and continued to stare at the floor. The German gave him a contemptuous glance, as though he could not waste time talking to such an illiterate oaf when he still had the whole train to examine, and passed on down the corridor.'[19]

Dormer and Birch both successfully made their way back to England; the remaining five men in their team were all captured.

Yvonne Baseden, code name 'Odette', wireless operator with the 'Scholar' network, was arrested only four weeks after being parachuted into France in March 1944, when the location of their safe house – a cheese factory in the Dôle region – was given away by a member of the network who had been arrested and tortured:

'We had sat down to lunch with the concierge and his wife when the man keeping watch at the window suddenly said, "*Le Boche!*" We were horrified and swept everything off the table. There must have been nine of us there and we had decided that if anything like this happened we would hide within the depot. We dispersed as quickly as we could to various hiding places. There was a main hall plus another floor above and I happened to be on the floor where I could hide quite quickly, with one other man, a Frenchman. We could see a little bit of what was going on through a gap, but of course we couldn't talk or communicate in any way.

'The first part of the search was not particularly thorough and after a while the Germans went away, just leaving one sentry on duty. As the hours went by, we began to think that with the approach of darkness some of us might be able to escape, but unfortunately the water system made a noise which seemed to convince the sentry that there was someone there and he called the Gestapo back to do a proper search. We heard all these cars drawing up around the depot and waited. I was able to see what they were doing and I realised that they were going to search from one end of the depot to the other. There were at least twenty of them.

'Eventually we were found, one by one. I was one of the first because I had been hiding quite close to where they arrived. They got us out by dragging us by our hair on to the floor. In the course of their searching, at one point they shot through the ceiling in exasperation and it was only when blood came dripping through the ceiling that they realised there was someone hiding above. That is how they found Lucien [*Baron Gonzagues de St Genies, leader of the network*]. We were lined up until they decided they probably had all the group, which I think they did, except for the Swiss concièrge, who had managed to escape. We were brought down to the front of the building and handcuffed two by two. I saw the body of Lucien being brought down handcuffed to another man. The rest of us were all alive, but had been beaten up in various ways. We were put into horse-drawn carts and taken to Dôle, where there was a small prison. The two women – the concièrge's wife and myself – were put into one cell and as many men as they could put in the next. Then we just waited for what was going to happen next.

'I can't remember exactly how much time passed, whether it was one or two days, before it was decided to transfer us to Dijon where we were dispersed into different cells in a very big prison overlooking the railway station. Over the days that followed, we were brought out singly for interrogation by the Gestapo, who assumed that I was just one of the French helpers in the group. There was no indication that they had found my radio or that they thought maybe I was the radio operator. Before we left England all agents were given the possibility of taking with them a poison pill. I said I wouldn't and Lucien said he would and he explained to me later that because he had been a prisoner in the hands of the Germans before and had escaped, he couldn't be arrested again because they would identify him and therefore the whole of the mission could be put on to his shoulders. He said if anything happened to him he would immediately take his poison pill and when I saw his body was being brought down, I realised that he had taken his pill.

'After the transfer to Dijon we realised that this was going to be a very difficult time. The interrogations varied a lot. On one occasion they decided surely I wasn't telling the truth, so I was taken down to the cellars and put in a cell in the dark and left there. Eventually, after, I don't know, maybe a couple of hours, two Gestapo people came in, one was in uniform and was armed and they started interrogating me about what the group was doing. Because, of course, I wasn't all that anxious to answer, they started shooting around my feet. For some reason I realised that this was just a put-on. I can't say I was particularly frightened, in any case – I was quite weak at that time and I really didn't mind what was going on. So not only didn't I answer very much, but I said I didn't know very much about their plans or anything, because the man who'd died was the person who was responsible. Then I was dragged back up to the second floor – I could hardly climb up the stairs – past an office full of people in uniform typing reports. It was very extraordinary, a sense of being someone else. Then I was taken back to the office and asked the same sort of questions again.'[20]

Yvonne Baseden was eventually sent to Ravensbrück concentration camp from where she was repatriated at the end of the war.

In July 1944, Roger Landes used his pistol for the first and only time in the war – to shoot the wife of André Grandclément, code name 'Bernard', the former leader of the 'Scientist' network:
'We knew that Grandclément was a traitor – he had admitted as much to me in September the previous year when he tried to persuade me that communism was our real enemy, not Germany. I wish I had shot him then and I would have done so had there not been two women in the room at the time. He was turned by the Germans after being arrested earlier. They convinced him that France's best interests lay in siding with Germany to present a united front against communism and from that moment on he abandoned the Allied cause. We managed to capture him in July 1944 by persuading him that an aircraft was being sent to take him back to England. He really believed he would be able to talk his way out of trouble.

'When I heard that he was being held by a group in Bordeaux, along with his wife and a bodyguard, I made arrangements to go straight there. We had a Citroën car, the kind the Gestapo used. We removed the permit and changed the registration number and set off for Bordeaux to the house where the group were keeping them. Some of my friends wanted to shoot the three of them at once, they had been responsible for the deaths of so many, but I insisted that we should have some semblance of a trial because I didn't want us to be accused of murdering three people out of hand after the war ended.

'I interrogated them for about six or seven hours. Grandclément admitted he had worked for the Germans, but said he had only done so to save the life of his wife, who had also been arrested earlier by the Gestapo. But he said he hadn't told them everything he knew and only gave them snippets of information, trying to put the blame on others. I didn't believe him. When we had finished the interrogation we discussed what to do with them. Everyone agreed they should be executed immediately. What could we do with them? We had no prison to keep them. Grandclément still believed they were going to be sent to London. I remember he said to me, "Can you give me your word of honour that I am going to London?" I didn't want to tell a lie, so I said "I give you my word that you are leaving this house." I told him that as the aircraft was on its way he would have to be separated from his wife and travel on different routes for their own safety.

'We drove in two cars to the Le Muret area, where a Maquis was based. Killing Grandclément and the bodyguard was not a problem, but nobody wanted to kill the wife. I said I would do it; I was in charge and didn't feel I could order anyone else to kill a woman. We couldn't let her go, you see, because if we did the whole of our group would probably have been arrested. I was responsible for the lives of my men, it was my duty to protect them, and unfortunately in a war sometimes innocent people get killed.

'I said that when I heard the shot that killed Grandclément – we had separated them by then – I would kill her. The moment I heard the shot I lifted my Colt .45 and shot her in the back of the head. The bullet went through her head and a jet of blood a yard long shot out. The members of the Maquis then buried them. She did not know she was going to be killed. It was my duty to kill her. I was the commanding officer. No one wanted to kill a woman, of course, so I had to do it. I didn't sleep for a week after that . . .

'On the way back to Bordeaux we came across a road block. We thought we might have to shoot our way out, but fortunately we were driving in a black Citroën similar to those used by the Gestapo and so as we came up to the road block one of our men wound down the window, stuck his head out and shouted, "*Heil Hitler.*" We were waved through. When I got back, I radioed London with news of what we had done and got a reply saying "Good work".'[21]

SOE plan to create a 'Rumour Organisation', dated 9 March 1942 and classified 'MOST SECRET':

RUMOUR ORGANISATION

The best way to describe the organisation of rumour-spreading is perhaps to detail the method adopted in one country. For this purpose we will select Turkey.

A chief whisperer was appointed who passed on the rumours to agents working among all classes.

The Turkish public was divided into three categories:

1. The Intelligentsia
2. The Middle Classes
3. The Lower Classes

Agents were appointed to deal with each category, and they in their turn appointed sub-agents. These sub-agents need not be conscious that they are being used to spread rumours at all. In Class 1 the agents included an M.P., several students, a professor and a pensioned officer. Class 2 included businessmen, civil servants, journalists and junior officers. Class 3, hairdressers, waiters, shop assistants, newsvendors, merchant seamen, tailors, etc.

The procedure was for the organiser to pass the rumours to a head agent for each section who was responsible for disseminating it in his section. The head agents received a monthly salary. The sub-agents may have got a tip or present occasionally but were not regularly on the payroll.

PART 1

Organisation

Those responsible for Rumour Organisations should bear in mind the following points:

1. They should not whisper themselves, but should select sub-agents.
2. These sub-agents should be chosen for their connections in various circles.
3. It should be remembered that most of the rumours will be designed to travel from the country in which they are spread, to an enemy or enemy-occupied country.

4. Special channels should be sought for 'smoke-screen'
   rumours and these channels should be very sparingly
   used.

PART II

The technique of whispering
Whispering consists in not talking yourself, but in making
other people talk. They will do this only if the whisper
interests them and this is more important than that they
should believe it. Whispers can be started in the following ways:
1. By sub-agents repeating the story by word of mouth.
2. By repeating the story in a loud voice in front of third
   parties. It was found in Turkey that German-speaking
   Poles were successful in communicating alarmist stories to the German colony by repeating them to each
   other in public and in German. Talking in front of
   servants, hairdressers, waiters, etc., is often more
   effective than direct repetition, because the person
   overhearing the story imagines 'he is on to a good
   thing'.
3. Jetsam, i.e. notes left in telephone boxes, letters sent to wrong addresses, waste-paper baskets
   in hotels, etc.
4. Faked Stop Press! announcements in newspapers. A valuable trick because it can always be claimed that the
   announcement was 'hushed up'. It is also easy to fake
   the printing of the Stop Press.
5. Talking on telephone wires known to be tapped or taking
   advantage of the chance of crossed lines, when it
   occurs.
6. Press and radio, where any control is exercised over
   these, may be used to support whispers but are not
   themselves to be regarded as whispering channels. A
   more round-about way of using the Press is to secure
   publication in a small local paper and telegraph this
   by secure means to London, where quotation can be
   arranged in other papers, these quotations in their
   turn being used to spread the rumour more widely.
In all these methods it should be remembered that a story
travels better if it is tied up with topical events –

scandal, horrors or whatever it is people like to talk about . . .

GUIDANCE FOR THE PRODUCTION OF RUMOURS

The following notes are based on rather more than a year's experience of the machinery for producing rumours which has been set up in England, and are intended as a rough guide for those who may be asked to undertake this work elsewhere. They are therefore very general in form, and do not attempt to enter into details which could only be applicable to individual territories.

1. Planning

The first essential of a rumour is that it should serve a definite purpose. It may seem childish to emphasise this point at the beginning, but experience has shown that there is always a great tendency in composing rumours to select or accept stories simply because they are brilliant improvisations as stories. The attitude of 'wouldn't it be a good idea to spread such and such a rumour?' is a dangerous one and the inventors of rumours should discipline themselves to decide first what effect they wish to produce, and then begin working out rumours which will produce it.

Rumours for general consumption (and this paper does not deal with rumours intended to deceive the enemy intelligence service) may be intended either to produce definite action by the general populace, or a modification in its mental outlook which will produce appropriate action at some later moment.

The type of individual action which can be effected by rumour is almost entirely economic. Rumour, for instance, plays an enormous part in producing inflation, hoarding, black-market transactions, etc. We have clear evidence that in one country a rumour transmitted through us caused a three-day run on the banks.

In preparing the populace for action, rumour can do much to improve or destroy morale; in fact, the greater the present distrust of official information which is spreading over the world becomes, the greater the effect of rumours will be. In general such rumours should suggest the essential strength of one's own side, and the weakness of the enemy.

A note on certain pitfalls in devising this type of rumour will be found in paragraph 3.

2. *Qualities of a good rumour*

A rumour must be such that it will spread. Essentially this means that it must be such that anyone to whom it is told will almost certainly repeat it not once, but several times. It must therefore give pleasure to the teller. It is not necessary here to go into a detailed exposition in modern psychological language, since the main factors which give pleasure to the teller of rumours have been the common stock in trade of comic writers for at least the last two thousand years. In general the teller derives this pleasure from the sense of power which repeating the story gives him. This indeed is the basis of all careless talk. Specific subjects which will make a rumour pleasurable to repeat, are enumerated below.

a) *Self-aggrandisement* i.e. 'I am in the know, you are not.' This explains the large number of stories about what Churchill said to Eden yesterday.

b) *Horror* People will always enjoy making their listeners' flesh creep, and also their own.

c) *Sex* Those who have little opportunity for sexual experience consistently enjoy talking about it. Good, sexy rumours also have the advantage that they are told and listened to in a more emotional frame of mind than many people realise, and they have therefore a deeper effect.

d) *The amazing coincidence* The conviction that if two one-legged men are simultaneously struck blind at different ends of the earth, this would have some immense significance, seems to be quite ineradicable. Any story linked to such semi-occult events has a very good chance of spreading. This is the advantage of all astrological, prophetical, mysterio-religious rumours.

e) *Wishful thinking* This always carries, but is dangerous (see paragraph 3).

f) *A scandal about the great* Rumours are mainly disseminated by people in low positions. Anything that bolsters up their pride by telling them that those in high positions are no better than they ought to be, will always be popular.

g) *Jokes* A good joke will usually travel, but it has the

disadvantage that unless it is a very bitter joke, it is repeated in a frivolous state of mind and has little or no proper effect. The Germans hardly bother at all about anti-Nazi jokes circulating in Germany, and they are probably right.

3. *Some disputable points*

a) *Credibility* The balance of evidence seems to show that though it is better for a rumour to have some basis in fact, this is not absolutely necessary. It should, however, have what I may term an emotional basis in fact, i.e. it should fit in with the *sort* of thing which people believe likely or want to happen. Among ignorant people, technical credibility is not of much importance. It was, for instance, believed in Morocco that amphibian tanks under their own power had crossed the Atlantic and it is widely held in Europe that letters are held up for months in order that they may be disinfected for typhus.

b) *Wishful thinking* There is an obvious danger in disseminating stories about our own strength and intentions, if the reaction caused when they are found out not to be true is too immediate. It is therefore better in such stories to refer to events comparatively far distant in time or space and when speaking of what is near at hand to emphasise rather that we are heroic than successful. The technique of spreading hyper-optimistic rumours about their own success among the enemy in order to cause ultimate dismay by disappointment is one which may occasionally prove useful.

c) *Horror stories* It should be remembered that atrocity stories are extremely dangerous. Among a people determined to resist or among a people oblivious of their danger they may be very valuable, but where morale is already shaky, atrocity stories sometimes only contribute to a paralysing fear.

d) *Sex* Everyone must gauge for themselves how dirty a sexual story can be. There is a danger of making stories so revolting that a large proportion of the hearers will never repeat them. On the other hand in certain classes you can go very far, and it should be remembered that the more lurid the setting, the more firmly the rumour conveyed will stick.[22]

5

The Heavy-Water Raid

I*N FEBRUARY 1942, Allied intelligence reported that the German war machine had ordered the production of 'heavy water' at the Norsk Hydro plant at Vemork, in the Norwegian province of Telemark, to be stepped up to 10,000 pounds a year. 'Heavy water' – deuterium oxide – was a vital component in the production of nuclear energy. Concerned that Germany was racing towards the development of an atomic bomb, plans were made to destroy the Vemork plant. On 18 October 1942, four Norwegian agents – Jens Poulsson, Knut Haugland, Claus Helberg and Arne Kjelstrup – parachuted on to the desolate Hardanger plateau. Their orders were to prepare the way for two gliders carrying thirty-four British commandos, who would carry out the attack.*

Claus Helberg:
'I understood when I got into SOE there would be a possibility that I could be sent back to Norway to do jobs behind the enemy lines, getting information, spying or sabotaging, so I was very pleased when in the autumn of 1942 I was told I was being sent back in connection with an action at Vemork.

'Our mission was to find a landing place for the gliders, that was task number one, and then to do a reconnaissance in the Vemork area. The first step was to move all our equipment from the landing place quite a far distance, about a hundred kilometres, in very poor conditions. When we landed there was no snow at all, but two days later it was winter, with a lot of soft, wet snow, making for very difficult skiing conditions. Our equipment was very heavy, we couldn't bring everything in one trip, so we had to go back to get more stuff, bring it back and so on. This lasted about four weeks.

'After that we went down to the plant to do the reconnaissance, to see where there were German posts for instance. The plant was in a deep gorge running from east to west with high mountains each side. We came down the north side opposite the plant and reported everything we saw back to Britain by wireless.

'We got the message that the Freshman mission – the glider operation – was going to land, I think that it was the 19th of November. We had had many messages that said they are not coming tonight, not coming tonight, but then we got the message they are coming tonight. And that night we went down to the landing place we had found, we placed our lights in the snow, but no one arrived. We went back to base, in a hut not far away, and the next day we got a message from headquarters in Britain asking if we had any information, because one plane and both gliders were missing.'[1]

On 19 November 1942, two Halifax bombers towing Horsa gliders set out across the North Sea for the 400-mile journey to Norway – the longest glider tow ever attempted at that date. The first Halifax crossed the southern coast of Norway at 10,000 feet, but was unable to locate the landing zone. Low on fuel, the pilot turned for home but ran into turbulence so violent the towline parted. The glider crash-landed on the side of a fjord – eight commandos were killed and four seriously injured. The second Halifax, attempting to stay under storm clouds, crossed the coast too low and crashed into a mountain ten miles inland. A total of twenty-three commandos survived the crashes. They were rounded up by the Gestapo and later executed as 'spies', even though they were all in uniform.

Knut Haugland, radio operator:
'First, we got a message that the gliders had come down not too far away and we were told to search for them. Then we were asked to wait for another message and we got the sad news that both gliders had crashed. I think that was the worst moment for us all and in a strange way it made it more important to us that the operation should eventually succeed. We were instructed to stay in the mountains and wait for further orders.'[2]

Diary of Jens Poulsson:

> *20 November:* London's radio message about the glider disaster was a hard blow. It was sad and bitter, especially as the weather in our part of the country improved during the following days.
> *18 December:* To make matters worse, everybody except myself went sick with fever and pains in the stomach. We were short of food and were obliged to begin eating reindeer moss. The

W/T operator found a Krag rifle and some cartridges. I went out every day after the reindeer, but the weather was bad and I could find none. Our supply of dry wood came to an end.[3]

Claus Helberg:
'We had contact with the headquarters and we were informed that they would try a new attack, not with gliders this time, but with a small raiding party of Norwegians. The idea was that the new group should go down to Vemork and blow up not the whole factory, but the cells where they produced the heavy water. So now we had a new waiting period. We settled down in a small, rather primitive hut; this was in the beginning of December. We were far above the timber line and we had hardly any food left, just some porridge and some flour. I went out on skiing patrols in the huts around the Hardanger plateau but during the war you couldn't find much food in the huts because there was a shortage of food everywhere in Norway. I remember I found some fish, some trout, in one hut, and I took that. We could manage from day to day but we were a little afraid of the future, for how long the rations would last and when would we be able to shoot the first reindeer. I remember we started digging into the snow to get reindeer moss. It was our leader, Jens Poulsson, who said we'll try reindeer moss; the reindeer could eat and survive by eating reindeer moss, so we could do it. I'm not quite certain if that gave us any nourishment, but we managed. Then about Christmas time our leader shot his first reindeer, so that was a happy Christmas: we had Christmas Eve, music from the wireless and got news from the BBC from London. I remember we had a little wood we found near the hut so we could heat the hut in the stove by the wood, so it was a good time.

'We waited for a long time for a message about this new group to come and in January we got the message, they are coming tonight, so we went out, placed our torches out in the snow, waited for them, but nobody came. They hadn't found us so they returned, went back to Britain, and they could parachute only when there was moonlight so we had to wait for the new moon period, February, so that was a long waiting period, for four weeks. In the meantime, we shot another reindeer and I went on reconnaissance tours to get further information about German activities at Vemork, which had increased because of the glider disaster. The Germans knew that something was going to happen, knew that an attack on Vemork had been planned.'

★   ★   ★

On the night of 16 February 1943, six Norwegian SOE agents parachuted on to Hardanger plateau in an operation code-named Gunnerside. They were almost immediately trapped by the worst blizzard any of them had ever experienced.

Joakhim Ronneberg, leader of Operation Gunnerside:
'I was a training officer in sabotage and demolition up in Aviemore when I got the first message from London saying that I had been picked to lead an operation to Norway. They never spoke about nuclear weapons at all, they just mentioned heavy water, that it was important in war production, but they never told me what it was used for. We had less than three weeks to prepare, to plan our retreat to Sweden, choose the route, get hold of all the maps and intelligence about the target. That bit was easy because we had the Freshman operation [*the failed glider attack*], which had more or less laid the ground for us. We went straight to their models and their drawings and their information. They had built mock-up models in full scale and we could just go in there and train. It was actually very impressive because when you left there you could get a piece of paper and you could draw up the whole situation at Vemork. You had never been there but you knew it exactly, how the buildings were placed compared to each other and where you could get cover and so on. It was really amazing. I remember being told, well, if you need a room to lock up the Norwegian watchman, the key for the lavatory is on the left-hand side of the door when you leave the high-concentration room. It was the last thing inside I saw, that key hanging there. I don't think I say too much if I state that there has never been any operation done in continental Europe with so good information on the target as we had.

'When you are waiting for air transport you're always waiting for the weather reports and during the war the weather reports were not very reliable. When we left on the 16th of February the weather forecast was very good. We had asked just to be dropped on a certain spot on Hardanger. Conditions were very nice when we landed, but during the day they got worse. We found a hut in the neighbourhood and decided that we would start from there at about six o'clock in the afternoon. Well, the weather conditions, they got worse and worse, and before the night was over it was a real blizzard and there was no question of leaving the hut at all, we just had to stay put until the weather improved. That took four days. I remember we had some ventilator on top of the chimney that was broken loose and I climbed up to try to fix it and I was twice lifted by the storm from the roof and thrown over on the other side of the hut. That tells you a little bit about the strength of the wind.

'When we flew in, we had asked to be dropped on a certain spot that was about fifty kilometres away from the headquarters of the Swallow [*reconnaissance*] party. Well, we jumped out and we came down on the ground but we were not on the spot where we had asked to be dropped. The distance to the Swallow headquarters was about the same but the countryside between those two positions was very much more difficult, uphill and downhill and so on. As we were walking towards their position we came down a hillside and suddenly saw two skiers, in the distance, apparently looking for somebody. It was Claus Helberg and Arne Kjelstrup. I remember Knut Haukelid went to try to make contact and we were still laying in cover and watching and we heard a happy yell. It was a great moment, actually.'[4]

Claus Helberg:
'The day after we heard they had landed we got a heavy storm and that lasted for about a week and we knew that it was impossible to move on the Hardanger. They couldn't have started finding us and we didn't exactly know where they were, but after six or seven days the weather cleared, it was calm, good weather, so two of us went out to look for them. We had heard by the wireless they had landed further west from us, so we went into that direction to find them. I think we stopped for a while, talking a little, and then we heard someone shouting "Hello" and that was Knut Haukelid and the other men. We were, of course, very, very happy to see them. It was a great moment. They gave us things like chocolate and raisins and other civilised food and we offered to serve them reindeer, but they didn't appreciate it much. I'll never forget that meeting on the Hardanger plateau.'

The attack was planned for the night of 27 February. The Norsk Hydro plant, on the side of a steep gorge, could only be approached three ways: via a narrow suspension bridge spanning the gorge; along a single-track railway hewn into the side of the ravine and running directly into the plant; or from above, down steep steps along pipes which fed water into the turbines from a reservoir at the top of the mountain. The saboteurs decided to scramble down the opposite side of the gorge under the cover of darkness, cross the river and then climb up to the railway line, which was not guarded as the gorge was thought too steep to negotiate.

Joakhim Ronneberg:

'We left our advance base at about 8 p.m. We started on skis, but were later forced to continue on foot. It was very difficult, steep country, and we sank in up to our waists in snow. Skis and sacks were hidden close to the cutting from which we began a steep and slippery descent to the river at 10 p.m. On the river, the ice was about to break up. There was only one practicable snow-bridge with three inches of water over it.

'From the river we clambered up a sheer rock face for about 150 yards to the Vemork railway line. We advanced to within about 500 yards of the factory's railway gate. Carried on a strong westerly wind came the faint humming note of the factory's machinery. We had a fine view of the road and the factory itself. Here we waited until 12.30 a.m. and watched the relief guard coming up from the bridge. We ate some food we had in our pockets, and once more I checked up to make sure that every man was certain about his part in the operation and understood his orders.

'Cautiously, we advanced to some store sheds about a hundred metres from the gates. Here, one man was sent forward with a pair of armourer's shears to open the gates, with the rest of the covering party in support. The demolition party of four men stood by to follow up immediately. The factory gates, secured with a padlock and chain, were easily opened. Once inside, the covering party took up temporary positions while the demolition party opened a second gate ten metres below the first with another pair of shears.

'I stopped and listened. Everything was still quiet. The blackout of the factory was poor and there was a good light from the moon. At a given sign, the covering party advanced towards the German guard hut. At the same moment, the demolition party moved towards the door of the factory cellar, through which it was hoped to gain entry. The cellar door was locked. We were unable to force it, nor did we have any success with the door of the floor above. Through a window of the high-concentration plant, where our target lay, a man could be seen. We were afraid of knocking out the window because then we would tell the men inside that we were coming.

'I had been told there was a cable tunnel leading underneath the cellar and that you could get in that way. During our search for the tunnel, we became separated from one another. Finally, I found the opening and, followed by only one of my men, crept in over a maze of tangled pipes and leads. Through an opening under the tunnel's ceiling we could see our target. Every minute was now valuable. As there was no sign of the other two demolition party members, we two decided to carry out the demolition alone. We entered a room adjacent to the target, found the door into the high-concentration plant open, went in and took the guard completely by surprise. We locked the double doors between the "heavy-water" storage tanks and the adjacent rooms, so that we could work in peace.

'My colleague kept watch over the guard, who seemed frightened but was otherwise quiet and obedient. I began to place the charges. This went quickly and easily. The models on which we had practised in England were exact duplicates of the real plant. I had placed half the charges in position, when there was a crash of broken glass behind me. I looked up. Someone had smashed the window opening on to the backyard. A man's head stood framed in the broken glass. It was one of my colleagues. Having failed to find the cable tunnel, they had decided to act on their own initiative. One climbed through the window, helped me place the remaining charges and checked them twice while I coupled the fuse. We checked the entire charge once more, before ignition. There was still no sign of alarm from the yard.

'When we were nearly finished putting up the charges we started talking about the fuses in Norwegian and the Norwegian guard suddenly said that he would be very pleased if he could have his glasses because they were so difficult to get in Norway those days. The natural answer would probably have been, damn your glasses, we haven't time for those details now, but instead we dropped what we were doing and started searching round in the room for his glasses. In the end I found the glasses case and said, here you are, and he said, thank you very much indeed. I was down on the floor with insulating tape and so on, making up the last of the charges, ready for blowing and he said, well, I am sorry but the glasses are not inside the case, and I had another search and I found them as a bookmark in his logbook. It's amazing what you do in that sort of stress situation.

'We lit the fuses. I ordered the captive Norwegian guard to run for safety to the floor above. I remember telling him to keep his mouth open, otherwise he would damage his eardrums. He did, because I spoke to him two years later and his hearing was all right. We left the room and twenty yards outside the cellar door, we heard the explosion. The sentry at the main entrance had been recalled from his post. We passed through the gate and climbed up to the railway track. For a moment, I looked back down the line, and listened. Except for the faint hum of machinery we had heard when we arrived, everything in the factory was quiet.

'The next thought was, now we have to walk to Sweden!'

Jens Poulsson:
'I was in the covering party. To us it seemed that the demolition teams had been gone for hours. We couldn't understand what had happened. Then we heard this very small, muffled bang. I thought it had not worked; it could not be the real thing. At that moment a German soldier came out of the hut with a torch and started to shine it around where we were hiding. I was very tempted to shoot him, but I looked at my companion and he shook his head. It was a very good thing I didn't kill him, because the alarm had still not been raised. After looking around a bit with his torch, he went back into the hut and shut the door.'

Claus Helberg:
'The only thing I was thinking about was what I would do if or when a German guard came. Should I hide myself and let him pass, or should I shoot? Of course, it would have been very dangerous to start shooting, so the idea was to avoid contact with any patrolling German guards. It was a great relief when I heard the explosion. It wasn't a loud explosion because it was inside this large concrete building.

'After the explosion I just waited for a few minutes and then I heard the voices of the demolition group. They had a password, I think it was Piccadilly and the other group should say Leicester Square but I'm not quite certain if that was said, I can't remember. Anyway, we ran away from the plant and through the gate and down the railway line to the point we had come up from the gorge. We crossed the river, and then clambered up on the road and found our skis and then we skied down towards Rjukan [*the nearest town*] and then up a narrow zigzag road all the way up to the mountains.'

Joakhim Ronneberg:
'After we coursed down towards Rjukan everything went our way, more or less. We started on the zigzag road leading up to the Hardanger plateau and it took us about three hours I think. Then we walked for ten kilometres before we took a rest. It was sunrise, a lovely morning, excellent, and we were sitting there, all nine of us, knowing that the job was done, nobody had been hurt on either side, we hadn't even loaded our guns. We were sitting there eating chocolate and raisins and biscuits and things and nobody said anything at all; they were occupied by their own thoughts I think.

'On 18 March we crossed into Sweden and that was an extreme feeling, to be able to shake hands and say, well done, thank you very much, it has been a pleasure, it was a really good feel-ing.'

Claus Helberg:
'I separated from the others at Rjukan and didn't see them till I got back to England. I was glad to be by myself. I was at that time quite a good skier, so I had quite a high speed and this was an area where I had skied every winter for many years, so I loved it. I saw the sun rise, the skiing conditions were very good and it didn't take me a long time to get away.

'Three weeks later I was ordered to go back to the depot where we had stored our weapons and ammunition. When I got to the hut, I saw there were lots of ski tracks outside. I was rather suspicious, but I still went inside. I was a fool, of course. Then I looked through the window and saw nine or ten Germans approaching the hut. I ran out as fast as I could, jumped into my skis and sped off. Fortunately, I still had my rucksack on my back. They started shooting, shouting and shooting. I remember I thought, this is the end, this is the end of my career.

'Two of them started to chase me, but after about twenty minutes maybe, there was only one. After a while, I realised I was faster skiing uphill and he was faster downhill; probably he was heavier or had better skis maybe. In one long downhill he got quite close to me and shouted, "*Hände hoch.*" I turned round, drew my pistol and fired one shot from my Colt .32. Then I saw, to my joy, that the German only had a Luger, and I realised that the man who emptied his magazine first would lose, so I did not fire any more, but stood there as a target at fifty metres' range. The German emptied his magazine at me, turned and started back. I sent a bullet after him; he began to stagger and finally stopped, hanging over his ski sticks. I turned back to get clear away as the others might come at any time.'

Signal to London from Gunnerside team:

Operation carried out with complete success. High-concentration plant completely destroyed. No suspicions aroused and no shots exchanged. Greetings.

The attack caused extensive damage to the plant and destroyed around 1,000 pounds of precious heavy water, more than three months' production. By working day and night, the Germans were able to restart production, further convincing the Allies that they were intent on producing an atomic bomb. A massive bombing raid caused more damage to the plant and early in 1944 the Germans decided to move their entire stock of heavy water to Hamburg on board a commandeered ferry, the Hydro. *Knut Haukelid, a member of the original heavy-water raid, was still in Norway. He was ordered to do whatever he could to stop the* Hydro.

Report by Knut Haukelid:

At 1 a.m. on the morning of Sunday, 20 February, I myself with three colleagues left Rjukan in a car which had been procured for the purpose. I went on board the *Hydro* with two men, whilst the third stood by in the car on shore. Almost the entire ship's crew was gathered together, below, round a long table – playing poker, rather noisily. Only the engineer and stoker were working in the engine-room, so there was no question of going in there. We therefore went down to the passenger-cabin, but were discovered by a Norwegian guard. Thank God he was a good Norwegian. We told him that we were on the run from the Gestapo, and he let us stay.

Leaving one man in the cabin to cover us, the other men and I wriggled through a hole in the floor and crept along the keel up to the bows. I laid my charges in the bilges, hoping that the hole in the bows would lift the stern of the ferry and render it immediately un-navigable. I coupled the charges to two separate time-delay mechanisms tied to the stringers on each side. These time-delays I had had specially constructed out of alarm-clocks. I reckoned that the charge was big enough to sink the ferry in about 4 or 5 minutes.

I set the time delay for 10.45 a.m. the same morning. This was the time which (as I discovered on a previous reconnaissance trip aboard the *Hydro*) would bring the ship to the best place for sinking. By 4 a.m. the job was finished, so we left. The car took us to Jondal and we were in Oslo the same Sunday evening.'[5]

At precisely 10.45 a.m. on Sunday 20 February, a huge explosion ripped open the bow of the Hydro *in the middle of Lake Tinn. She keeled over and sank within minutes.*

The 'heavy-water raid' was perhaps SOE's most daring and exciting operation of the war and would later be made into a Hollywood movie, The Heroes of Telemark, *starring Kirk Douglas. It was thought at the time that the success of the raid hampered German atomic research sufficiently to guarantee the Allies winning the race to develop the first atomic bomb, although it later transpired that Nazi scientists were probably on the wrong track.*

Report by Lieutenant Frans Larsen, code name 'Frits', dropped into Denmark in February 1944 to set up operations in Copenhagen, posing as a secretary at the Ministry of Agriculture:

On 29 August, 1944, I moved into a reserve living house. One of the group leaders of the Holger Danske [*a Danish resistance group*] had contacted me and asked me if I could supply him with a pistol which he wanted urgently. I wrapped this pistol up in some wrapping paper I found in the cellar of the house. While wrapping the pistol I noticed that the paper had the name and address of the previous occupant of the house on it, and I scratched this out carefully with a pen-knife. I then took the pistol to the Lost Luggage Office and left it there for the Holger Danske man to pick up. I did this at 8 o'clock in the morning and the Holger Danske man was supposed to call for it before 12 o'clock.

Unfortunately, two hours after I had deposited the pistol, the Gestapo carried out a snap raid on the Left Luggage Office for the first time in three months. They were suspicious of the parcel and on opening it, found the pistol. I had scratched the name and address off the label, but had left the label itself still attached and had not noticed a small invoice number on the top of it. The Germans went to the shop and from that small invoice number, got the name and address of the house in which I was staying.

Meanwhile, I had returned to my house at about 5 o'clock. I started to write out my accounts for the last month, which I kept disguised as household accounts. I sealed them up in an envelope and left them on the table. I then started working on some plans of the Free Harbour as I was organising the sabotage of several ships there at the time. I also had about 6,000 kroner on me, which had been given to me by Muus [*a local resistance leader*].

At about 8 o'clock, I heard the doorbell ring and as I was expecting a man who was coming to collect some money from me during that evening (this man had phoned me an hour previously), I went to the door, leaving my coat with my L tablet [*suicide pill*] in it over the back of the chair. I looked through the peephole and on seeing an ordinary-looking man with a hat on, opened it. Immediately five Gestapo men jumped on me and forced me back into the house. The first thing they appeared to notice was that my hair was dyed. They then searched the house and found the accounts, the money and the plans of the harbour. It was impossible for me to explain these things away and it was clear that they would not believe my cover story of being a secretary to the Ministry of Agriculture!

I had a very good hiding place for all my compromising material and I am of the opinion that if this had been hidden in the hiding place and not on the table, the Germans would not have discovered it and I would have got away with my cover, as the Germans were primarily looking for weapons and I had none in the house.

They phoned up the Gestapo HQ and received orders to bring me in. They escorted me to their car, which was parked about 400 yards down the road. One Gestapo man walked beside me and three behind. When they reached the car, the Gestapo man beside me bent down to unlock the door and as the others were a short distance behind, I hit the man in the face with the suitcase I was carrying on the orders of the Gestapo and knocked him out. I then jumped over a hedge and ran for it as hard as I could.

The Gestapo of course immediately started shooting and shouting. However, they did not hit me. I had quite a good start and was gaining ground rapidly, when unfortunately, on jumping down onto the railway track, I hit my knee so badly that I could no longer walk. The Gestapo picked me up and took me back to the house, beat me up for running away and then for the first time, hand-cuffed me.

I was taken to the fifth floor of Shell House [*the notorious Gestapo headquarters in Copenhagen*]. A senior Gestapo man approached me and tried to be friendly, explaining that I was not in the hands of barbarians, but at the same time pointing out to me that they realised I had important information which they intended to get, one way or another. He then told me that if I did not give him the information they required, I would be taken to some other people who might not treat me as kindly as he was prepared to do. I was then left alone for a quarter of an hour and then five or six senior Gestapo men entered the room. One of them said to me "Good old Frans, how are you? You arrived in Denmark on such and such a date." This was my real name and the date was correct. This shook me considerably and I don't know to this day how they knew. They also had a full description of me and knew that I was a friend of Muus's, whose name they did not know at that time. They referred to Muus as Joergen and were particularly anxious to know his whereabouts, and a number of addresses. I refused to answer any of their questions.

They pointed out to me that just as I was working for Denmark, they were working for the Fatherland, and that unpleasant though it might be, I had so much information they were determined to get that information in some way. I refused to comment, so they took me to another room, placed me on a table and beat me with rubber truncheons. They stopped at intervals and repeated their questions, asking for names, addresses and agents in the organisation and addresses of depots. I told them nothing and the beatings continued with interruptions for the introduction of fresh men to carry on beating and questions to be repeated.

There was also an interruption while Hershend [*another agent*], who was working with me and had been arrested at 11 o'clock at night at the same house as I was, was brought in. I denied that I knew him and I believe Hershend denied that he knew me. At this stage of the proceedings, I was in a very bad state and could not remember what happened between Hershend and myself, but I do not think that the Gestapo was very interested and were probably using Hershend as a bluff to make me talk.

I finally gave away a few addresses, some of them important and some not important. One was the house where the charges for the ship sabotage were stored. This caused the arrest of the store-keeper. At about 4 o'clock in the morning, I gave the Gestapo the address of the house outside Copenhagen which I knew Muus to have occupied at one time, but which Muus had informed me that he had left two or three weeks ago. The Gestapo drove me out to where I told them the house was and on finding it empty, were furious.

They drove me back to the Shell House, and before asking any further questions, they wrapped a towel round my face so I could not be heard, as it was daylight by this time, and said that they would give me a hundred strokes with a rubber truncheon to teach me not to be so funny in future.[6]

Eventually, after further repeated beatings, Larsen began to give away information leading to a number of arrests, but no blame was attached to him by SOE after he was repatriated at the end of the war. SOE's attitude was that few, very few, agents would ever be able to withstand the enemy's brutal interrogation techniques. It was for this reason that suicide pills were standard issue.

6

Boffins and Back-Room Boys

*T*HE CONTINUING *safety of agents in the field depended to a considerable extent on the back-up they received from a small army of experts, technicians, decoders and dogsbodies toiling at home in top-secret research stations spread around the United States of America and the United Kingdom. First, the agent had to be equipped with a suitable wardrobe for the country to which he, or she, was assigned. Their clothes, hats, shoes had to be wholly unremarkable, not just appropriate to the country they were in but to the social station of their false identities. Next, they needed convincing forged papers, without which their arrest was almost inevitable. Then there were the 'boffins', the scientists dreaming up the kind of gadgets with which Q equipped James Bond – 'sleeve guns' and 'thumb knives' – along with rather more mundane secret weapons, like exploding rats and sugar beet, itching powder, invisible ink, edible paper, Chianti-bottle bombs and incendiary cigarettes. Most important of all were the decoders, who were required to make sense of vital, but sometimes hopelessly garbled, messages transmitted from the field by wireless operators often working in great haste and under the most stressful conditions.*

Douglas Everett, one of the team of scientists working at Station IX, SOE's 'dirty tricks' department, based at the Frythe, a former private hotel in Hertfordshire:
'Station IX was the Research and Development arm of SOE. It consisted of three main groups: there was an experimental group to which I was assigned, there was an engineering group and a radio group. One of the nice things about working at Station IX was that one was able to use one's imagination. It was a bit like playing with adult toys, and I think that feeling of playing with toys – inventing ideas, why don't we try this and so forth – helped to create the atmosphere there.

'Many of the activities of agents were intended to be more pinpricks than major operations. One of the things we had an operational requirement for was a means of etching glass shop windows with rude messages about Hitler. We produced a paste which when smeared on glass would etch it. It was provided in two forms, either as a mock skin cream, or as a mock toothpaste, and these were really quite useful if you wanted to cause a little annoyance locally. Unfortunately, a whole batch of the toothpastes were sent out to North Africa without proper instructions and it was issued to agents as real toothpaste.

'There was one very general problem and that was the reliability of time fuses. The deviation between the stated time delay and what happened in practice was rather wide. In fact, we had one or two cases where agents had reported that a ten-minute time pencil had gone off in three to four minutes and this was very worrying. So we had a fairly major research programme to try and establish why there were these variations. It turned out that one had to specify the quality control of the manufacturers and check up more closely on the materials used. In a sense this was a rather dull job, the systematic studying of all the variables and so on, but I think from the point of view of SOE it was probably one of the most important things we had to do, making these fuses more reliable.

'The other thing which I got particularly concerned with was the problem of reception committees and ways of getting containers to them. We did quite a number of trials on the ground, in which we tried different layouts of lights and so on to try and find out the best layout and the best colour and so on. Another problem was finding the containers once they had landed. We had an ambitious project in which the container sent up a spray of droplets which were chemiluminescent, so you got a sort of purple cloud above the container. Scientifically it was the cleverest of all, but it turned out in the end that it wasn't really practical, so our attention went over mainly to bells which were actuated on impact. We got to the stage of manufacturing, and had requisitions for hundreds and thousands of them, but whether they were ever produced I don't know.

'We also had the problem of disruption of rail traffic. There again we did a whole series of trials using, interestingly enough, genuine French and German railway track which had somehow been acquired by the army, to discover what size of charge was needed to damage rails of different kinds. These trials were carried out in January near Aldershot. It was a bitterly cold day, and we thought we had established the size of charge needed. But then reports started coming in saying the charge wasn't big enough, the point being that rail at minus five is much more brittle than rail at plus twenty. Now, perhaps we ought to have known that, but it was one of those things we didn't take into consideration. I think one of the things we were particularly concerned with was that the devices which we tested were safe in use, that a chap with frozen fingers and shivering all over was able to operate them safely. So a lot of our user trials were made under the most unfavourable conditions, mud and cold and wet and so on.

'We also had a pharmacologist at Station IX who was in part responsible for the suicide pill. We knew perfectly well what would go inside – cyanide – but it had to be made of a suitable rubber so that when it was crushed it would in fact break. We were concerned with those sort of mechanical problems, whether it was something which could be held in the mouth and whether biting it really would work.

'We had a constant stream of devices from Station XV [*SOE's camouflage research outfit*] – explosives hidden in dung and various other booby traps – that we were asked to evaluate and test, but while they were all very cunning, on the whole they were not very robust and often not very reliable. One of their important tasks was to find a way of destroying incriminating documents. They produced a number of different ideas – incendiary briefcases and suitcases and packets and so on – but none of which actually performed the job. They would singe the papers but wouldn't destroy them completely. We had a very firm requirement from up high that what was needed was something which would completely destroy the contents of secret files, and we gradually developed a solution which got more and more complicated.

'First decision was to have a lock that was very difficult to pick. We first enshrouded a lock with a lead jacket so you couldn't see how it worked under X-ray. Then we had a double metal container with insulation between so that if you tried to saw through the lock with a hacksaw it shorted and off it went. There was at least one other anti-interference device and we were very proud of the end result. When it became known to the bomb disposal people, they asked to have a go at opening it. I was instructed to take one of these things to Lord Rothschild's office in St James and I said to him, for God's sake, don't start fiddling with it, be very careful and so on. So I left it with him and the next morning had a phone call to say that his office floor had a hole in it where the thermite incendiary mixture had burned right the way through.'[1]

Private Albert Adlington, technician at Station XV in Hertfordshire:
'I was a plasterer by trade. I went into the infantry, the East Surrey
Regiment, and stayed with them until 1942 when we were up at
Thetford, under canvas, and one of my friends, he was a sergeant
major, came over and said, "'ere, Bert, get your kit laid out, you're
posted." I said, "Well, I haven't asked for a posting," and he said,
"Well, whether you've asked for one or not you're posted." I said,
"Where have I got to go?" and he said, "You've got to report to
84 Baker Street, London." "Oh," I said, "that suits me down to the
ground, that's marvellous," and I remember him saying to me, "Well,
'ere, Bert, if there's any opportunities for me, let me know, will you,
I'd love to get to London." I said, "George, I see enough of you here,
I don't want to see you there." So anyway, I reported to 84 Baker
Street with my rifle, fifty rounds and my full kit and I saw a Major
Rawlinson and he said, "Well, look, take all this gear home, you don't
want this. Now tomorrow morning," he said, "you report to the old
carpenter's shop at the back of Victoria and Albert Museum and ask
for Captain Wills." Well, eventually I found this place, a rickety old
place up a dirty old wooden staircase, and banged on the door and a
little window opened and a civvy bloke said, "What do you want?"
I said, "I've got to report to Captain Wills," and he said, "Oh,"
and he shut the window, opened the door and said, "Wait there."
Eventually, he came back and took me into this other room where
there were some blokes mucking about with dead rats and I thought
I don't like the look of this outfit very much! Anyway, he took me
through to Captain Wills and I saluted him and he said, "Oh, cut
that bullshit out, we don't want none of that. You're here to work;
we know what you can do and that's what you're going to do."

'So he took me out into the workshop and introduced me to
a Sergeant Bull and the first job he gave me was to mould a
knob of coal which I did, in a two-piece gelatine mould with a
plaster case. I thought, what the hell do they want lumps of coal
for? Well, I soon found out – they were going to fill 'em with
plastic explosive and trundle 'em off to wherever they wanted to
blow something up, so I did this quite happily. We also made
big turnips which we cleated together like we did the coal and
stopped the joint around so that nobody could see it's ever been
anything but one whole thing and then we had ATS [*Auxili-
ary Territorial Service*] girls come in and paint them. Although
we'd cast them in as near as we could to the colour which they
originally would have been, we couldn't do it exactly, so the
girls came and painted them, put blotches on them and when

they were finished you couldn't tell the difference, they were marvellous.

'Another job they gave us was to make a box of skittles which they filled with grenades and the ball was filled with detonators. Then the skittles were painted with caricatures of people like Churchill, Stalin, de Gaulle, all the famous Allies. They were horrible caricatures but you could recognise who they were and these were stuck on the skittles. They were done like that in case a German sentry suddenly found them in a car or something and asked what was in the box and they'd pull one out and look at it, and see this picture of de Gaulle looking really horrible and would shriek and hoot with laughter. As far as I know they were shipped off to Italy, where the partisans wanted them, broke them open and got the explosives out to use against the Germans.

'One time we went to London Zoo and picked up some camel shit which we used to make casts in papier mâché, which the ATS girls painted. They all disappeared and apparently whatever they used them for – probably blowing up tanks or something out in the desert – was very successful because I was sent back to the zoo to see if I could get a bigger pile. I went in a little truck and Captain Wills said to me, "Now, once you're at the zoo and you get what you want, *nobody, but nobody* is allowed to look in there, and if anyone does, here's a revolver, shoot them." I thought, Christ! Anyway, we're coming through Hyde Park on the way back and we're stopped by two redcaps on motorbikes and they wanted to know what we were doing and I said, "I'm sorry I can't tell you," and one of them went to walk round to have a look in and I said, "If you touch those buckles I shall shoot you," and I would have shot the bugger. I said, "Look, if you want to know what's in the back, follow us to where we're going and ask at the other end, will you?" And this is what they did.

'When I'd done everything I could do in the plaster shop I was sent back to London to work on ageing. The first thing I was given to age was a briefcase. What you had to do was put it in lukewarm water which softened the leather up and brought out the creases in the leather that were there naturally. Then, when you'd done that, you'd take it out and you'd let it dry and rub it over with fine sandpaper to take any bloom that was left off of it and then you rub Vaseline over it with a sprinkling of what we called "rotten stone" and you'd sort of rub it on, getting into the little cracks and crevices and then you'd wipe it all off and then dust it again with rotten stone and it looked just like an old case. To make the metal parts look old, I used a mixture of methylated spirits and . . . I'm not sure if it was sulphuric acid or nitric acid, the weaker one of the two. I know it gave off a dense vapour which probably didn't do my chest any good. Anyway, you'd get this on a little piece of wood, or an old brush, and just brush it on the metal parts and wipe it off straight away and it'd take the shine off all the metal. Sometimes it took some of the plating off the metal which didn't matter. Then we found this system was also good for suitcases, so we used it on that as well. You'd kick the suitcase up and down the workshop a few dozen times, get a few rust scratches on it and then you'd treat it exactly the same as you would the briefcase and it looked really old.

'One day I was asked to age a bundle of new banknotes. We were locked in this little room and there was a bloke stood outside on guard, no one was allowed in there. I told the staff that was going to work with me that I didn't know what they were wanted for, but we'd got to make them look old. So we filled the sink up with water, put in some black aniline dye and bundled these notes in this water and we left them in there for a little while, then we strung wires across the room and hung these notes out to dry. Before they got completely dry, we would screw them up in our hands and then open them out and hang them up again. We'd fold them to make out they'd been in somebody's wallet and after a couple of days they looked beautiful.

'We had a tailor, an old German who managed to escape the Nazis, and he was an absolute artist in his work. He could look at a suit and he could tell you where it came from, Czechoslovakia, Italy, Spain, Germany. So if an agent was going off to Germany he'd make him a suit in the German style but that had to be aged, too. There were no new suits in Germany, only for the real higher-ups, so the suit had to be aged. Well, sometimes we'd put that suit on and go to bed in it and keep it on for a week. It stunk to high heaven at the end of it 'cause you never had a shower or nothing! After it had got creased naturally, we used to gently rub a very thin film of Vaseline over the creases, so that when you hung your jacket up you got a dirt mark where the creases had been. You used rotten stone again to dust on them to take the newness out of them and on the lapels like you'd use a bit of very fine sandpaper to take the gloss off of them. In the end you turned a suit that was twenty-four hours old into a suit that looked six months old.'[2]

Joyce Couper, aged twenty, technician at Station IX:
'I was on the underground switchboard at Western Command and I was bored stiff with it. I wasn't interested, so I applied for something

else. I wrote to the CO and said that I had an artistic background and I was enquiring if there was anything in that line that I could do towards the war effort. I got the reaction that yes, certainly there was, and I was sent to Baker Street where I had an interview and told them all I could about myself. Then I was sent to the Thatched Barn on the Barnet bypass. They wanted to know if I could paint and silkscreen, things like that, design labels. I actually hadn't had much experience of that but they said they thought I could do it and took me on.

'I arrived there with two other girls and saw the most beautiful place with a swimming pool and everything, it was gorgeous. My companions were all similar to myself. We all had had a bit of artistic training – they were a very nice crowd of people. The men, well, a lot of them, were tinsmiths and they used to make tins to look like tins of tomatoes or peaches and fill them with grenades or detonators.

'One of the things we had to do was make hollow logs in plaster with little bits of leaves sticking out and paint them, paint all the rings where the wood was sawn across. They were filled with grenades and detonators and sent off to France and put on peasants' carts, the odd one thrown in with the real thing. Every so often you'd hear that such-and-such a load had got through and done its job. And then there was great joy and everybody cheered. The next thing would probably be beetroots and we'd do the same thing. Then there would be what we called "tyre busters". French people would send a little bit of rock from certain areas and we'd have to sit down and copy it exactly, every little bit of marking and colour. It had to be the exact replica of that little bit of stone and they were made in plaster, and inside were the tyre busters. If the German cars ran over them, they blew up! Then they'd get dead mice and rats, scoop out the insides and send the skins over to us and we had to fill them with plastic explosive and fasten them up again. The idea was that agents would drop them into the coal bunkers of steam engines, they would get shovelled into the furnace and blow the engine up. The girls didn't like doing that much because it was pretty messy, so the men took over, handling the dead rats and mice.

'We used to make little silk maps to go inside handbags between the lining and the bag, or roll up and put inside fountain pens, to help prisoners escape. The maps were probably the most difficult things I did because they were so fine and they had got to be very accurate.

'We met some of the men who had got out of France and we had to disguise them so they could go back into the country again. We used to puff out their cheeks and dye their hair and give them humped backs – we padded their jackets for hump backs with cotton wool and meshy stuff, flock or furniture stuffing. The materials were the very best, we had the best of everything that could be obtained from all over the world, to use as we wished in any way we wished, and if it was wasted, it didn't matter.'³

Claudia Pulver, a dressmaker and refugee from Vienna, was recruited by SOE to make suitable clothes for agents going into the field:
'I was trained as a designer, generally speaking, anything to do with fashion. I had had very, very little practical training; it was all what we used to call *Fingerspitzengefuehl*, it was all in the fingers. I was working for a small company run by refugees called Leroco, in Margaret Street, London, when we were approached by a Major Kenmore, who appeared in full British uniform and asked us if we could find Continental clothes. He didn't tell us why. We went round a lot of the refugees we knew to find suitcases, overcoats, some with fur collars, Homburg hats, gloves, ties, everything – mostly male things to start with. Of course, we gave them new ones in exchange and they were quite delighted. We didn't know very much as to why or where everything was going, although we had our ideas.

'Eventually, I was called up for war work and I wasn't too eager to go into a munitions factory, so I suggested to my boss that perhaps we could start making garments for whoever needed the suitcases. That was accepted and we were made to sign a secrecy document, and we opened a little workroom round the corner in Great Titchfield Street. We had two large rooms, one was the cutting room and the other was the stitching and ironing room. I imagine we had two cutters, a number of machinists, some finishers and pressers. It was a proper professional outfit which got better as we went on, a nine-to-five operation except for the times when we had to dive under the table because there was an air raid, which was quite frequent.

'We started making shirts. I would imagine we had an output of, well, anything from a hundred to two hundred shirts a week, it could even have been more. To start with, we got old shirts from refugees and we took them apart, looked at the various collar shapes that were fashionable at the time, looked at the way they were manufactured, looked at the seams. There certainly was an enormous difference between the side seams that were made on the Continent and those that were made in England; we did what was called a French seam. The shape of the cuffs was different, the position of the buttonhole on the under collar was entirely different and sometimes the plackets of a shirt were different. We made a lot of patterns, different patterns of European shapes and ways of doing things, so that we would have a library for people to choose their own shapes when they came to us.

'Labels were taboo, my goodness labels were terribly taboo. I remember the only mistake we ever made and that wasn't in a shirt; it was a pair of gloves which went across and the agent came back saying you made a mistake. I turned them inside out and there was a "Made in England" label in one of the fingers.

'We had all these lovely young men coming in and I was quite young and enjoyed all these handsome dashing officers from all sorts of countries like France and Canada. We had to take their measurements and we made about four or five shirts for each of them. It was quite fun talking to them. They weren't supposed to talk to us, but of course they did because we had lots of girls working there.

'Eventually, they said could we make something for women and of course we could, so we had a lot of girls coming in. One of them was Violette Szabo [*an SOE agent taken prisoner in France shortly after D-Day*], who was probably the most beautiful girl I'd ever seen. I remember making black underwear for her – God knows why she needed black underwear – among other things. Most of them knew exactly what they wanted because they'd been living abroad in France and knew exactly what the fashion was in France, something we wouldn't have known any longer in wartime, so we made clothes for them to suit whatever their style of living was over there. We got quite friendly with them, they used to chat to us and we used to take them out for a drink, none of which we were supposed to do. So we did find out a little bit, but these secrets were terribly safe with us because for us this was more important than anything else, you know. We worked as if our life depended on it, which it probably did!

'We also had quite a lot of prostitutes from the brothels in Paris coming in. We made appropriate underwear for them, very provocative, whatever they needed. They were very important to whoever was in control of them because their clients were a lot of German officers and they got quite a lot of information out of them. They were the ones that came backwards and forwards more often than others, because I think possibly they had to bring their information back personally. We had one who I know went backwards and forwards ten or twelve times and survived, only to die of a botched abortion after the war, which was quite sad.

'I remember an Irish girl, Paddy, who was quite wild and used to go round France with a wireless tucked in her bag. When the Germans stopped her and asked her what she had in her bag, she said, it's a wireless of course. She got away with it and survived the war. We had a French countess who was pregnant and came across in a rowing boat. Then there was a girl who had to have most unusual and very elegant clothes, a riding outfit and an evening dress I remember, because she was being sent into an elegant position, totally different to the girl who was pushing a bike around with a wireless in the saddlebag.

'We could never understand how they could be as brave as they were. They were incredibly contained and distant and somehow you felt that there was something very special about them. I mean, for a woman to go into this kind of work really took something, and as for their reasons for doing it, it's very difficult to understand at all, but, you see, this was wartime, we were all living from one day to the next, so it wasn't that unusual at the time that anybody would do something quite so brave. There were an awful lot of people being terribly brave all the time.'[4]

Claire Wrench, a clerical assistant at Orchard Court in London, where agents were fitted out before being sent into France:
'Each agent was furnished with papers to identify him with his cover story and clothing was provided to match him with his role. Meticulous care was taken that every article of clothing and all accessories should be an exact replica of items manufactured in France. The whole procedure was a model of thoroughness and every article that an agent brought back from France was studied and copied to the last detail. I remember one of the two tailors who were summoned to our flat from time to time demonstrating to me how even the buttons on the men's suits needed to be sewn on in a special French style. I had not the slightest inkling of the source of all the phoney French equipment but it was incredibly comprehensive, even down to French matches and Gauloise cigarettes.

'As far as our office was concerned, it was policy to speak French all the time. I believe that the aim was to reduce the likelihood of any agent, and many were British, coming out with an English exclamation or expletive if caught off guard in France. This policy enormously enlarged my French vocabulary and included the French for every item of men's underwear, not to mention the French for "pimp" and other such useful information. Finally, I learned that "merde", which we always said to departing agents by way of wishing them "Good Luck", had an additional and more basic meaning. This occurred when I used the word on a formal French occasion. When I was taken aside and the literal translation was revealed, it caused me acute embarrassment.'[5]

Evangeline Bell, a diplomat's daughter, fluent in French, worked on the French desk in London, processing OSS agents for the field:
'It was our job to transform ordinary Americans into Dutch long-shoremen, French factory workers, even a member of the Nazi SS police. One mistake, and our people could be executed. Their lives depended upon what they wore or carried, either manufactured by us or collected from refugees who had fled occupied Europe. If I was outfitting a French farmer, I looked for patched blue work clothes, heavy hand-knitted socks, sabots, a beret. Even his buttons were sewn with parallel threading rather than in the American cross-stitch style . . .

'Stamps were important. People couldn't move around occupied areas without proper identification. Stamps had to fit an agent's cover story and his credentials. He needed permits to own a bicycle, for food rations, or travel orders. C&D [*Cover and Documentation*] even had a facility for dirtying up French franc notes, always in small denominations, such as a French farmer would stuff in his shoes. Sometimes, women in C&D were asked to wear the notes in their brassieres to soften them. Agents were instructed how to smoke French cigarettes, right down to the stub. One agent had been spotted by an alert Gestapo guard because he tossed away a half-smoked cigarette, something no frugal French *paysan* would ever do . . .

'A hospital certificate for a recent illness would explain why you were not at work or in the army. A letter from a friend deploring the death of a family member would tell why you had traveled from your home. Civilian apparel bought from refugees to the United States was shipped back to OSS in London and studied for American laundry marks that might betray the wearer. OSS New York was asked to search second-hand shops in the Lower East Side for German fountain pens, battered suitcases of European manufacture, even religious symbols.

'We never knew who the agents were, and only our radio reports from behind the lines indicated that they were in place. It was a terrible responsibility, knowing that one small mistake might cost them their life.'[6]

Pauline Brockies, a secretary at Station XIV, SOE's secret printing works in Roydon, Essex:

'I was driven through the gates of what was obviously a large country house and up a drive about a mile long. You didn't see anything of it until you actually got to the house and then it was all very quiet and, well, just like a country house. I was absolutely astonished when I found out what was going on, because I had absolutely no idea, no idea whatsoever. Station XIV was the place where documents were forged for agents – we called them "bods" – going into the field.

'The cover story at Station XIV was that we were a mapping research station. I think most of the sergeants were in the Royal Engineers. They were obviously picked for their capabilities and what their jobs had been in civilian life, because they were all highly skilled, every one of them. They had to be, because people's lives depended upon what we were doing there. I was a sort of dogsbody. I suppose I was like a technical secretary, anything that was going I did, from cutting out French ration cards and using rubber stamps to stamp the things with.

'I worked in the same office as Sergeant Gatwood, who forged all the signatures on the documents. He was a much older man than all of us, more like a father figure I suppose you'd say, and he was a very kind and gentle man. His skill was absolutely fantastic. He had the largest inkstand you've ever seen, with all sorts of coloured inks and things and different kinds of pens. I never ever saw him practise. He wrote straight on to the card, or whatever it was that he was signing, which I think was remarkable. Having filled them in, the documents then had to be rubber-stamped, or in some instances they would have to be rubber-stamped first, because sometimes they'd have to be signed across the stamp.

'Before anything was printed, people would have to look at the genuine documents to see how they were printed. The Germans were very clever in their printing. What they used to do, they'd have a paper and then they'd have what they called a cross-screen. You'd have two lots of printing over the top and what you had to do was to get down, first of all, to the colour of the paper, then work out what colour the cross-screening was. The *Fremdenpass*, for example, was a foreign worker's pass. It had a red, bright scarlet, cover with a big black German eagle on the front. The paper, I believe, was grey, but it took a while to work this out because of the cross-screening. The cross-screening on it, I think, was black and red. The black would go down first and then the red would go over the top of it, or vice versa. It was highly technical to find out these things, because in point of fact we were working back to front. You see, we'd got the original and then we'd got to sort of take it back and print it, so it was a different way of doing things. We had a Sergeant Collins who actually drew the screening on a piece of glass.

'One of the things that was most important was, of course, the paper, because it had watermarks and things on, so that had to be specially printed. Rubber stamps had to be made. Everything was made at Roydon, except for the paper. The work was very, very painstaking. They went to the absolute nth degree of everything.

'Sometimes if an agent had been pulled up and had his documents checked and got away with it, a memo came down from head-quarters. There was one occasion where we had done some papers for a ship and one of the German officers that boarded the ship said he recognised the signature on one of the documents because it was his friend. In point of fact, it wasn't his friend at all, because they were papers from Station XIV. So that just shows that they were perfect, doesn't it?'[7]

Leo Marks, head of SOE's deciphering section:
'My official brief was to keep an eye on the security of agents' traffic. It wouldn't be difficult to underestimate professionalism in the code room when I joined SOE because there wasn't any. Coding at that time was a total disaster. We had inherited a system of coding from SIS, Britain's peacetime intelligence organisation. They resented SOE, resented our very existence. They did everything they possibly could to close us down or at least impede our progress. Codes were not taken seriously by SOE, but what really stood in our way was that SOE's head of signals had implicit faith in the judgement of SIS. They said poem codes were right for agents, so they must be right, according to him.

'This was how poem codes worked. From a poem you select five words, you give each letter of those words a number and from those numbers you transpose your message. You then do that process again, allegedly for security – that's what is called double transposition – and then you transpose it a third time. It was a tedious, laborious, ugly and altogether farcical method of coding, particularly if the agent chose a well-known poem. An intelligent Boy Scout could break the code and mathematically reconstruct the words of the poem.

'One agent, for example, actually used "God Save the King" as his code. If the enemy had intercepted his message and broken the code, it was such a well-known quotation that they wouldn't have had to look very far for the other words and thereafter they would have been able to read all his messages. So, the first step was to try and substitute original compositions for published poems so that if the enemy broke one message at least they wouldn't automatically know the rest of the words and we'd buy a bit of time for the agent.

'When I got on to the various Country Section heads and asked them to write me some poems, a rumour went round that there was an outbreak of insanity in the code department. Without any authority, I began recruiting girls to make codes by hand, and although I certainly do not regard myself as a poet I wrote about fifty original compositions. One of them, which I ultimately gave to an agent called Violette Szabo, became rather well known: "The life that I have / Is all that I have / And the life that I have / Is yours . . ." When I gave it to this stunning-looking slip of mischief, Violette Szabo, she said, "Who wrote that?" And I said, "I'll check up and let you know when you come back," feeling that she never would, but she did.

'The problem was that agents in the field, surrounded by the enemy, petrified sometimes, would make mistakes when they tried to do their coding. They'd have no squared paper, there'd be no electric light, the Germans would be all round them while they were transmitting, and if they made a mistake in their coding and London couldn't read it, London would say, re-encode that message on your next schedule. Well, you could get caught doing that.

'So I made a rule: there shall be no such thing as an indecipherable message. Agents had signal schedules which required them to come on the air to transmit their messages at certain times, and the Country Section heads were quite merciless and adamant that if they had messages that were indecipherable they had to be broken by the time of their next sched or the agent would have to retransmit. Sometimes that sched was only forty-eight hours away, so I got a team of girls to help me and we would work round the clock. We would have a sleepless forty-eight hours, literally sleepless, because there was no greater failure in the code room than to know that an agent has risked his or her life coming on the air to send a message and because we couldn't read it he'd got to come on the air again.

'Agents without electric light and in a state of extreme tension would have considerable trouble with the laborious process of numbering transposition keys. So that numbers which should read, for example, 4, 6, 9, 12, would read 4, 12, 15, 6, and that would take an enormous lot of reshuffling to break. Another extremely common problem was when agents misspelled words or misremembered them and we would have to reconstruct the kind of spelling mistake the agent had made and that is where having access to that agent's early messages and mistakes he made in training was absolutely essential. Then the information was filtered through to the girls.

'We exhausted, if necessary, 100,000 permutations of probable errors. Each girl would have so many keys to try herself by a certain time, they'd work round the clock. It was exhausting, sometimes immensely tedious, because they never met the agents and they never quite understood the content of the messages. They just knew they had to plod on with trial and error; it was a grim, grim effort, because it was always against the clock.

'If an agent was captured, it was essential that he should be able to tell us, so that we would know if the enemy was sending traffic on his behalf and take necessary steps to rescue him. In a poem the security checks were pathetic in their amateurism. For example, some agents had to make a spelling mistake every third or fifth or eighth or tenth letter – that was supposed to be a security check. If they failed to make the spelling mistake, we were supposed to know they were caught. They were given another check which they were supposed to give the Germans to show how genuine they were. So each agent was given a bluff check and a true check. He was allowed to say, for example, I've got to make a spelling mistake every twelfth letter. His true check was that he was supposed to insert a "D" or an "X" or a "Z" in the letters at the end. They were hopeless as security checks. The enemy had only to break one of his messages to see what the agent was up to. Many agents tried gallantly to use their security checks and London often didn't even spot them.

'Another compounding difficulty which the Country Sections didn't really understand was that very often atmospheric conditions would be very bad for transmission and the code groups would arrive mutilated because of atmospherics, which made it almost impossible to identify the security checks even if they were present. We still tried and many an agent did his damnedest to tell us he was caught, but the sheer ineptitude of the poem code system made it impossible for us to know, that's why the system had to change, but it was a nightmare to persuade SOE to change it.

'My concept was to give every single agent a code individual for that agent, printed on silk with all the work done for him, with all the transposition keys worked out for him. So he had no numbering to do, and when he'd finished a message, he would cut it away from the silk and burn it, so there was no point in torturing him for it. If he lost his silk, he could still fall back on a poem in emergency. But our priority was nil and SOE had to use every ounce of its influence to get hold of the silk and to get the printing done. It took almost a year before the silk codes were working in the field and poems were relegated to extreme emergencies.'[8]

Patricia Jones, a decoder at Station 53A, a country house at Grendon Underwood, Buckinghamshire, requisitioned for use as SOE's 'listening post':
'I joined the FANYs in '42, I think. My cousin Veronica had already joined. I thought we were all going to drive generals about, or drive trucks or something or other, so I was slightly surprised when I was made to learn Morse and various other things.

'The whole of Grendon revolved round Veronica. I shared a little hut with her and we sat side by side decoding. She was extremely good at it and I wasn't half as bright as she was, so I did the easy ones. Anything difficult was passed on to Veronica who was absolutely obsessive, firstly to help the agents and secondly because she liked any form of puzzle, so she virtually worked round the clock. She was very involved with Leo Marks and he helped her along when she got stuck.

'I would think for an old lady the living conditions would have been appalling, but we were all young and frisky and were living in far more luxury than other people who were doing war work. We always remembered who we were working for, the agents, and the conditions they were living under, being hunted nearly every night. I remember the first month I was there, I couldn't sleep because when it got dark I thought of people being hurtled out of Lysanders into the unknown, doing things in a hundred years I couldn't do.

'I remember the great excitement all round when a message came from someone who we hadn't heard from for a bit and I remember, of course, the nights when even Veronica, who was a dab hand at decoding, couldn't get a message right. You could go back over their messages because you roughly knew who the agent was, how he wrote, but some were very, very difficult to decipher. Veronica would work all through the night on them, looking whiter and whiter. We chain-smoked, of course. It would go on for twenty-four hours. Veronica might hop into bed for a couple of hours and back she'd go again, until I presume Leo Marks came to the conclusion that it wasn't decipherable, but I think those occasions were fairly rare.

'When an agent was trying to get some message through to you, the least you could do was your very best to try and find out what he wanted or what he was doing. These were life or death messages we were trying to decode. We knew perfectly well the conditions under which the agents were operating, where they were going and where they were being dropped, because of the messages we were sending out. We knew roughly when they were going over the other side and we knew when they arrived when a message popped up. It was very exciting when one found they were fine.'[9]

Barbara O'Connell, decoder at Station 53A:
'Nobody told us who we were getting the messages from, or who we were sending them to, but after a bit we gradually got an idea of who we were working for – agents in the field. We gathered from the messages that came in that they were in sabotage of some kind and it was extremely dangerous work and therefore the quicker we got on with the message, the better it would be for them. We knew that the agents must be under considerable stress, because from time to time they just disappeared or they'd be sending a message and would break off in the middle. You knew then that the DFs [*direction finders*] had homed in on them and they'd had to stop.

'Many of the messages that came in gave us great satisfaction because we could see that they were doing wonderful jobs. It was also equally upsetting when we heard that somebody had been caught. Although they were all given code names, somehow we usually knew who they were, because a sort of relationship built up between us. They used to send love to so-and-so and we'd often, although we were not meant to, say love from somebody in our messages. I mean, it was very silly really to do it, because they obviously didn't want to spend longer decoding the message than they had to. We didn't add whole loving messages, we just said something to make them feel that there was somebody on the end taking an interest in them.

'Apart from the messages that we put in that we probably shouldn't have done, we were also given messages from their families: "Simone sends her love and is very well", or "Timothy's had his second birthday", little sort of touches like that, but obviously they couldn't be too long because it was dangerous for the agents to be on the air for any longer than they had to be.'[10]

In March 1942, the Germans captured Hubert Lauwers, an SOE wireless operator working in The Hague, in the Netherlands. It had long been the ambition of Nazi counter-espionage officers to 'play back' a captured radio transmitter – an operation they referred to as 'Englandspiel' (the game against England) – in order to pass misleading information on to London and receive in return details of Allied plans. Lauwers was interrogated by Major Hermann Giskes, a clever and resourceful Abwehr officer, who eventually persuaded him that the only way he could avoid execution was to reopen communication with London. Lauwers finally agreed, but attempted to warn London that he had been captured by omitting his security checks. Disastrously, the omissions were not picked up. During the course of the next eighteen months, the Germans took complete control of SOE operations in the Netherlands, playing back more and more transmitters as more and more wireless operators were captured. Before Englandspiel ended, no less than fifty-two Allied agents were dropped straight into the arms of the Gestapo, more than 4,000 messages had been exchanged with London and 350 resistance workers had been arrested. In addition, 350 containers of supplies were dropped to the waiting enemy.

Leo Marks was instrumental in first raising the alarm:
'For reasons I could not fathom, I had a feeling of unease about the traffic from Holland. I could not define it, I just felt there was something about it that wasn't right. One particular day I was being given hell by the head of finance because he had found out I was employing two girls without any authority. I told him that these girls were helping to break indecipherables. I showed him what an indecipherable message was and explained why they were so dangerous for agents if we couldn't break them. He said, well, it will be dangerous for you if you don't come to me in future to get permission if you want to employ somebody . . . and suddenly, I don't know why, I realised what had been worrying me about the Dutch traffic. I shook his hand and thanked him and rushed away from the office to see if I was right. What I discovered was that we had never received an indecipherable message from Holland due to mistakes in coding. Why not? Why were they so good?

'I took my suspicion to the head of the signals branch. He saw the significance of there being not a single indecipherable due to coding but said, "We cannot expect the Dutch to cancel their operations on the strength of this. I cannot go to the Executive Council with this. Bring me further proof, further reason for believing that the Dutch are blown." I was then almost in despair. How do you get further proof? I went to my favourite thinking hole, my father's rare bookshop at 84 Charing Cross Road, and came up with a plan. Without telling anyone else in SOE, I sent a message to Holland that was deliberately indecipherable, something only a trained cryptographer could break. If it had been received by an agent, he would have no alternative but to ask London to repeat it. If it was answered without a request for a repeat, the only explanation was that it had been deciphered by a trained cryptographer – and only the Germans had access to trained cryptographers. That is what happened. There was no request to repeat the message and we received an answer. The only explanation was that the wireless operator to whom it had been sent was in German hands. There was no other, none.'

Towards the end of 1943, two agents escaped from a Dutch prison and made their way back to England to warn SOE what was going on in Holland. Even then, some SOE officers refused to believe their story, since Giskes had sent a message to London warning that the two escapees were double agents, having been turned around by the Gestapo. But Giskes soon had to admit that Englandspiel was over and on Saturday 1 April 1944 – April Fool's Day – he sent a final, sarcastic message to London:

To Messrs Blunt [Blizzard], Bingham & Co, Successors Ltd, London. We understand that you have been endeavouring for some time to do business in Holland without our assistance. We regret this the more since we have acted for so long as your sole representatives in this country to our mutual satisfaction. Nevertheless we can assure you that, should you be thinking of paying us a visit on the continent on any extensive scale, we shall give your emissaries the same attention as we have hitherto, and a similarly warm welcome. Hoping to see you.[11]

POISON PEN TECHNIQUE

As a means of harassing or even destroying enemy personnel the use of Poison Pen or anonymous communications presents certain advantages over more direct action. Furthermore, if successful, the victim is not martyred as in the case of assassination, but is discredited amongst his fellows by what appears to be his own ignominious acts. There can be little doubt that a carefully planned 'frame-up' resulting from 'planted' evidence is capable of utterly destroying even the highest of official enemy personnel and no safeguard can be devised to frustrate a determined attempt. No reprisals can result from such action and no danger besets the operator . . .

Disguised handwriting or block printing and the use of commonplace notepaper provide sufficient safeguard for the operator and additional safety is gained by posting such communications from various areas.

The similar techniques which can be carried out on a fairly large scale would include anonymous communications to the wives of enemy officials in which an accusation of infidelity, sexual or moral misconduct is made. Similar communications addressed to the officials with respect to their family will have a demoralizing effect. In spite of the frequent statements of high-minded persons that they would entirely disregard an anonymous communication, the information received thereby cannot be erased from their mind and no matter what trust exists between members of the family, such allegations will demoralize.

In this instance and as part of the general technique anonymous denunciation and allegation will carry increased weight in direct ratio to the factual content of the mis-sive. It would, for example, do little good to denounce the wife of an enemy official as being unfaithful on a certain occasion when the wife can prove an airtight alibi, such as being in the company of her husband at the time in question. If the operator had knowledge of an out-of-town visit by either man or wife the alleged incident should be timed to coincide with such absences so that proof of innocence might be difficult to obtain.

Another method of harassing the enemy will be found in the writing of extortion or threatening letters to official persons . . .[12]

7

D-Day

*A*T LEAST *a year before D-Day, OSS and SOE were cooperating in the development of an ambitious plan, code-named 'Jedburgh', to train three-man teams which would be parachuted into France to provide liaison and support for local resistance forces. It was decided at a high political level that the teams would be tripartite – American, British and French – and that they would go into action in uniform, creating a visible presence completely at odds with the clandestine operations OSS and SOE had previously conducted. Ninety-three Jedburgh teams were dropped into occupied Europe immediately after the Allied invasion. Their orders were to cause maximum disruption and discomfort to the Germans by destroying communications, blowing up roads, bridges and railways, sabotaging transport and generally creating mayhem behind the German lines. The Jedburgh operation was one of the great successes of D-Day – by effectively delaying the German response to the invasion, the Allies gained vital time to build the bridgehead in Normandy. Their training mostly took place at Milton Hall, near Peterborough.*

Major Thomas Macpherson, Cameron Highlanders, twenty-three years old, leader of Jedburgh team 'Quinine':
'Milton Hall was an exceptional place as a training school, or indeed as a way of living in wartime Britain, because the French somehow procured a certain amount of very drinkable wine for the mess and the Americans of course had copious rations of the sort that British households hadn't seen for years during the war. We had our standard rations which were good enough, if somewhat predictable, but mixing the three together produced a standard of food which gave us a good deal of pleasure.

'We completed our training on schedule and by the end of April we were on standby to go into France at any time, because of course none of us knew when D-Day would take place.'[1]

Captain B.M.W. Knox, OSS, leader of Jedburgh team 'Giles', got the strong impression that they were being trained for a suicide mission:
'While we were wonderfully trained in the most advanced techniques of clandestine work, we were not privy to what the high command planned. We never quite knew what our function was beyond the mission prescribed for us in our operational orders. If we were part of some larger strategic scheme, we did not know it. Neither was it desirable that we should have known; we might have been captured and forced into talking. But it was quite clear to us that our unit commanders did not expect us to come back. You know how careful the military is in making you sign for anything of value – binoculars, prismatic compasses, special watches, rum, wireless sets, special pistols, fishing gear, that sort of thing? When I went to the stores to draw my special equipment, the officer concerned said he was not too bothered about a signature as it would not mean much. That was a sign that we were regarded as lost – together with our equipment – the moment we got on the plane. But none of us had the slightest doubt that what we were doing was absolutely right and, of course, that carried us through; nobody, not one man, bugged out. They were baying to get into the field.'[2]

Captain Stanley Cannicott, British member of Jedburgh team 'Alan':
'Training at Milton Hall near Peterborough, the ancestral home of the Fitzwilliam family, partly Elizabethan and partly eighteenth century, was a unique and memorable experience. French, American and British were all thrown together cheek by jowl under the same roof for over nine months. We differed in temperaments, background and experience; foreign legionnaires, taxi drivers, ne'er-do-wells, university lecturers and some almost hot from school. Our physiques differed too, from American college football giants to fighting bantam cocks. Surprisingly, we got on very well. Of course, there were cliques and arguments, but no punch-ups. We worked hard and played hard but all held together by one dominant aim: to get behind enemy lines.

'We learned how to lay out a dropping zone and to use special secret systems for beaming aeroplanes in, such as the S-phone [*portable transmitter/receiver*] and the Eureka Rebecca set [*early radar device*]. We practised raids on airfields, factories and railway lines. Then, of course, there was the perpetual physical training. I remember one occasion when we were dropped some way from Milton Hall and told to make our way home as quickly as we could. It was expected that we should do this within about twenty-four hours. This we all managed only to arrive at Milton Hall and find there, sitting in the great hall by the big Elizabethan window, one team beautifully dressed, shaved, washed and drinking their rum and ginger wine. How had they done this? "Simple," they said. "We walked onto the railway line and held up the train with our carbines."

'Then there was living off the land. After a long cross-country march we would bivouac in a wood and a truck would arrive out of which would be thrown one live sheep and a bag of flour. "That's your supper" we were told. Actually, we ate very well indeed because we had not only the ex-chef of the *Queen Mary* with us but also several French Foreign Legion types who were quite au fait with the killing and preparing of sheep. A big game-hunter gave us numerous lectures on living off the land. I still have some of his lecture notes which make quaint reading: "It is important to reject all prejudice and every consideration except the bedrock necessity of getting food somehow in order to keep going. Rats and mice are both palatable meat. Rats, in fact, cooked in a stew might be mistaken for chicken. Dogs and cats provide excellent food and they are worth much trouble in capture by friendly advances. The liver, in particular, is excellent; it can be stewed with leaves and provides an excellent meal. The hedgehog would be a lucky find in a dry ditch. Turn it on its back, tickle the body lightly with a stick or the fingers. It will then poke out its head and neck which can be severed by a stroke, skin and cook as suggested for dogs and cats." Although these lectures were most interesting and he was a great chap, I think we took them all with a very large pinch of salt.

'A Jed team was self-selected, that is, after some weeks of general training, two officers of different nationalities would pair off. This was quaintly called "getting married". There were a few divorces! The two officers would then choose a sergeant wireless operator as their "child" and the team, after that, trained together as much as possible.

'Briefing was in a flat in Baker Street where we spent a day poring over maps, checking our special code system and counting out our mission money – 100,000 francs each and one million for the whole team. The drop was to be that night but, on arriving at the airfield, the mission was cancelled for the night. "Trouble at the dropping zone," they said; not good for morale. So we returned to London to find the office closed. Our dispatching officer didn't really know what to do with us so he gave us some cash and told us to go and find our own digs and to report back to the office in the morning.

I don't think he realised at the time that we were festooned with weapons, equipment and battle smocks plus helmets. Looking like a fair imitation of Mexican bandits, I led the team to the portals of the Park Lane Hotel late at night. The bar was closed but the staff looked at us and wrongly assumed that we were just returned from action at the front. We were treated as great returning heroes, the bar was opened, free drinks were served and we were given an excellent suite. We left that night.'[3]

General Donovan himself insisted on landing on D-Day, 6 June 1944. He was accompanied by the London chief of OSS, Colonel David Bruce:
'When we finally got ashore in Normandy, I had maladroitly, in taking evasive action when fired upon by enemy aircraft, fallen on the general and gashed him badly in the throat with my steel helmet. It must have cut close to the jugular vein, for he bled profusely. At this time he wore, and it was the only occasion when I knew him to do so, the ribbon of the Medal of Honor, in those days everywhere recognizable. We sauntered inland to an American battery, the furthermost position occupied by our people in that sector. Beyond was a huge open field, enclosed at the far end by a tight hedge. In the field, three presumably French peasants appeared to be digging up roots or vegetables. Donovan approached the battery captain and said he was going forward to question his three French agents, who were expecting him. The captain, looking at his bloody throat and the Congressional medal, warned him this was dangerous but let him proceed.

'As we progressed, our alleged agents disappeared. Donovan and I came to a halt in the lee of a hedgerow that was being subjected to intermittent German machine-gun fire. Flattened out, the general turned to me and said, "David, we mustn't be captured, we know too much." "Yes, sir," I answered mechanically. "Have you your pill?" he demanded. I confessed I was not carrying the instantaneous death pellet concocted by our scientific adviser. "Never mind," replied the resourceful general, "I have two of them." Thereupon, still lying prone, he disgorged the contents of all his pockets. There were a number of hotel keys, a passport, currency of several nationalities, photographs of grandchildren, travel orders, newspaper clippings, and heaven knows what else, but no pills. "Never mind," said Donovan, "we can do without them, but if we get out of here you must send a message to Gibbs, the hall porter at Claridge's in London, telling him on no account to allow the servants in the hotel to touch some dangerous medicines in my bathroom."

'This humanitarian disposition having been made, Donovan whispered to me: "I must shoot first." "Yes, sir," I responded, "but can we do much against machine guns with our pistols?" "Oh, you don't understand," he said. "I mean if we are about to be captured, I'll shoot you first. After all, I am your commanding officer."'[4]

Major Sir William Crawshay, aged twenty-four, dropped into Indre, near Nantes, two days before D-Day as part of Jedburgh team 'Hugh':
'The drop went perfectly, no complaints, no problems. We were able to bury the chutes. We found our comrades with no problems at all. We had been told to find a junction of paths in the forest and to take cover, watching the junction, which we did. Somebody was supposed to come to the junction, light a cigarette upon which one of us was supposed to emerge from the undergrowth and give the password, which was "*Bonjour, monsieur, est-ce qu'y-a-t-il une maison dans le bois?*" Bloody stupid and needless to say, the chap never turned up! We then put a watch on a big farmhouse nearby, counted all the inhabitants and when we reckoned they had packed it in for the night, we burst open the two doors and told these terrified Frenchmen not to be worried, we were Allied troops. They gave us the contact which put us on to the Maquis chief.'[5]

Thomas Macpherson and his team dropped near the town of Aurillac, in southern France, on the night of 8 June 1944, two days after D-Day. A member of the reception committee ran to warn the local Maquis that a French officer had parachuted in, accompanied by his wife. Actually the 'wife' was Macpherson, but it was a perhaps understandable mistake: he was wearing a kilt:
'The briefing we received before our initial flight was of a most general nature and we were totally unaware of the limited number of people in France who were active supporters of the Resistance and the serious danger of French people betraying their own countrymen or any British officers or French officers who turned up. Our arrival in France somewhat depressed us in that we came into a dropping zone under the management of the local mayor, whose entire team consisted of two or three neighbouring farmers, who turned up with their carts and their oxen, and a group of about seven *résistants* with ages ranging from fifteen to sixty-odd.

'We arrived at about two o'clock in the morning of June the 9th and it didn't take me long to assess, on waking up from a brief sleep, that we had an inactive group, inactive from lack of knowledge, equipment and real leadership. So I made up my mind that we were going to show them we had arrived and give them confidence by carrying out a sabotage, against a railway bridge, immediately that first night. We loaded up the *gasogene* [*gas-driven*] lorry with what I thought, from the description of the bridge, was an adequate amount of plastic explosive. When we got to the bridge, I set out some perimeter guards and the work of planting the explosives took about ten minutes. I set the things with a five-minute delay, we got in our *gasogene* and chugged away, and to my delight, and to the morale boost of my French companions, we heard this enormous bang as we moved off.'

Captain George Millar, SOE agent:
'When the Jedburghs arrived by parachute on our dropping zone at Vieille, we lit fires and I was able to talk the aircraft into the zone on a thing called an S-phone, which was a small transmitter with which the parachute organiser could talk to the pilot of the aeroplane. I think there were eight people altogether, some of them were Gaullists who were on their way to Paris. They were all very undisciplined because when you parachuted you were supposed to collect your own parachute, bring it in and give it to the organiser of the parachutage, but none of these odd bods from Paris behaved properly and they left their parachutes lying on the ground.

   'One of the Jeds was a mad American by the name of Bassiter who would say things like, "George, let's go out of these woods and bag ourselves a Kraut." He was a stockbroker before the war. He lived in Claridge's when he was in London and every time he asked the doorkeeper to find him a taxi he gave him a ten-pound note. When I had to go back to England he asked if he could have the use of my big Citroën and my driver. What he did was drive to the Cote d'Or, which is the best burgundy country in France, and loaded the car with vintage wine.'[6]

Major William Colby OSS, leader of Jedburgh team 'Bruce', parachuted 14 August 1944:
'Landing was made in gardens amid houses and adjacent to a main street. There were luckily no injuries to members of the team. Assembly was rapid and contact was made with civilians aroused by the noise of the containers falling among the buildings. The civilians advised us that we were in the town of Montargis, which was located approximately twenty miles from the announced DZ. The civilians also informed us of a German garrison in the nearby town and we decided to leave immediately, leaving our equipment

and radio behind due to the fact it was so scattered and to hunt for it would merely gather a large crowd and alert the Germans.

'Just before daylight we hid ourselves in a small ditch alongside a wood and about fifty yards from a main road. We lay there all day and watched the Germans pass, going to Montargis to assist in the search for us. We learned later the town and the surrounding villages were given a thorough going-over by the Germans in their search for us.

'When dark came we moved off on a compass bearing towards our safe-house contact. A storm came up and it became necessary to attach ourselves to each other by means of our pistol lanyards. After several hours of struggling through the mud in this fashion, we heard voices ahead of us. The lightning flashes revealed a lone house, so the attempt was made to contact whoever was in it in the hope of receiving aid. Lieutenant Favel knocked on the door while the other two members of the party covered him. We discovered that this was a Resistance radio post with an operator who had come from London eight days before.'[7]

Major Sir William Crawshay:
'The biggest problem in working with the Resistance was probably general disobedience, overenthusiasm; people would go and blow up trees just for the fun of blowing up trees. They never had any problem with having an Englishman with them. First of all, I spoke fluent French and then they realised that we were the boys carrying the goodies. First request, before anything else, was always cigarettes. Second request was for boots.

'One day, about two o'clock in the morning, I went for a well-earned rest in the chateau cellars and I was woken up by an orderly who said the Germans are here, they have surrounded the chateau. One reacts very fast. You are trained to. I took my radio operator down to the cellar and covered him with coal and then I opened the door of the cellar next door, which was the wine cellar, returned to the coal cellar, left the door ajar and turned off the light as the Germans rushed in. They must have been a very second-class lot, because you could hear the officers, who were obviously reserve schoolmasters, I should think, saying, "Come out, come out. Don't waste my time." In fact, what happened was that the German who was about to come into the coal cellar hesitated because it meant stepping into the dark. Then German Number Two said, "Look, what's here, there's a wine cellar," and they all went down to the wine cellar until one heard this frustrated little officer saying, "*Raus,*

raus!" and he eventually managed to get them out. I can tell you, I have never needed a drink myself more than then.'

Thomas Macpherson:
'The second morning after our arrival I was tucking into a meagre breakfast, which was local peasant brown bread and some chestnut purée on top, when there arrived a middle-aged French officer in immaculate full cavalry uniform who requested my assistance by arranging a drop of weapons for an assembly of FFI [*Forces Françaises de l'Intérieur*]. I listened to him and then refused completely. I said to him the best thing he could do was to disperse these people immediately. It is the absolute antithesis of guerrilla warfare to group people together, because the moment they're grouped together, they're easy meat for regular forces to mop up. He went away down-hearted, assuring me that the British weren't pulling their weight. What I'd predicted exactly occurred: they were surrounded by regular forces and were routed. Happily, the loss of life was not very great, but they lost all the weapons, ammunition and equipment that so many people had risked their lives to bring in to them and it was quite wrong.

'He had hardly gone, when a ragged but impressive chap came in on a bicycle with the news that there was heavy German movement going north to the Normandy front and could we do anything about delaying them? It was only subsequently that I heard it was the Das Reich Division [*one of the German Army's most formidable fighting formations*]. This was much more our job – sabotage, ambush, the lot – and so I said, right, we'll go. It was a great help having the chap who had come in from there because he was able to give us ideas of how we could approach. He took us along a dust-covered track that ran parallel to the main road and went from farm to farm. We parked up at one of the farms, hid our *gasogene* vehicle, and I went up with one other chap to have a look at the road. There was a lot of traffic, trucks, half-tracks, armoured cars and supply vehicles going north. There were woods scattered along the road which seemed to give us our best opportunity both of approach and of doing something. Some of these woods had really large trees close to the road and we conceived the idea of blowing them down so they fell across the road and doing that repeatedly over a certain distance to have a cumulative delaying effect.

'In the first area we blew two pretty large trees down close together and fortunately we were able to arrange the charges so that they fell across each other. This was quite a formidable barrier that certainly couldn't be moved by a light vehicle. I left one chap there, about a hundred yards behind it, so that when he briefly made himself known he would have the maximum surprise effect. We got into the vehicle again and moved to another farm which was about two miles further up the road. When the Germans came up to the first barrier, at first they thought it was just trees that had fallen across the road. The column was led by an armoured car, followed by a half-track with some troops in the back. Some of the troops got out, walked up to the barrier, scratched their heads and talked to the armoured car chap. The armoured car tried to push it out of the way and of course couldn't, it was much too heavy, so this caused a long delay. They had to send messages back for the type of tank that is used for engineering work, with a bulldozer and scoop. With some difficulty, they eventually cleared the trees. The whole thing must have taken well over three hours. Then the tank was told to go in the front of the column and the troops who had been watching this operation with interest walked back to get in their half-track. At that time the man I'd left behind opened up with his Sten gun as they walked along the road. That created some alarm and despondency. Other vehicles in the column opened fire, but they weren't at all sure where it was coming from, so my chap was able to skip into cover, disappear down the hill and get away safely.

'Having by good luck predicted more or less what the German reaction would be, what I did at the next barrier was to use the same technique, putting down two trees across the road, but I put our only two anti-tank mines underneath them, well camouflaged with dust and gravel. The tank came along and this time they paused because they realised there might be a chap with a gun somewhere around. Two lorryloads of soldiers dismounted and swept the area each side of the road for about half a mile in front of the road block and for about a quarter of a mile behind. All this took a nice lot of time. Then they gave the all-clear and the tank ploughed forward and I'm happy to say there was a nice big bang. The tank lost one track, slewed around and blocked the road. That was an illustration of that extreme rarity – things going to plan. It meant a very long delay while they sent for another heavy vehicle.

'None of this I saw because we hadn't left any personnel there at all. We had gone on to make a third block at the next suitable place, which was about three miles up the road. We again blew an almost identical pair of trees down across the road and this time, in a crude and elementary way, booby-trapped it. We left a couple of standard hand grenades balanced precariously in the branches, so that the moment they were dislodged, they would blow. That we thought would serve as a degree of discouragement and I believe it did, and again it was some hours before they got their column on the move again. During that time, we did our last fling, which was a pure dummy. Along the road we were running out of woods, but there were two areas with some trees beside the road, about a mile apart, and we blew a couple of light trees down on the ground and we thought they would be sufficiently cautious to sweep the sides, look underneath and all the rest. Then we legged it.

'Our contribution to delaying the Das Reich Division going north to Normandy was in essence trivial, but cumulatively, if you could imagine this in various degrees going on the whole 800-mile length of France, it contributed to about a ten-day delay in the projected arrival of these heavy reinforcements and it must have had a considerable effect in allowing us to stabilise our bridgehead.'

Sergeant Robert Kehoe, aged twenty-two, OSS wireless operator with Jedburgh team 'Frederick':
'One evening during dinner there was a knock at the door. We were alarmed. It was nearly dark, and sentinels should have alerted us. A young woman entered, ready to collapse from fatigue. She was immediately recognized as Aïde Richard, an important link in the communication network. Aïde had bicycled many miles to report a disaster some distance to our east. A group of men had been eating dinner in a farmhouse, before preparing for an airdrop we had arranged for that night. The door swung open, and they were greeted by a volley of gunfire. All were killed, and the house was burned by a platoon of raiding German soldiers.

'Aïde, posted nearby, had planned to carry any messages following the airdrop, but when she received the details of this tragic raid she set out immediately to bring us the report. She was forced to bicycle in the dark and frequently had to hide in woods or fields to avoid patrols and checkpoints. She was distressed, having been personally well acquainted with some of those killed. Only after delivering her report did she break down. Exhausted as she was, she insisted on returning the next morning to carry information and directives for the *résistants* in the area, who were terrified by the night's events.

'Aïde's report should have alerted us about our own security. The raid she reported was attributed to informers. This may have been the case, but overconfidence and carelessness also played a part. One morning, a sentry came to report a small truck moving slowly in an easterly direction from St Nicolas du Pelem, following the main road

just south of us. Scattered reports came in from farmers about an
unusual amount of movement along the nearby roads. Despite these
warnings, we proceeded with our regularly scheduled transmissions.
Maquis throughout the area were pressing us to arrange airdrops, and
we were struggling to meet the demand. This meant that I had to
ask London for extra transmission time and stay on the air much
longer than either the rules or good sense recommended. Nearing
the end of a transmission, we suddenly heard several bursts of rifle
fire coming toward us, apparently from only a few hundred yards
away, quickly followed by machine-gun fire. I seized what I hoped
were most of the enciphered messages, the radio crystals, and as many
of the cipher books as I could reach. As the bullets came raining
in, there was bedlam. We all moved fast, but the radio was left
standing. It is difficult to comprehend our failure to plan for this
type of emergency. But we had not done so, and now we were all
on the run, only seconds ahead of our pursuers.

'Our group of six split up, seeking to get out of the area. The
French civilians merged into the local farms. The three of us, being
in uniform, could not do that; instead, we ran downhill into a wooded
area along a small stream. The volume and proximity of gunfire were
ominous. We feared running into another patrol coming from the
opposite direction, which would have happened a few minutes later.
Fortunately, the German soldiers, though numerous, were distributed
over a broad area. Their intelligence on the general situation was
good, but it was not precise. Otherwise, they would have taken us at
the cottage. Also, as usual, they were cautious about surprises from the
woods or from behind the hedgerows. In addition, they undoubtedly
were diverted by the discovery of the radio. Dreadful as this loss was
to our operations, it may have saved us because the enemy stopped to
search the cottage and surroundings, picking up our radio equipment
and possibly one or two cipher books. Also forgotten in the panic to
get away was a map posted on the wall containing information on
drop sites and on some of the Maquis, identified by a simple code that
German counterintelligence could easily work out. We were able to
warn headquarters about these losses through another network and
thus prevent London from using contaminated information.

'When the first volley of rifle fire came at us, we grabbed our
weapons. I was wearing a .45-caliber pistol on my belt, which I
regularly did during transmissions. Wise and Agueric [*the other
members of the team*] each had carbines as well as .45s. We also had
a bundle of hand grenades; this time, we feared we might really need
them. Judging from gunfire and shouting, it was evident that we were

soon to be surrounded by enemy patrols coming from all directions, along the trails and across open fields. We could not possibly outrun them or move out of the area. Our only choice was to hide, hoping that we might be able to move at nightfall. We crawled into a thick briar patch immediately adjacent to the trail we had followed from the cabin. The trail was regularly used by people and livestock, thus making visual detection of our tracks difficult. A major fear was dogs. Trained search dogs, or even ordinary farm dogs, could easily give away our location.

'Throughout this long afternoon, we remained motionless in the brier patch. People passed frequently on the adjacent dirt road; most wore cleated boots, which identified them as enemy soldiers. Frequent rifle shots rang out from all directions, some from patrols passing directly in front of us. Surprisingly, none fired into our briar patch, aiming instead at locations all around us. It apparently did not occur to them that we could be so close. A favorite tactic of such search missions was to skim over the hedgerows with rifle or machine-gun fire on the assumption, often correct, that this would cause the partisans to make a run for it.

'Our most frightening moment occurred when a patrol of perhaps a dozen men moved slowly down the trail and halted directly in front of us. We were only a few feet away, and it was easy to hear them speaking. Had they remained silent, they would have heard us breathing. They were speaking in German, but we did not know enough of the language to understand what was said. We were overwhelmed with fright but remained still, and the patrol finally moved on. It searched the area and let loose several volleys of rifle fire, but the Germans did not fire into our hideaway or poke into it with bayonets, another technique commonly used to flush partisans out of their hiding places. We stayed quiet, while keeping weapons ready to fire. If discovered, we planned to fire at the attackers and then run. In our desperate situation, our only advantages would be the element of surprise and our knowledge of the area. Had such action been necessary, we probably would have been annihilated. We had all agreed not to be taken prisoner.

'For me, that afternoon provided an interesting personal experience. We three lay on our bellies on the ground in the briar thicket, weapons loaded and cocked. I had only the .45-caliber pistol. I held it in my hand outstretched toward the trail a few feet away. I was unable to prevent my hand from shaking constantly. Curiously, however, whenever a threat approached, the shaking stopped as my whole body became tense and alert. The body hormones apparently knew their job and did it well. We tried to maintain absolute stillness. I waited an interminable time before turning slightly to the side to urinate – the noise sounded like a cataract.

'As evening approached, the sound of shooting, which had come from every direction, decreased and eventually stopped. We backed out of our hiding place and soon spotted a farmboy driving some cows. He knew little, except that the whole area had been saturated with enemy patrols throughout the day. He had not seen any in the last half-hour, however. We speculated that the Germans were leaving the contested area before dark, and we decided to move without delay. We moved slowly and cautiously, keeping under cover of brush or woods wherever possible and watching the hedge-rows carefully to observe any movement. Our short-term objective was to move eastward, crossing the road which ran north–south through Canihuel and which had been one of the access routes for the enemy attack.

'The few people we met were agitated, fearing reprisals against themselves and their farms. From their reports, it appeared that most of the patrols had withdrawn. This encouraged us to move speedily. We did so, crossing the road without difficulty. We did not return to the cottage to search for the radio because we assumed that everything had been seized and that it might be guarded. After dark, we stopped for supper and information at the home of a farmer who had worked with us. We then departed for a wooded spot a few miles away, where we bedded down in the brush for the night, hoping to regain contact with our colleagues in the morning.'

Captain Desmond Foster-Smythe:
'Our arrival in town was always an excuse for a party, with lots of champagne, much patriotic singing and drinking of toasts. I remember one particular feast where the local members of the Resistance roared out a rather drunken version of the "Marseillaise" and then my chum Charles and I stood up and sang "God Save the King". After this, everyone looked expectantly at our two OSS colleagues. To their great embarrassment, they did not know the words of "The Star-Spangled Banner", so we had a quick conference and agreed a plan. I announced in French that the Americans would sing a specially composed anthem of international goodwill. The two OSS officers clambered to their feet, put their arms across each other's shoulders and to the tune of "Hark The Herald Angels Sing" delivered a word-perfect rendition of a song then popular in pubs in London. I can't remember it all but I know it began "Uncle George

and Auntie Mabel, Fainted at the breakfast table . . ." It was a great success. All the French got up and saluted.'

Major Oswin Craster, aged twenty-eight, leader of Jedburgh team 'Stanley':
'You had to be very careful where you had an ambush. You could never have it near a village because the Germans would go afterwards and round up everybody in the village and shoot them, so we had to choose places well away from villages. I think I must have set up about half a dozen ambushes around Boussière, Grenon, Sole and Belmont. Belmont was on a side road that took the Germans up from the south in a general north-easterly direction, back towards Germany, so a lot of people were coming through. It was a very wooded part of the country, minor white roads. My early Boy Scout training meant that I was quite good with a compass and in the woods they had these *sanglier* [wild pig] tracks and if you bent down very low you could make your way through the wood very easily, keeping your head down.

'We ambushed a German paymaster and the odd German car, people moving on through, soldiers on foot who immediately shot back at you and made all the leaves on the trees fall down round you. In an ambush, on our side, you might get about ten chaps. Now, they had no shoes, or so they said, and so you couldn't march them anywhere. We had an old lorry that ran by charcoal gas, but it took some time starting up. You parked the thing some way from the road and then the charcoal had to sort of pre-heat somehow, there was a little fire under the lorry, and then you pulled a lever and it went tick–tick–tick–tick and you hoped it would start. And sometimes it would not start. Then all you got was a loud bang and a cloud of smoke and dust, so you had to start again. It was very nerve-racking sometimes.

'We sent a lot of information back but whether anybody had any time to listen to what we were sending, I rather doubt.'[8]

Thomas Macpherson:
'Acquiring transport was one of the very early priorities. The group that I went to had only one vehicle when I arrived. This was a *gasogene* lorry of about two-ton capacity, driven by a boiler, literally a boiler that you stoked, which made its own gas and made the most appalling smell and appalling noise. It went along rather slowly, but it got you around. So I had to get our French friends – fortunately one was the owner of the local garage – to commandeer some vehicles. The first one I had that was any use was a tiny little bubble car called

at that time a Peugeot 202. I rapidly discovered that the quality of the wartime tyres was quite appalling and so we had to carry three spare wheels. We wouldn't have had time to risk changing a tyre, so we had to have the wheels: rather like Formula One, we got down the changing of a wheel to about three minutes.

'From there I moved upwards through a couple of other cars until the final triumph when we captured two cars from the French Milice, which was the armed part of the collaborating French police. They were the best cars of the day, long sleek black Citroëns, front-wheel drive, extremely roadworthy and probably the fastest vehicle around. That car covered a good few miles for me. Two of the local ladies, the wife of the garage proprietor and the wife of his brother, made two pennants and I put one on each wing, again for propaganda reasons. One was the Union Jack and one was the French flag with the Cross of Lorraine in the middle of it and both of them they surrounded with gold tassels – it was very smart indeed!

'Like in all of Europe at that time, because of air raids cars had shielded headlights with only a pinpoint of light coming through. We left our headlights open, so that if we ran into trouble we'd blaze away with full headlights which could blind an ambush if we ran into it, which we did on occasion. When we ran into trouble, this could be of two types really. One was you ran into a fixed road block, which would happen at a crossroads. The other was the accidental one, where you just happened to run into an enemy column going the other way. The latter only happened to me once and by great good fortune it was in a wood and very near a turning. We converged from opposite sides of the crossroad and we did a very smart left turn and disappeared down the other road at a high rate of knots, pursued by a certain amount of noise, but there was no way they were going to catch us unless they achieved an accidental hit.

'The fixed road block was mainly intended for catching clandestines and messengers and things like that, so it was usually around a particular bridge or crossroads which they wanted to block. If we spotted it first, which we generally did, we reversed very sharply out of it. There would be an exchange of fire, but it's surprisingly difficult to hit a car moving at reasonable speed. We did have one occasion where, at night, we ran into a road block. I think they were a bit somnolent because it was in the early hours of the morning and we simply crashed it. They hadn't properly blocked the carriageway, there was a light barrier across and we switched on our full headlights, which dazzled them so that their shooting was not very good, and crashed straight through.

Some forty miles later we came to a fut-fut stop because we found they had in fact holed the petrol tank, firing behind us and the fuel had leaked away.

'One of the problems of motorised banditry was, of course, getting petrol. We made a deal with the Communist FDP that in return for some of the help we had given them they would ensure that we got a regular supply of petrol from Decazeville, a town just to the south of us. The Germans who normally garrisoned the place had become sufficiently wary of the RAF that they never had the garrison and the relief garrison in town at the same time. The garrison would move out and then there would be a gap of some hours before the relief garrison came in. I wanted to demonstrate during this gap that the Allies were around, not only to raise French morale but to discourage those who thought of helping the Germans. I went down there, met the mayor and the deputy mayor, all in their Republican sashes and so forth. The mayor offered me a cup of coffee and we were quietly sipping our coffee on the balcony, looking at our watches and thinking we had an hour or so to spare before the garrison was due, when suddenly we saw, at the far end of the street, two German armoured cars, clearly the forerunner of the garrison. Fortunately, I and my driver were quite quick off the mark and we got back into our car with remarkable speed. The Germans didn't fire but sent one of the armoured cars to pursue me. There's a long hill out of Decazeville and they were a long way behind and we were much quicker up the hill anyway, so we thought we'd risk a bit of fun. There was a cutting in that hill with a rickety sort of footbridge across it. As we drove up, I manufactured in the car something called a gammon grenade, which is a terribly simple device. You took about two pounds of plastic explosive, enclosed it in a rubber bag, put a detonator and a percussion device in the top and if you hurled it at something, with luck it would go off. I told my driver to stop and I went up on the bridge with this gammon grenade and waited for the armoured car to come up. Fortunately, there was only the one and at the appropriate time I leaned over the bridge and dropped it. My aim was not perfect. I should have hit the open turret in the front, but fortunately it just clipped the engine and went off very satisfactorily, blew the engine to bits, set the car on fire and enabled me to get back comfortably to my own vehicle.

'I hadn't been there very long before the Germans put up posters in various towns offering enormous rewards for my apprehension. That I took as a compliment.'

Sergeant Eric Grinham, aged twenty-six, wireless operator with Jedburgh team 'Stanley' in the Cher area of France:
'There was a scare one night when a German soldier who was injured when his convoy was shot up staggered into our camp and was caught. The following day, the Maquis made him dig his own grave and shot him. They shot him simply because he was a German soldier. They had suffered very badly in that area and two nurses had been raped so the Maquis were unmerciful. I didn't see much of him, but I believe he wasn't beaten up, just questioned, and I then saw them lead him away with a spade and not long after I heard the rattle of Sten guns and then they came back. I saw bloodstains afterwards and a little stick to mark where they had buried him.'[9]

John Ellis, aged twenty-three, wireless operator with Jedburgh team 'Minaret':
'We stayed ten days in Lespareux and then started to go into civilisation more, firstly to Lasalle and then on to St Hippolyte du Fort, where we grouped up a little bit while the Germans were chased out of the area. The Maquis had great fun shooting them up and I had my best radio office of the campaign there, it was in the wall of an old castle that had been converted before the war, into basic living quarters and this particular room had been the holiday home of a British clergyman and had electricity and, what is more, it had a bog, which was unheard-of in that part of France! I also got excellent radio transmission from there. That, to me, was a little bit of a holiday.

'Going from St Hippolyte du Fort back to Lasalle, I had a little bit of a contretemps. I had a little Fiat 500 car to carry all my gear, which just about staggered along, and I missed a road and ended up in another village about ten miles away, near the main route down the Rhône Valley, and the people there couldn't believe I was British. They thought I was a German infiltrating them, or trying to escape or something like that. They were going to shoot me probably. They went and got some Maquis people but they, unfortunately, were communist Maquis and they had no doubts about me at all – they were going to take me out and hang me. Fortunately, during all the argy-bargy, a lad suddenly came into the village in a car who was in our Maquis group and was also the son of one of the local people there and said, "Ooh no, he's our British sergeant!" And as the Fiat had by now conked out, he towed me back to Lasalle.'[10]

Captain Duncan Guthrie, aged thirty-three, leader of Jedburgh team 'Harry', made contact with a Maquis in central France but had to prove his identity:

'We had this system of "*messages personnelles*" every night on the BBC. We all had a personal message which we could tell people to listen out for if there was any doubt as to our authenticity. So fortunately I was able to say to the leader of the Maquis, "Listen tonight on the British wireless and you will hear them say '*Le docteur a des cheveux gris*' and then you will know that I am OK." They listened and, sure enough, the message came up and they knew I was all right. I say fortunately because they decided, rightly or wrongly, that the Belgian who had led me to the Maquis was a plant and they shot him in the middle of the night. I woke up in the night and heard a shot and next morning they told me they had shot him. If my *message personnelle* had not come through, they might very well have shot me too. I only saw him for an hour, but I found him an unattractive person, fat and greasy, but that was not enough reason to shoot him. Things happen in war.

'Sometime in August, a local French farmer came in with a boy who was having a holiday on his farm. He was a Parisian and when the farmer's wife went to make up his bed, she had a look at his suitcase and he had armlets with the French version of the swastika and all sorts of flags and things. They had him arrested and brought him into our camp. He admitted that he was a member of the Nazi Fascist organisation in Paris, but he was only about eighteen or nineteen and a very presentable young man. We looked through his correspondence and I was very struck by the fact that he wrote to a friend in Paris, obviously someone of about the same age, and said, "We had a lovely evening last night, we picked up a couple of girls and they were very nice. I have been reading recently an awful lot, and I have been reading Kipling and what a wonderful writer he is." I thought, well, I don't know, I am not a Kipling fan but some of his writing was lovely and at that age I think I, too, would have liked Kipling. This was a chatty sort of letter and it made him very human to me.

'They had this little trial and he was found guilty. And there were we in the forest and I remember there was one chap, whom I did not like very much, from Marseilles, who was a busy chap in the Resistance and as tough as old boots and very brave and fierce and all that sort of thing, and he came along and gave the boy a shovel. I suppose he knew he had been condemned to death. I said to Gapeau [*another member of the team*] "We can't shoot him," and he agreed and so I said, "Let's go to the commanding officer and say so," so we did. We said, "You can't really shoot this chap, he's only eighteen. What's he really done? He just had some badges in his luggage." The commander said, "No, all right. But what can I do with him?" I didn't know what to say. I knew that we couldn't look after him, we couldn't have prisoners when we were living under the trees in the forest.

'He said, "I will give you an hour. You come back in an hour and tell me what I can do with him and we won't shoot him." Gapeau and I sat down and we couldn't think of anything to do with him. So, after an hour, he had his shovel and he dug his grave and a few minutes later, two shots rang out. I wasn't there, I couldn't face it but a Frenchman who was there said how brave he had been.'[11]

Major John W. Summers, OSS, leader of Jedburgh team 'Horace', parachuted into the Brest area on 17 July 1944:
'From the date of our arrival in the field until 25 July, we attempted to establish contact with the Maquis in and around Brest, but due to strong German mop-ups the majority of the Maquis leaders had been caught and executed, and the units dispersed. Finally, on 24 July we decided to go to Brest ourselves and establish contacts. The leader of the Brest arrondissement disclosed a plan to get us into this area by hiding us in wine barrels for the trip. On the evening of the 25th, two Frenchmen came to us saying they would hide us in wine barrels and deliver us to our area. The two men were very much in a hurry as their truck permit was good only up to nine o'clock, it was a two-hour trip and it was then six thirty. I immediately made the decision that we would go. It was a truckload of wine being delivered to the Germans in Brest. The wine had just been emptied from three of the barrels, and we placed ourselves in these. The forty-mile trip was made in two and a half hours, during which time we were completely miserable in mind and body. The truck was stopped several times by German patrols but the drivers' papers were in order and it was allowed to proceed. After what seemed years, we arrived at our destination in a wood about five miles north-west of Brest. We spent the night in a foxhole in the wood. A German observation tower was very near and there were other positions all around. Although we had reached our area, the situation did not seem too good.

'We left the following evening for a safe house about three miles north-east of Lesneven. Again we rode in the wine barrels, and this time the truck had a flat tyre in the middle of St Divy, which was held by a strong German garrison. As a matter of fact, a German patrol helped the driver change the tyre. After what seemed a very long time, we finally started moving again and arrived at our destination. It was still daylight and so we put on civilian clothes to make the last part of the journey to the safe house.'[12]

Report by Capitaine Le Zachmeur, member of Jedburgh Team 'François', on the death of SOE agent Major Ogden-Smith and SAS officer Maurice Myodon after German troops surrounded the isolated farmhouse where they were sheltering near Quimperle, 29 July 1944:

The Major was seriously wounded in the stomach by a burst of fire and, unable to move, gave himself some morphia and applied first aid. The SAS officer, wounded by a grenade (fracture of the leg and arm), dragged himself in front of the Germans in order to allow his comrades to retire. He fired four magazines, killing and wounding quite a number of the enemy. Being then out of ammunition he shouted to the Germans as follows: 'You need not be afraid, I have got no more ammunition.' The Germans then approached and ordered hands up – they got hold of him, fired a burst of sub-machine gun into him and finished him off with a bullet in the temple. The major was then deliberately shot by the Germans. Both Major Ogden-Smith and Myodon were in uniform and wore the insignias of their rank.

The Germans burned the farm, killed the farmer, a Mr Fiche aged 72 years, with a bayonet in his back, took away all the farmer's goods and drove off the cattle. The Germans stole everything off the corpses in the way of jewellery, money, boots and effects. They forbade their burial and exposed the bodies the whole day in front of the farm. The next day, the Germans came back, buried them but forbade them to be taken to the cemetery.

We were given away by a Belgian *collaborateur* who lived a few kilometres from there and who whilst walking in the country, had seen us. He sent his wife to Quimperle to inform the *Feldgendarmes*, and it was her who was in the car leading the detachment to the spot. The Belgian, his wife, and his eldest son were executed on my orders, by patriots, two days later.[13]

Captain George Millar:
'One time Maurice and I were coming back from Besançon where we'd been inspecting the bridges which the Germans had mined, of course, so they could blow them up when the Allies came through.

We'd interfered with the blowing-up arrangement and just wanted to make sure that our interference hadn't been tampered with. On the very edge of the forest we met a German NCO, a *Feldwebel*, on patrol with his Schmeisser sub-machine gun across his chest ready to fire. One of the best things I had done during my SOE training was to make myself into a crack pistol shot. I could shoot through my pocket quite accurately at close quarters and always carried a Browning .45, which was heavy but it was a killer. You knew if you hit a man with it, he went down, no matter where you hit him, the shock was so terrible from the concussion. Maurice was behind me when I met this German pretty well face to face. I was wearing my usual blue overall trousers and a blue overall jacket. I had my Browning in the right-hand pocket of the jacket and I shot him twice, as we were trained to do, caught him in the middle of the chest, bang. Down he went as if he'd been pole-axed. Maurice and I hauled him into the undergrowth because there was a lot of shouting and movement in the forest and we had to lie beside him for, oh, a couple of hours while German patrols went past. Thank God they hadn't seen our ingress into the shrubbery. It was horrible lying there with a dead man because the bluebottles were terrible and they sort of dipped themselves in his blood and then came to sun themselves on us.'

Captain Geoffrey Jones, OSS agent with a Maquis in Grasse, was asked to carry out a reconnaissance of the harbour in Nice in preparation for the invasion in the South of France:
'Just before we occupied Nice, General Frederick called me in late one afternoon and said Admiral Hewitt [*the naval commander*] had asked us what we could tell him about the harbour facilities in Nice because he'd been in some minor skirmishes and some of his ships needed repairs. He wanted to know if he could use the harbour for this purpose. General Frederick then looked at his watch and said, "It's now five o'clock. Can you get me this information by tomorrow morning? I'm having breakfast with the naval liaison officer and I want to show him just what we can do."

'I went back to my tent and looked at the wall. I wasn't sure what I was going to do because we had already had radio contact with our operatives in Nice and were not due to reach them again until the next day. Just at that moment, as luck would have it, two of my men came in who had just returned from a mission behind the enemy lines and one of them was the grandson of the harbourmaster in Nice.

'I explained my problem to him and he immediately offered to go back and get the information I needed. But as I was telling him what I needed to know – harbour depth, location of installations, possible presence of submarines, mines et cetera – I could see I was asking too much of him. He was only about twenty or so and all this talk about precise naval information was completely strange to him, so I shrugged my shoulders and thought, to hell with it, I'll go with him.

'So I put on a blue civilian suit and we took my car and left it in the woods above the River Var. The bridge across the Var to Nice had been bombed. There was a temporary pontoon bridge, but you could not get across it without a *laissez passer*, but the river was not very deep in the summer, so we waded across, holding our weapons above our heads. By this time it was already midnight and we had to get in and out before the sun came up, so we had to get a move on. Near where we crossed the river was a farmhouse and every farmhouse has bicycles. We snooped around in a barn, found a couple of bicycles, borrowed them and peddled into Nice.

'Naturally, there was a curfew in the city and no one was supposed to be about, but the beautiful thing about German patrols was that they always wore hobnailed boots and you could hear them a mile away, so it was not hard to avoid them. We heard, rather than saw, a couple of German patrols as we skirted the city. By the time we got to the harbourmaster's house it was one o'clock in the morning. He lived on the fifth floor with a nice balcony overlooking the port, but of course the front doors were locked. The kid began to throw rocks up to the top of the house but made so much noise that people began to call out, "*Qu'est-ce que tu fais la-bas? Fiche-moi la paix.*" ["What are you doing down there? Give us some peace."] Then, all of a sudden, this wonderful apparition appeared on the balcony. I almost strangled keeping myself from laughing out loud. I swear to God, it looked like he had stepped straight out of Dickens. He was wearing a nightshirt and a sleeping hat and had a long white beard. When he demanded to know what was going on, the kid said, "*Titine, Titine, c'est moi! Ton grandfils.*" The old man suddenly realised who was out there and hurried down to let us in. We explained what we were doing and what we wanted and he was perfectly happy to help. He got out all the charts for us, showed us where everything was, where the bomb had blown up the harbour, where the submarine had been sunk to block the harbour entrance and even traced an overlay on the charts with everything marked on it. I bundled them up and put them under my coat, thanked the old man profusely and off we went.

'Peddling furiously out of Nice, I heard the sound of a truck coming up behind us. I knew we wouldn't be able to out-peddle it and there was nowhere to hide at that moment. In training we had always been told to act confidently and never let anyone know you are scared. If a policeman looked at you suspiciously, for example, we were told to go right up to him and ask for a match or directions to such-and-such a place. I knew that if we were seen peddling furiously out of town we'd look suspicious, so with a sudden flash of inspiration I said to the boy, "Turn round, we're going to pretend we're going into town. If we're stopped tell them we're worried about our relatives as we've heard the Americans are coming." We turned round just as a German truck came into view. Of course we were stopped because it was well after curfew.

'The boy could speak a little German and I knew enough to understand what was going on. He was very good. He explained that he had heard the Americans were coming and that we wanted to make sure our parents were safe. By indicating he was frightened of the Americans, he got a more sympathetic reaction from the Germans in the truck. They reprimanded us for being out after curfew and told us that under no circumstances could we go into the town. We told them we lived in the farm where we'd borrowed the bicycles and they told us to put our bicycles into the back of the truck and they would give us a lift "home".

'So we climbed into the back of the truck and rode with the Germans back to the farm, with me holding tightly on to the charts under my jacket. At the farm we thanked them politely and they drove off. We returned the bicycles, waded back across the river, found my car in the woods and were back in Grasse before dawn. We woke up one of the girls who translated French for us and asked her to type out our report. At seven thirty that morning I went in to see the general who asked me if I had had any luck. "I think so," I said, and handed him a complete report with all the information he wanted, including maps and overlays and so forth.'[14]

Hélène Deschamps-Adams joined OSS as a field operative in France in 1943 after becoming disillusioned with the political wrangling and rivalry between various factions of the French Resistance movement:
'At 11 a.m. on August 17, 1944, my adopted sister Jackie, who was also in the OSS, and I met Petit-Jean [*code name for the senior OSS agent in south-east France*] at the Café des Deux Garçons in Aix-en-Provence. Three days had already passed since the landing on the Mediterranean coast. Orders were given to locate units of the SS Panzer Division, which had come up from the Atlantic coast, near Bordeaux. We also had to estimate the strength of the German

infantry escorting the tanks. Any details, no matter how small, should be reported, we were told. We had to leave immediately. Petit-Jean was to meet us next morning at eight o'clock in the village of Pertuis, almost thirty kilometers from Aix. We then would move to Apt, meet our radio operator and give him the intelligence data.

'As Petit-Jean was leaving the café, he intentionally left the local newspaper. Inside the folded pages were passes with falsified German seals and stamps which would allow us to pass German posts without too many problems. There were also miniature printed booklets giving information on enemy insignia, matériel and troop descriptions, and he had added a few bills of French currency for an emergency.

'By noon we were on our way with the only transportation available to French civilians – bicycles. Beyond the hamlet of Venelle, we spotted an enemy ammunition train camouflaged under tall plane trees. We immediately paused near the tracks, leaning busily over Jackie's bike, and while she forced some air into the tyre, German guards came to investigate. Reassured that we were no threat, they offered to help, while I methodically listed in my mind the number of boxcars and their locations.

'We left again, heading towards Pertuis. Coming in the other direction was a German convoy composed of several trucks, light machine-gun vehicles and a number of foot soldiers. At the same time, a P-47 aircraft appeared out of nowhere and began raking the convoy with machine-gun fire. We tossed our bikes into a ditch and threw ourselves into a sunflower field while the fighter plane made several dives, strafing the convoy. The German machine-gun vehicles were hit first, then several trucks. They must have been carrying fuel, because there were explosions everywhere and a long column of black smoke ascended into the sky. The plane left and, taking advantage of the confusion, Jackie and I crossed the field until we reached the main road again, a kilometer or so beyond the convoy.

'We knew that we had to cross a bridge over the Durance River. It was supposed to be guarded by German soldiers, but when we came near, there was not a soul around; the bridge had been bombed. Leaving our bicycles on the riverside, we started crossing the bridge, moving with great difficulty along the damaged rail, holding on to one of the sagging cables.

'As soon as we stepped foot on the other side, we were surrounded by a group of men in civilian clothes, carrying guns. They wore the FFI armband. They searched us, found our papers with German stamps, and took us prisoner. Forced to march to Pertuis with guns at our backs, we were taken to the town hall for interrogation. We tried to explain our mission to Mr Martin, the tobacconist in town and the man in charge, but they only laughed. They locked us in a pigsty for the night and placed a guard at the door.

'Around 1 a.m. there was a violent scuffle outside, accompanied by vociferous shouts. The door flew open, and our guard was knocked down with the butt of a rifle. Men wearing FTP (Communist) armbands prodded us with their weapons and ordered us to follow them to their camp on the other side of town. Less than an hour after our abduction, Martin, the FFI chief, presented himself to the rival camp, accompanied by a dozen men armed to the hilt. They looked furious and launched into a barrage of vile obscenities, dire threats and vulgar gestures. The Communist leader made the mistake of pointing his weapon at Martin and was kicked to his knees by Martin's bodyguards. Following a long pause, the FTP man gave us back to the FFI. "We'll meet again," he hissed angrily, "I'm not finished with you bitches."

'Brought back in front of a makeshift tribunal, the trial was conducted with dispatch. I knew by now the chances of our survival were slim; the underground had a reputation for carrying out its verdicts with speed and alacrity. Martin listened to the reading of the charges. "You are collaborators," they stated, "the proof is undeniable. The papers you carried have German seals. You have been found guilty of treason. The penalty is death."

'We were paraded through the town, past hundreds of hostile villagers. A sort of frenzy seemed to possess them. From the everyday housewives to the petit-bourgeois merchants, these self-appointed "patriots", who had never lifted a finger during the occupation, cautiously hiding in their homes, were now out in the street, demanding justice, spitting at us as we walked by. We reached a café-restaurant on the market place and were told to sit on a bench and wait. Neither of us could utter a word. I wanted to cry, but it was too late for that.

'We were jarred from our nightmare by sharp-cut orders. The beaded curtain of the bar parted and in came Bibendum [*code name for another OSS agent*]. He came forward and made a broad gesture of relief. "I came in time!" he exclaimed. "Some FFIs on the road boasted to have captured two girls."

'Martin showed up behind him, a bottle of red wine in one hand and glasses in the other. "No hard feelings?" he asked with a broad smile, as if an insignificant misunderstanding had just been settled.'[15]

OSS THEATRE REPORT

1 JULY 1944

Achievements

1. On 25 June 1944, 180 B-17 aircraft carried out a large-scale daylight operation for the purpose of delivering supplies and equipment to 4 Maquis areas in central and southeastern France. Each aircraft carried 12 containers loaded with various types of arms and ammunition. 177 planes completed the transmission, delivering 2088 containers.

2. During the month of June 223 tons of arms and supplies and 43 bodies were dropped to resistance groups in France for the SI Branch. In addition, 8 agents and 17 containers were delivered to France for the SI Branch.

3. The Forces Françaises de l'Intérieur (FFI), if adequately supported, may eventually gain control of large areas of central and southern France. Although the unprecedented air operation of 25 June will help to extend and strengthen the fighting capacity of the Maquis, it is obvious that many of the resistance groups in France will not be able to survive unless such assistance is continued during July and August.

4. Thirty-three American agents attached to Special Forces Headquarters were in the field at the end of June. These men have taken an active part in bitter fighting and sabotage work, including successful attacks on trains, bridges, communications lines, and supply dumps. A number of SO agents have supplied valuable intelligence reports. All of them have worked closely with the resistance groups in the areas to which they have been assigned.

5. On the night of 24/25 June 1944, two PT craft under the direction of Cmdr. Guest of the Maritime Branch completed a successful ferrying mission which delivered 4 SI agents with equipment to the north coast of Brittany. These men were dispatched at the request of the Third Army and FUSAG to obtain specific tactical information. They will operate

as two separate missions of two men each, known as 'Monkey' and 'Giraffe'.

6. On the night of 16/17 June, the 14th Sussex team was delivered successfully by an SOE operation. This two-man team established its first W/T contact through Station Victor on 21 June. Communication has now been established with all except 2 of the 14 Sussex teams that are behind enemy lines. A total of 86 messages have been received from the Sussex teams, of which 62 have been intelligence messages.

7. The counter-intelligence information prepared by the Italian Division of X-2, London, helped to facilitate the penetration of the extensive enemy stay-behind intelligence and sabotage network in Rome. Approximately fifty enemy agents have been captured since the city capitulated and penetration of the enemy network continues.

8. Since the 31 X-2/SCI unit landed on the beach-head in France on 10 June, certain individuals have been apprehended. The resulting interrogations will facilitate future work of this nature and furnish further information concerning enemy intelligence networks in France.[16]

8

Stirring the Balkans Cauldron

A GENTS ASSIGNED *to the Balkans soon discovered that the confusing and turbulent politics of the region created an additional burden which made their lives even more stressful. Frequently, the partisans they were supposed to organise and support were less interested in fighting the enemy than they were in preparing to fight each other for power after the war had ended. In Albania, for example, there were more than fifty guerrilla bands in existence, some fiercely nationalist, some fiercely communist; Allied support for one group immediately antagonised all the others. In Greece, rivalry between competing clandestine forces led to a bitter civil war; when an agreement was reached to end the infighting, at least until peace was declared, the strongest political group, ELAS, promptly set about forcibly disarming some of the smaller groups. In Yugoslavia, then as now, the Serbs, Croats and Slovenes were at each other's throats; the Allies first supported General Draža Mihailović, leader of the nationalist Chetniks, then discovered that he was using weapons dropped from Allied aircraft to fight the communist partisans, led by Tito. By early 1944, the Allies had switched their allegiance to Tito.*

While the various resistance movements in the Balkans played an important role in Allied strategy – sabotaging supplies and communications and tying down troops to prevent them being deployed in more decisive battles being fought elsewhere – both British and American governments, already concerned about the post-war balance of power, were decidedly reluctant to nurture communist partisan groups, even though they were often the best trained and disciplined. Thus it was that OSS and SOE agents in the Balkans found themselves in a maelstrom of conflicting aims, trying to accommodate the shifting political and strategic requirements of London and Washington while dealing on the ground with hot-tempered, ill-disciplined, antagonistic and largely ungrateful underground armies whose hatred for the enemy was only exceeded by their hatred for one another.

Report by Captain J. McElroy, SOE, on operations carried out in the Drama region of Greece, January to November, 1944:

I was dropped onto the hills of Chol Dag, near the town of Drama, on the night of 10th January, 1944. Fortunately, for all concerned, heavy snow, about 1½ ft deep, made the landing a comparatively easy one. The first Greek to meet me was Petrakis, whom I had previously met in training, and whom I got to know and appreciate much better in the months to follow. Then followed dozens of large, whiskered Greeks, who threw their arms around me and kissed me on both cheeks.

I was then escorted to a large tree nearby, where I was introduced to my first real Andarte [*guerrilla*], Capetano Anontones, who later became leader of the Nationalist bands in that area. The setting was rather romantic, sitting cross-legged by a large fire, bristling with bullets, bombs and knives. There followed our first hike to the village of Kastanotis, three to four hours away, which was reached just before dawn.

Some time during the day I, with the others, Major Kitkat, Captain Pike and Corporal Campbell, wakened to find ourselves the exhibits of the entire village. One could not, thereafter, even perform the more intimate actions of one's normal life, without having a large and admiring audience of both sexes and all ages. The house, which in the moonlight appeared quite presentable, now took on a different aspect in daylight. Almost every house was a tumbledown affair with no glass in the windows and a leaky roof. Most of the houses contained several rooms, one for living in and the rest filled up with the junk of generations; almost invariably, the lower rooms were occupied by the family's livestock. The bathroom arrangements left much to be desired and fell rather short of those on view at the 'Ideal Home' exhibition. In this particular house a small hole existed on the verandah, which overlooked the entire village and was devoid of cover of any sort. The lice and bugs which thrive on conditions like this made sleeping in the open a pleasure. The problem of refusing the hospitality of a house was later solved by the Bulgars [*Bulgarians fighting on the side of the Axis*], who burned all the Andarte villages. This was the most useful thing the Bulgars ever did.

Owing to the possibility of activity by the Bulgars, it was decided to set up camp in a less inhabited area. This was carried out the next day. The only cover we had then was a parachute, and the cold was intense. Finally a stove arrived, which faithfully produced nothing but smoke: the necessary warmth was provided by blowing one's head off trying to keep the stove alight . . .

It was three weeks before contact was made with Cairo, as no batteries had been sent with the wireless set. The Andartes, however, solved the problem by holding up a car and removing the batteries from it. By this time I had constructed a hut, with stone walls bound together with mud, and roofed with corrugated sheets. Although the hut had two fires in it, the cold was almost unbearable.

This part of Greece had been given to Bulgaria by the Germans and most of the men had preferred to take to the hills rather than collaborate with the Bulgars. The condition of most of them was appalling. Their clothes were literally in rags, sometimes so many patches existed that it was impossible to tell the original cloth. Only a very small number had shoes or boots, most of them had only a piece of leather bound round their feet. Socks were non-existent. No medical supplies existed, and past wounds had to heal as best they could. The women, too, were poorly clad, and children were born with no medical attention whatsoever. Several women were about to become mothers when we left, with very little hope of a doctor as they were still in the hills.

Recces were rather different to elsewhere in Greece because Bulgar families had been brought in to settle in all the villages in the plains; even in the villages in the hills at least one Bulgar family resided and reported on anything suspicious. The most disastrous recce was one near Kavalla, carried out by myself with Sergeant Chatterly as interpreter. We started off in good spirits with about 12 Andartes, one of whom said he knew the way. We found, however, that immediately he left the valley where our camp was, he was lost. We carried on as best we could, but Andartes will never, at any time, pass a dangerous spot without either having an argument, coughing, spitting, lighting a cigarette or firing off a spare round. This recce was no exception. Instead of crossing over the main road, which was patrolled, they stood in the middle of it and had a long and loud discussion as to which direction to go.

Finally we crawled into a village and tried to knock up a Greek who would guide us to the next village. It took an hour before the door was opened, and the sight which met our eyes goes to prove the terror that the Bulgars had instilled into the local Greeks. In the middle of the floor the owner of the house was down on his knees praying and begging us not to kill him and his family, while huddled in the corner was his wife, with stark terror in her eyes, clasping her children to her. When we finally convinced him that we were not Bulgars disguised as Andartes, as apparently they sometimes did, he got up and kissed us all, and also our rifles.

He then put a map of Greece on the floor, but his mutterings were unintelligible. Finally, however, he took us to the next village, where we got another guide. This new guide was a bit better, but very windy, as the next village we were going through had about 12 Bulgar police. The guide decided to go by the road which just skirted the village, instead of by-passing it, which would have meant several hours' detour. Unfortunately the dogs heard us about two kilometres away, and by the time we got near the village every dog in the country was barking. However, just as we reached the first house, lights began to flash, and the guide, with one shout of 'Police!', dashed off in the direction he happened to be facing, which was across the open plain, and was never seen or heard of again.

In a split second we were all away. My own line of retreat happened to be up a steep hill, where I was abruptly stopped by a 4ft high wall. Fortunately we had all run in the same direction, except the aforementioned guide, and the Andartes had moved so quickly that they had not even taken time to drop our kit. I decided then that to carry on this recce with such a band was useless, so gave orders to return and collect a fresh lot. Alas, the second lot was as bad and I came to the conclusion that 99.99% of all Andartes were a patriotic crowd of useless 'old women' – an opinion I still hold.[1]

Captain Julian Amery, SOE liaison officer in Albania:
'The classical, rather old-fashioned, theory about guerrilla warfare is that you find a movement which already exists and you send one or two officers to advise and guide them and help them with money and arms. But [Orde] Wingate, who was one of the greatest guerrilla leaders of World War Two, said it was awfully difficult to get them – even with money and arms – to do the right thing. They take the money and they take the arms and go off and fight private civil wars of their own.

'So, if you want them to do what you want to do, you want to have a striking force under your own control. And so I said to myself in Albania, where a civil war was going on and neither side was doing much against the Germans, could I get a striking force? And I found that there was a battalion of Soviet soldiers, from eastern parts of the Soviet Union – Turkomans, Uzbeks, Kazaks – who had, I was told, killed their Russian officers and deserted to the Germans in the early stages of the war, but the Germans had taken them prisoner and hadn't trusted them enough to put them in front-line service.

'I got in touch with these chaps through a Turkish-speaking priest and sent them a message, saying, "You're on the wrong side, the Germans are losing the war. You ought to kill your German officers and come over to me!" I sent several messages like this and one morning, about five or six o'clock, I was sleeping in the woods with a guard of about half a dozen people and I was woken and my bodyguard said, "There's a Chinese to see you." So I rubbed my eyes and propped myself up and a man came in with very Mongolian features in a German uniform. He sat down beside me and he had a big green handkerchief in his hands and he opened the green handkerchief and there were six ears and he indicated that these were the ears of his German officers. "We've done what you said," he said to me in very broken German.

'Well now, ears look much alike and I wasn't at all sure that they were German ears – they might have been the ears of some wretched Albanian peasant – so I asked him how many had come and he said two hundred had come over with their arms. And I thought that the only hope is to blood them at once and get them to attack a German post. But the question was, was it a trap for me? I spent about half an hour trying to make my mind up and decided I better had take the risk. So I went over to where they were encamped, about two miles away, had some difficulty in communication with broken German, a little bit of broken Russian, and put the plan to them that the next morning they were going to attack a German post and they said, "Splendid." And so we reconnoitred the post that evening and the next morning we set off.

'The question is, how do you lead men when you can't talk to them? You have to lead them from the front. So I set out at the head of this column, and as I advanced, I thought to myself, they killed their Russian officers, they killed their German officers and now I am their officer! And I couldn't help looking round at them over my shoulder. We got to the camp. The Germans had seen us coming because they opened up and I got very slightly wounded, enough to fall over, and I thought, my God, now these chaps will run away. Not a bit of it. They waited to see what happened to me. I got up, took off my hat and said, "Come on, charge!" and they went like wolves, bounding down into the camp and wiped it out. I think they killed a hundred people or so, stripped them of their watches, boots, any valuables they could see. And that was the initial action. They then stayed with me for two or three months until we had to leave the country. They were a cheerful lot, quite tough soldiers and there was a good deal of entertainment at night, singing and dancing.'[2]

Major Monty Woodhouse, commander of an SOE mission parachuted into northern Greece to destroy a bridge over the Gorgopotamos River:
'The plan to demolish the bridge was to make it impossible for Hitler's troops to go by rail to North Africa, because this was the only route from Germany down to the south of Greece. We needed a considerable force to blow it up, because it was a long and strong bridge. We had an excellent team of New Zealand engineers and Greek guerrillas and so on, but I could see that we were going to need to have help from local partisans in order to have enough men for the operation.

'I made contact with Zervas, the guerrilla leader, who greeted me in Greek with the famous remark: "Welcome to the bearer of good tidings." Zervas was rather taken aback to learn that Ares Veloutiotes, the communist leader, was on his way to the village because there was no friendship between them. However, Zervas made it clear that he would come with me to the railway line and I hoped that Ares would be doing the same. While Zervas and I were having a meal, Ares and his band arrived in the village. The ordinary rank and file in these guerrilla bands weren't really enemies, but Ares Veloutiotes was different – he would without hesitation shoot one of his own men who didn't agree with him. However, we needed Ares for our operation, otherwise he would fight us.

'We set off for the bridge with Ares's band and Zervas's band more or less in step together, until we got to a certain village, I can't remember the name of it, which was clearly a meeting place of the communists. Ares stopped there and conducted a private meeting with his own fellow communists at this village. Zervas and I went on. I didn't know whether Ares was now going to desert us, but he didn't, he followed us a day or two later. Obviously, the leading communists in the area had told him to go ahead and help us, and not to sabotage our operation.

'When we were approaching the area of our operation, Ares's men captured a wretched gypsy gangster. Unfortunately for him, he was carrying an Italian card and admitted that he was paid by the Italians to report on the resistance. Ares insisted that he should be hanged, and that I witness the hanging. There was no doubt that this wretched youth was a spy, he had accepted money from the Italians, and if we let him go, he would go back to the Italians and give us away. He was a perfectly worthless creature. Nevertheless, I felt bloody about it; I can only say I felt very ashamed.

'The bridge was guarded by an Italian unit; there must have been about eighty to a hundred men at different points on the bridge, mainly at each end, where they had concrete pillboxes. The first thing that our side had to do was neutralise the pillboxes at each end of the bridge, so they began with hand grenades thrown into the pillboxes. And of course a lot of Italians burst out, a lot were killed and a lot came out. Two or three miles up the line, there was an armoured train which was available to come out whenever called upon. Marinos, our very reliable Greek leader, took twenty or thirty men to blow the line and make it impossible for it to reach the bridge.

'The bridge itself was about two or three hundred yards long, perhaps more. There were stone pillars which we could not demolish, but there were two massive iron girders at the south end of the bridge and we had first-class engineers, New Zealanders, to plant the charges. The leading New Zealand engineer controlling the whole operation fired a Verey pistol when he wanted us to lie flat on the ground to avoid the flying fragments, but I couldn't bear to miss the scene. There was a pause of about thirty seconds and then came this wonderful sight of the steel lines floating up in the air and crashing on to the ground. I remember vividly the three of us – Zervas, Ares and myself – joining hands and dancing round in a circle and singing a well-known Greek hymn which had no meaning but just seemed pleasant to listen to. And then we walked home in triumph.

'After the Gorgopotamos Bridge was blown up, the Italians took some hostages, fifteen or sixteen villagers, completely innocent people who just happened to be walking round. They took them to the bridge, sat them down by one of the broken pillars and shot them. That really was bloody-minded. It was a terrible, terrible war.'[3]

Captain Edgar Hargreaves, SOE, parachuted into Yugoslavia in May 1942 to work with the Chetniks but was captured the following year and driven to Belgrade:
'I was taken into what appeared to be an office building and told to

sit down and wait. I was guarded by a soldier. And then in came a civilian wearing a black leather overcoat – it was the first time I had seen one of these – and he took some details. And as he was typing my name, rank and number, I happened to notice on the top of the paper the *Geheimstaatspolizei*, so I knew that this was the Gestapo.

'Then I was taken downstairs to quite a modern sort of jail and all my clothes were taken away, everything was removed, and I was put into quite a small cell which was right next to the heating equipment for the building and it became absolutely like an oven. I was kept there, I think, for two days with no food, no water, nothing at all; by that time I was completely dehydrated. Then I was taken out and I was given a shirt and a pair of trousers and taken upstairs into some very elegant surroundings, a very nice office room where they had some form of restraints on the wall for putting your hands and arms into. Then one or two Germans came in, including some women, terribly smartly turned out, very civilised-looking and they ignored me completely, talked among themselves. And then I was asked quite a lot of questions. One's answer was always to begin with: "According to the Geneva Convention all I've got to tell you is my name, rank and number which I'm very pleased to do." But it was all rather silly really because they seemed to know more about us than we knew ourselves. They had a complete copy of all the messages we had ever sent, which they seemed to have been able to decode.

'After that first interrogation I was taken downstairs and my clothes were taken away from me again. I was put into another cell this time. I maintained all the time as a British officer I was entitled to be treated according to rules of the Geneva Convention and their answer to that was that I'd not been in conventional uniform when I was captured, I was captured with a lot of sabotage equipment and therefore I was a terrorist. There was very little one could do to argue about that either. So I was taken down to my cell again and left there. A considerable time went past; occasionally I was taken up for interrogation and sometimes there was a fair amount of brutality.

'It was most extraordinary because they never used extreme brutality at all, but the idea seemed to be utter humiliation, making you completely without dignity. As I say, all my clothes were taken away, I was given no facilities for washing. The cell in which I lived was about five feet long, eleven feet tall and it had a light in the ceiling which never went off. I couldn't stretch my arms across it. All it had was a duckboard on the floor, an iron door with a peephole in it and no toilet facilities at all. If one wanted to use the lavatory you could bang on the door, sometimes someone would come and sometimes they wouldn't. It was just impossible to contain oneself at times and I had to just use the floor. And that always enraged them, which usually meant a few sharp blows.

'I was there over Christmas and there was a great deal of maudlin sentiment among the Germans. They kept crying and saying how miserable they were to have to be away from home and how they missed their families.

'Later, I was hung up by my arms behind my back in such a way that I could just take the weight of my body on my tiptoes. That immediately brought on terrific cramps in your leg and you couldn't stay there so immediately you had to put the whole weight of your body on your arms again. I think I spent nearly forty-eight hours like that before they eventually put me back in my cell. But it was not so brutal, it was painful and uncomfortable but it was not like having one's fingernails torn out or some of the other awful things one had heard about. Another thing they did was to put a bucket on my head and beat it with a pickaxe handle. What that was supposed to do, I don't know. I had parts of my body burned with cigars. But they were more sort of humiliating and niggling things rather than utter brutality. And at the same time you knew they were ill-treating a lot of other people far worse than they ever did me.

'I always insisted that I was a British officer and I always said, "Whatever you do to try and hide what is happening here, eventually it is going to become known and you are going to have to pay for it." Eventually they told me that I had been convicted of being a terrorist as I had sabotage equipment with me and that I was to be executed.

'They then transferred me to a military prison on the outskirts of Belgrade. I was in a cell there which was filthy dirty and there were rats in it and if one dozed off the damned things would come and bite you and leap onto you. People for execution were usually moved to cells on either side of a corridor leading to a courtyard, and on two or three occasions I was moved with them, but the following morning, when the executions were to be carried out, I was just left where I was and eventually taken back to the main part of the barracks. And then from there I was suddenly told one day that I was being moved. I said, "Where?" but they never gave you any great information. All I had was a shirt and a pair of trousers and I was handcuffed and we were sent off by train with two guards. Because of the disruption of the railways, there was a lot of changes of train and I sometimes had to be left on the platform while they went to find out wherever we were to go next. Usually I was handcuffed round a post, my arms on either side. It was midwinter and I was bloody cold, I had no shoes and just a pair of ragged old trousers and a shirt. By this time we were in Germany and the local population used to come along to belabour me and spit at me. Eventually, I ended up in Buchenwald.'[4]

Major Erik Greenwood, SOE liaison officer, parachuted into Yugoslavia, 17 April 1943:
'My mission was to liaise with the Yugoslav underground army under the command of General Mihailović, to support them and to arrange for physical support by air drops, and to organise two specific matters: one was the blocking of the Danube River, which was the main source of supply to the German forces in southern Russia, and the other was the interruption of the production of the bore copper mines in eastern Serbia. I was not trying to accomplish these things myself but to encourage the Yugoslavs to do it. I had with me one Yugoslav officer as a kind of ADC [*aide-de-camp*] and one wireless operator.

'After I landed I was embraced by everybody and kissed heartily on both cheeks and before we knew where we were we'd consumed several bottles of raki and slivovitz. That was the reception, they were simply delighted to see us and within, I think, possibly the next day or the next two days after that, there were two air drops of supplies, so I was regarded as a kind of magician. All I had to do was to arrive, open up my radio set and have my operator send a signal and an aircraft arrived, so I was extremely popular!

'Well, that didn't last. Initially, I was very much impressed by the fact that a whole army existed in an occupied country. Admittedly, they lived in very broken, heavily wooded, accentuated country and staying in the woods and forests is not difficult if you can keep alive, but there was a whole army organisation with internal radio communications operating in German occupied territory – to me almost miraculous. But as I got to know them better and was trying to get them to take some action, they kept putting things off for one reason or another and I became more and more disillusioned.

'Frustration creeps up on one. I wanted to move up closer to the Danube to reconnoitre, but there was always some reason why we shouldn't do it and it became quite apparent, quite quickly, that they didn't want to do it. I got more annoyed and started having arguments with them about it and said it was absurd that they should be so unwilling to do anything, when it was perfectly possible to do it in my opinion. All this tended to make me increasingly unhappy as the months rolled by.

'When we were moving around in the early days of my presence in eastern Serbia, I didn't know the country. So wherever I went, I either went with troops who were under the command of the officer to whom I was attached, or with a small body, two or three men, but with a guide we would find in the village. He would be sometimes offered money to take us and sometimes not, but almost invariably before we set off, he got drunk. I don't remember a move really where the guide wasn't drunk. A man would come forward and say, I know how to get to the point you want to go to, I'm very experienced on this journey, I do it all the time, my people live on the way, my cousin lives there, et cetera. This was nearly always untrue. He didn't have a cousin, or, if he did, he didn't know who the cousin was and he'd never been there himself. It was quite frequent in eastern Serbia to find people who had never been two kilometres from the place where they were born.

'Supply drops were difficult. My magical powers quickly disappeared because it took a long time for the next one and even longer for the ones after that. We once spent a hundred nights waiting for a single aircraft to appear and nothing came. From Christmas of 1943 until I finally left Yugoslavia, I think I saw one air drop in half a year.

'We spent a lot of time sending detailed signals of requirements, how many rifles were needed, what ammunition we needed for the rifles. The rifles we got were normally captured enemy rifles because we could rely then on getting ammunition. Once I asked for a drop of uniforms and what arrived were seventeen pairs of trousers, forty tunics, fifty pairs of old and very small boots and a few shirts. Somebody had risked his life to fly from North Africa to the middle of Europe to make that delivery. It was ridiculous, it should never have happened.

'So absurd things arrived. On the other hand, some wonderful things arrived. I got thirty letters from my wife on one occasion, all together. I got copies of *The Times*. I recall that I got a case of whisky on one occasion and it was very acceptable. So occasionally things happened that suited us, but on the whole we very rarely got one whole air drop which contained what we wanted. That was not due to any attempt to thwart us, I'm sure – it was due to incompetence. I suspect they were using Italian labour and the Italians didn't care what went.

'Our relations with the Serbs were not really worsened by the lack of supplies, because they realised that I could no more get supplies than they could. They grumbled about spending nights out in the cold and the rain waiting for some aircraft which didn't come, but we didn't have real friction about that. We had friction much more about their lack of willingness to undertake any action and that did cause real friction. At some meetings when we had a lot of officers present responsible for different areas, I would sometimes get quite angry and say, "Why can you not carry out the orders of the Supreme Headquarters?" and I remember on one occasion being interrupted by an officer saying, "Major, they're not orders, they're requests." They didn't regard themselves as part of the Allied armies and we would get quite heated. But these things always blew over. After the meeting, somebody would say, let's have a drink and it'd all be forgotten for the time being.

'It was not until towards the end of October '43 that I finally got the agreement of an area commander to attempt an operation. So with a few men and one other British officer, I set off for the banks of the Danube, two or three days hard walk away. On the way, a courier arrived with a long letter from the officer who'd agreed to the operation saying that he understood that I was going to the Danube to try to sink some barges and tugs and it must have been a misunderstanding on my part if I thought that he had agreed to it. I ignored his letter. I just read it and put it in my pocket and went on. The right bank of the Danube was extremely steep, almost precipitous, and we got ourselves into a position over the river during the night and at dawn the first string of barges came up under tug power. I had with me a former tug pilot from that very reach who knew exactly when to stop the tugs so that they would go aground. We opened fire on the leading tug and I presume that the helmsman took evasive action or was even killed, I don't know, but the tug almost immediately went out of control and so did the second one and all the barges behind them ran aground. That was exactly what I'd been trying to do for half a year. The result of that was that within a few days the Germans announced that they had taken a hundred hostages in Belgrade and shot them.

'That was the only action we ever undertook and the fact that they had these hostages shot was thrown in our faces by the local commanders. They said, there, we told you so, you can't do this sort of thing and have the poor civilians shot and that was difficult to gainsay really.'[5]

Captain Melvin O. Benson, OSS, dropped into Bosnia to work as a liaison officer with Tito's partisans:
'At two thirty in the morning of 22 August 1943, I parachuted alone

into Bosnia, in the area known as Metropolje. It was a great moment for me as I was the first American to begin work with Tito's partisans. A few days later I met and had dinner with Tito. He was most friendly and assured me that I would be given fullest cooperation and that he was pleased to have an American observer present. Tito said I would be given assistance in moving about the country to see things for myself and I was privileged to talk with anyone at any time. He thought that groups of Slovenes, Croats and Serbs in America, if accurately informed about the partisans movement in Yugoslavia, would give material support as well as moral. He spoke with bitterness about Draža Mihailović and the government-in-exile, branding them as traitors and criminals who were collaborating with the Axis to fight the partisans. Later events gave ample evidence to prove such collaboration. During our discussion we had been sampling the native plum brandy, raki. Tito chain-smoked using a miniature pipe as a cigarette holder. He was much pleased with some American cigarettes which I had brought with me.

'This meeting took place inside a forest of tall cedar trees. The makeshift table had large logs along either side for us to sit on and above was stretched a piece of canvas. Dinner was presently served by a plain-looking young woman who, aside from a small pistol, carried two hand grenades on the belt round her waist. Later I learned the grenades were for self-destruction in event of capture by the Chetniks or the Ustashi [*Croatians fighting on the side of the Axis*]. The large portions of mashed potatoes with thick gravy and large pieces of roast lamb were a special treat and were eaten without time for conversation.

'Having satisfied our appetites, the talk turned to recalling incidents both tragic and amusing. Tito displayed a large poster showing his picture and the offer of 100,000 marks in gold as a reward for his capture, dead or alive. He expressed great interest in the American tommy gun, which he knew about as a favorite weapon of gangsters. I made him a gift of the one I had with me, and several weeks later I saw him with it always within easy reach.

'Two days later we prepared to move to Jajce, a town known to tourists for its old Turkish fort and the beautiful waterfalls on the Vrbas River. We purchased two packhorses from peasants, paying them nine gold sovereigns for each one. All available animals were used for carrying equipment. We had one riding horse to share between five of us. Until dusk, we kept the column fairly well separated because of recce aircraft. Later, we closed up. After dark, the going became very difficult. We had climbed one side of a large mountain and were following a twisting, rocky trail down the opposite side. It was a stumbling job and went on for hours. All the time, the trail zigzagged through the large trees growing thick on the steep slope. Near midnight, having started early in the afternoon, we arrived at a small village where the packhorses were rested and we tried to sleep. The walking had made us warm, and now we froze. The altitude here was about 4,000 feet.

'Around two o'clock we were again moving. The country, as the sun rose, was extremely beautiful. Most of the walking was downhill now and at frequent intervals there would be pools of cold, fresh water from the inside of the mountain. Then we could see Jajce across the valley, still a long way away. Later, the trail turned into a country road which followed the Vrbas River. The yards around the neat-looking houses were orderly and clean. In the gardens were numerous plum orchards; vegetables, especially cabbage, seemed plentiful. At one place on the riverbank a woman was doing some washing and singing a cheerful song at the top of her voice as she worked.

'As we entered Jajce, the townspeople watched us with great interest. This was the third time the partisans had held Jajce. A vacant house was located for our mission, and after filling up on stew, we spread our blankets on the floor and soon were fast asleep.

'The old church in Jajce was opened the first Sunday after we arrived. It had been closed for two years. The church overflowed with the peasant women in their different native costumes who had come on foot many miles. That evening, a propaganda meeting was held in the cultural hall at which Tito with members of the Supreme Staff, Deakin [*Major Bill Deakin, a British liaison officer*] and myself were front and centre for everyone to look at. The speeches and singing were very enthusiastically received. The platform was decorated with a large sketch of Tito on one side, and Stalin on the other. The following day the main street was crowded with young farmers, eager to join up with the partisans.

'On the evening that the news of the Italian capitulation was received, Tito requested that Major Deakin and I proceed to Split at once to assist in obtaining arms and stores from the Italians. Within an hour we were underway with our wireless operator, Walter. We went by car from Jajce to Bugojno where we joined the First Proletarian Division, which was going to make a forced march to Split. Leading the column was a battalion of fairly well-equipped riflemen. Only a few had machine guns and the others all had Italian rifles with bandolier of ammunition clips. Then followed numerous packhorses and mules carrying hospital equipment, food supplies, the field kitchen and one small mountain gun. Most of the animals were being led by women. One elderly woman was herding along a flock of ten sheep. Also in the column were several cows, a bull and a couple of steers. There was a group of about fifty new recruits, still wearing peasant costume and without rifles. They looked to be fourteen or fifteen years old.

'With only occasional five-minute rest periods, we kept moving until three o'clock in the afternoon. We had been passing through sparsely wooded country and were now on the edge of an open valley. We established staff headquarters under some trees on a small knoll just outside a little village. A peasant woman came by with a bucket full of sour milk. This was passed around and we all had a healthy swig. Later, we had more food and a short sleep.

'At nine o'clock the brigade assembled again and an all-night march got under way, everything running smoothly without any shouting of orders or any fuss. The moon was high, and everyone seemed in excellent spirits. There was enthusiastic singing of partisan songs. We arrived in Mokromze at six o'clock the following morning, having passed through three villages which had been burned out several times by the Ustashi. At once we were assigned to an upstairs room in a house formerly the property of an Ustashi.

'The boys were busy unpacking the radio and putting up the aerial when we heard a burst of machine-gun fire. Looking out of our windows, we saw an Ustashi truck about four hundred yards down the road. Seven fellows jumped out and started running for cover. One was shot immediately, two others fell before they got off the road. Partisans with rifles appeared from all directions racing across the fields toward the spot. There were two more trucks coming up behind the first. Our boys cleared up the whole lot in short order and took the three trucks which were loaded with supplies.

'In order to hurry on to Split, we left at eight o'clock in the evening, and keeping a good pace we arrived at a place called Zadvarje at noon. Here, the local big shot put us up at a hotel. We were given plenty of good wine and food, and a chance to wash. While we were relaxing, at two o'clock our boys dashed in and shouted for us to run for it, that the Germans were entering the town. We grabbed our guns and, leaving all our kit except the radio, we ran a couple of blocks where we caught a lorry just getting started. As we were heading out of town in the direction of Split, a dozen Stukas circled around strafing the town and highway. We piled out and scattered in the ditch. It was a desperate scramble for the best cover. Explosive bullets came within a few feet. One direct hit on the rear tire of our truck put it out of action. We started running along the road, having to hide in culverts, the ditch or vineyards several times as planes came back to strafe again and again. Eventually, another truck happened along and carried us to headquarters just outside of Split.

'The following day, September 17, I attended, as American representative, a conference at which the terms under which the Italians turned their weapons and equipment over to the partisans was debated.'[6]

Captain James M. Goodwin, OSS, parachuted into Bosnia in January 1944 to act as liaison officer to the British mission:
'One of my functions as liaison officer was to encourage the partisans to keep the important railway line from Trieste to Ljubljana Zagreb cut sufficiently so that the enemy could not use it to transport matériel and troops to the Italian front. There were four main bridges on this line, one of which was the Litija Bridge. I suggested to the partisans that they destroy this bridge as soon as possible to continue our disruption of traffic on the railway line, which had been out of use for the Germans for three weeks, due to partisan activities. The Slovene staff agreed that the destruction of this bridge would stop traffic for at least two weeks, and probably longer, but that it was not a practical target because it was overlooked by a large castle which was used as a fortress to guard the bridge and this castle was heavily garrisoned by the Germans. I asked if they would undertake it if I could acquire air support and they agreed.

'Within a week air support was arranged and the partisan troops were in position for their attack. On September 17, John Phillips, a *Life* photographer, and myself, left the Slovene HQ and traveled with the partisans into German-held territory, which Hitler considered part of the Third Reich. During the night of the 19th we moved into a position about one mile from the bridge and waited for the aircraft to arrive. At 4.30 p.m., six Mustangs arrived and attempted to knock out the castle but because of the intensity of ack-ack and tracer fire they could not come in low enough to be accurate. Bombs fell in a radius of five miles from the castle and none came within three hundred yards of it.

'After observing that the castle was not knocked out, I thought it only proper that I request to go with the unit of about a hundred men that was to storm the castle. To my surprise this wish was granted. Immediately after the bombing we made our way toward the castle and after a considerable exchange of rifle and machine-gun fire, were forced to hold about 150 yards from the castle because a clear terrace remaining between us and the castle was guarded by three well-fortified bunkers. After about a half-hour of fighting, tanks were heard coming up on our right. The partisan captain in charge took fifty men and started out to meet them. I did not see him again but heard that he and his men knocked out two tanks with a Russian anti-tank rifle. This left the remaining fifty men to storm the castle in the command of one sergeant and one commissar. The sergeant and I crawled to a position where we could see the entire situation and plan an attack on the castle. It was in this position that he was hit in the shoulder by an explosive bullet and killed. I crawled back to the men and found that they, too, had been under heavy fire and a number of them were wounded.

'As a result of these unforeseen incidents, the units were now commanded by a young junior commissar, a kid of about seventeen years, who was so excited he did not know what to do. He tried to assemble his men two or three times and was trying to force them to charge the bunkers by firing at their heels with his sub-machine gun. Each time the men went out in the open they were driven back by fire from the Germans. After about an hour of firing into the bunkers, I noticed a lull in their return fire which made it apparent that now was the time to make the charge. I contacted the commissar and had him set up protective fire on the hill behind us and told him to order the rest of the men to follow me. He was so excited and worried that he would have agreed to anything.

'So I started through a barbed-wire fence with a group of the men to knock out the first bunker. As soon as we reached open ground, a partisan mortar opened up on us from across the other side of the valley and made us retreat. I then had the commissar send a messenger to the mortar crew and order them to stop firing. We realized this would take considerable time and from nowhere he produced a Verey light gun and fired a green flare up in the air and the mortar stopped. We again headed toward the bunkers and knocked the three of them out in short order, but we lost fifteen out of forty men.

'Once we reached the castle we were in a most dangerous position because we were now in view of both Germans and partisans, who could not distinguish us from their enemy. Our only alternative was to dash around the other side of the castle and try to get into the only door. To do this, we had to knock out another bunker at very close range with hand grenades. Upon knocking out the bunker, we were able to get inside a protective arch that gave us cover from rifle fire. The partisans yelled to the Germans to surrender and five of them came to us at once. We pushed four of them outside with two guards to take them back to our lines. The fifth German was arguing about something and would not go out. While he was talking, a German threw a hand grenade into our enclosure which landed at my feet and went off at the same time. The hand grenade wounded one man seriously and another man and myself with only slight wounds. The partisans carried me to their first-aid station and from there to a field hospital about two miles from the battle.'[7]

Captain Franklin Lindsay, an OSS officer parachuted into Yugoslavia on 14 May 1944 with orders to link up with a partisan group and lead attacks on railway lines in German-occupied territory, in the upper Savinja valley:
'All the towns and villages in the area were garrisoned by German troops. Food was always a problem, and sometimes a serious one. The higher we were in the mountains the safer we were, but the further we were from the valleys where food could be obtained at night. A foraging party we sent out one night into the valley for food ran into a German patrol; all of the partisans were shot.

'Our diet was varied, but not balanced. Occasionally on our marches the party would include an ox procured from a peasant farmer. It might be driven along with us for two or three days (at a very slow pace) until it was slaughtered. We would all live on meat for the next few days. Then it would be only fruit, then only potatoes, then only meat, and finally a return to the ubiquitous *zganci*, a rubbery ball of grain. On rare occasions a peasant wife would offer me a small bowl of *kislo mleko*, whole milk that had been allowed to sour to form a yoghurt. It was pure heaven.

'The food problem was worst in areas that were under German control during the day and partisan control at night. The Germans sought to deny us the food on which they knew we depended by confiscating the peasants' reserves for the winter. I remember vividly arriving one evening at an isolated peasant house. The family – father, mother and three children – had just sat down to an evening meal of beans and vegetables cooked in a single pot now on the table. There were no plates. They ate directly from the pot with spoons. When we came in, the family immediately stood up, greeted us shyly, and motioned us to take their places. Each of us carried a spoon stuck in his boot top. It was often called the partisan's secret weapon, and when we first arrived with the partisans we were cautioned never to lose our spoons; if we did we would starve to death. I dipped my spoon into the stew. It tasted marvellous. I knew that this was the family's meal and if we ate it they would go to bed hungry. I was determined to take only three or four spoonfuls but found it impossible to stop without one more and then a second. We did stop eating when there was about a third left in the pot, though the father and mother urged us to continue. It took the greatest will power to put the spoons back in our boots.

'While on the march one night, the head of our escort patrol heard the footsteps of men approaching us. At a whispered command, everyone went flat on the ground, guns ready. The other group reacted in the same way and the two groups found themselves about a hundred feet apart, each unsure whether the others were partisans or White Guard collaborators. After preliminary challenges, a shouted dialogue began between the leaders of the two groups: "Who are you?", "What village are you from?", "Who is your father?", "Where is your house?", "Who lives in the next house?", "When did you join the partisans?" Finally, each was satisfied that the other unit was also partisan and we continued on our way. It was a very effective way of determining friend or foe, since the leaders of the patrols were usually natives of the area and knew intimately the details of village and farm life, especially whether or not another person was a collaborator or a partisan. No false documents or cover story could be designed to stand up to this sort of questioning.'

Because SOE and OSS supported any guerrilla group with a will to fight the Germans, OSS and SOE officers occasionally found themselves caught up in the middle of internecine conflict.

Diary of Lieutenant E.R. Kramer, OSS, on an intelligence-gathering mission with the Chetniks in Serbia, September–October 1944:

September 17: This morning the partisans put in a light attack against some Chetnik villages. In the meantime, Colonel Kesserovic [*a Chetnik commander*] asked me exactly what my mission was and I told him and his officers that it was to evacuate Allied airmen that had been shot down, obtain information of German troop activity and also to obtain any other information available. They asked me if it would be possible for the Allies to prevent this civil war [*between the nationalist Chetniks and the communist partisans*], and stated that they had wanted to concentrate their efforts against the Germans, but every time they attacked or prepared an attack against the Germans, the partisans would jump on their backs. I sent a note by courier

to the local partisan commander, asking for a rendezvous with
the idea of stopping this local battle between Yugoslavs because,
while this battle was going on, large German columns were
passing through the Morava Valley from Prizren to Krusevac
and from there to Niš and Belgrade. The partisan commander
did not reply but he told the courier that the Americans had
no business becoming interested in the civil war in Serbia, and
that they had better get out; and, with that, he had the courier
beaten up . . .

September 18: At 6.00 this morning, the partisans put in a
heavy counterattack. The Chetnik commander of the brigade
with whom I am, Captain Gordich, asked me whether to
counterattack or retreat, and I replied that I was not the
commander of his troops, and therefore, could not advise him
but was solely here for observation. In the Chetnik ranks are
weapons of all calibres and makes. Many men go into battle
unarmed and wait for a man to get hit and then take up the
dropped rifle. A Chetnik soldier seldom has more than 35 or
40 cartridges for his rifle. The majority have no shoes and all
are dressed in peasant clothing. The only reason they fought so
stubbornly is to prevent the Communists from occupying their
villages.

September 19–23: On September 22nd, in a small village
eight miles north of Drenova, I saw the bodies of eight men
(civilians) who had been tortured to death by knife. The
older men had been slashed about the face with a knife and
then their skulls bashed in with a rifle butt. One young man
who had refused to join the partisans had been carved up
pretty badly by the orders of a partisan woman who stood
by.

I also found out from partisan prisoners that they had specific orders to kill and capture the American officer with the
Chetniks. Also upon my arrival back at Bela Voda, the peasant
at whose hut I had been staying told me that two hours after I
had left his place, a partisan lieutenant, two women and nine
guards came to his hut and asked of the whereabouts of the
American officer.

I never have much time to interrogate partisan prisoners
because if I do not get to them within half an hour after
capture, they are executed by knife. Prisoners are killed by
both sides. All partisans, dead or wounded are relieved of their
boots, shoes and serviceable clothing immediately, if they have

any. Hatred runs so high that I have seen men kick the dead after a battle.[8]

Sergeant Karl Svoboda, aged thirty-two, OSS wireless operator with the Wolfram mission to organise and assist partisans in north-east Moravia, parachuted into Czechoslovakia on the night of 13 September 1944, but failed to rendezvous with other members of the mission:
'After a night's sleep in the woods, I looked again for my colleagues, but without success. For four days I searched for my party in an ever-widening circle in the area of the arranged rendezvous. On the fifth day, I buried all my equipment and asked a Czech civilian how to get to a nearby village in order to get my bearings. The next night, I again slept in the woods. Waking up, I found that dawn was many hours behind me and getting to my feet, more asleep than awake, I raised my elbows in the air to stretch myself when I was pounced upon from the rear, my arms clamped behind my back by two SS men. These two were joined a few minutes later by the *Schutzpolizei*.

'The first question from the SS men after relieving me of my pistol and hand grenade was "Where is your poison?" With a tommy gun in my back, I handed over my "L" tablet. They then relieved me of my money and all other articles. They spoke to me in German and although I could not reply to them in the same language, I gathered that they were telling me that they knew all about me and that I was a parachutist. They accompanied their remarks by viciously striking me in the face. I was then asked where the other boys were.

'I told them I was a member of a party of five, and that I was walking ahead of the party, the others being a few hundred yards behind me, both these statements being false. The Germans told me that they knew the plane had gone over five days before and that it had done three runs. They even told me that the man of whom I had asked directions the day before had immediately given me away to the police.

'I was taken at once to police headquarters where one of them asked if it was true that England had cigarettes. I then proceeded to plan my story and alibis in order to cover my party. I told the police I thought the boys had made for Slovakia, so the SS called all their Slovak stations. In a few hours three Gestapo men arrived from Teschin. I got the impression very quickly that they knew as much about me as possible, and I was anxious for my own party, which I knew was not very far away. I was handcuffed and taken away by the Gestapo men to Teschin. Here at Gestapo headquarters I was taken into a room where there were seated one girl and one Gestapo officer. I was immediately blindfolded. They began asking me questions about my own life, all of which I answered. Again they asked me where my party was. I replied that they were five in all, including myself, and that I did not know where they were. They knew that the party was called "Wolfram". When asked for their names, I gave them only the Christian names, saying that we had seen very little of each other in England, and had not been given each other's surnames. The Gestapo officer said he did not believe me, so called in four Gestapo men who began to beat me with rubber bars and fists, while I was still blindfolded.

'All this time my hands were tied behind a chair. Then they stuck a thin hosepipe down my throat and turned on the tap. After taking out the pipe again, they asked me if I would now speak. Saying I knew nothing more, the men again stuck the pipe down my throat and turned on the tap. This time I lost consciousness. When I came to, they proceeded to push me over, my arms striking the ground under the full weight of my body and the chair. This they kept up for a long time.

'Next day my arms were twice their normal size. They then asked me what addresses the Wolfram party were going to, to which I answered that I had none as our operation on the first night had been a blind drop. Seeing that I was obstinate, the Gestapo men laid me against the wall and went for me, hitting and kicking me from all sides. Once more they asked me if I would speak. In reply, I begged them to kill me and get it over, to which they replied that I was not getting away as easily as all that.

'They kept this treatment up for about six hours, they then took the cloth off my eyes and released my arms. Then came a change of attitude. Into the room came the commandant of the Teschin Gestapo, who offered me a cigarette and charmingly asked me to take a comfortable chair. The commandant went on: "Tell me something about England." Then, for two hours, this officer asked me about English food, rations, cigarettes, America and American soldiers in England. I gave him an authentic report on English life which the commandant would not believe. Drawing the conversation to a close, the commandant said to me: "If you speak, you will save yourself." To this I replied that me and my party had been sent to Slovakia, where a Slovak rising was expected any day. I was then put in a cell, stripped naked and had to lie on a stone floor in the freezing cold. My wounds were now giving me great pain. My nerves were in a terrible state and in this new, uncomfortable predicament I broke down and cried. I was visited by a sentry every thirty minutes who gave me a kick on each occasion.'9

Interrogation continued intermittently for a further two months, during which time Svoboda became convinced that the Gestapo knew a great deal about OSS operations in Czechoslovakia. He was eventually sent to a concentration camp in Flossenburg, from where he was liberated by the Americans.

SOE was also active in German-occupied Crete and staged a particularly audacious operation in February 1944. Major Patrick Leigh-Fermor was parachuted into Crete with orders to kidnap General Kreipe, commander of the German garrison on the island. With the help of a band of Cretan partisans, he carried out a reconnaissance disguised as a shepherd and planned to strike on a narrow bend in the road between German headquarters and the general's villa:

'Several days' recce proved that he left for his house any time between dusk and nine o'clock. The plan was formed to carry out the operation on this journey, under cover of darkness; we then lay up and waited for the right moment. This was one of the most trying parts of the operation. Four evenings running he came back before dusk, as if he had got wind of the plan. On the fifth, however, night fell and he was still at his division HQ, so Captain Moss [*Stanley Moss, second in command of the raiding party*] and I put on German police corporal uniforms, and hastened with our party to the road fork. Elias [*one of the partisans*] was posted to signal one torch flash at the approach of the car, two flashes if accompanied. Moss and I took up our positions as military traffic police in the road, the other men, who knew each detail of the drill by heart, hidden in ditches on either side of the road fork.

'At nine thirty the warning single flash came, and three minutes later the car came slowly round the bend. Moss and I waved red lamps up and down, the car stopped and we walked towards the two doors drawing our pistols. I opened the right door of the car, flashed the torch inside, and saw the general was sitting beside the chauffeur. He was easily recognisable by his tabs, medals and Iron Crosses. While I asked for his papers in German, Moss opened the other door, struck the driver hard with a life preserver, took him by the shoulders, threw him out to the waiting Cretans, who quickly disarmed, handcuffed and bound him, and started off for the hills. Moss then jumped into the driver's seat.

'My party and I simultaneously seized the general, handcuffed and bound him, and put him in the back of the car. Paterakis, Tyrakis and Saviolakis jumped in beside him, with three sub-machine guns stuck out of the windows, and had the general covered by two fighting knives.

'The rest of the party dispersed at once. I put on the general's hat and sat in his seat beside Moss, who started up the engine and headed for Heraklion. The whole operation took just over a minute, and the Cretans carried out their part like clockwork.

'We drove into Heraklion market square, through the Canea Gate, the main German post in Heraklion, and out along the Retimo road. We passed twenty-two roadblocks in all. The sentry at one attempted to stop us by waving his torch up and down, but Moss drove straight on at the same speed. The other sentries saluted or stood to attention when they saw the two pennants of the car.

'We drove for about an hour and a half to Yeni Gave where Moss, Patrakis and Saviolakis got out with the general, who was then unbound, having volunteered his word of honour not to escape nor to draw attention to himself in the event of Germans being near. After the first shock, he seemed to accept the fait accompli fatalistically, and I informed him that he was an honourable prisoner of war captured by British officers and would be treated as such. They then set off up the foothills of Mount Ida in the direction of Anoyeia, a large and patriotic mountain village.

'We left a sealed letter addressed to General Brauer and all German authorities in Crete, stating that the general had been taken prisoner by British officers and by the time the letter was read would be on his way to Cairo. We then abandoned the car without destroying it, and left a British overcoat inside as corroborative detail. By this process we hoped to exculpate the Cretans living near the scene of abduction or suspicion. The ruse was successful.

'We then struck southwards towards Anoyeia and reached it as dawn broke. My German uniform caused looks of hate in this notoriously lawless village. During the afternoon, planes patrolled the northern coast constantly and a Fieseler-Storch hovered for three hours over every peak and ravine in Mount Ida, dropping hastily turned out leaflets stating General Kreipe had been captured by bandits, that his whereabouts could not be unknown to the population and that, unless he was surrendered within three days, all the local villages of Heraklion province would be razed to the ground and the sternest measures brought to bear on the civilian population.

'To the lasting credit of the Cretans, though hundreds knew his whereabouts, the secret was loyally kept.'

Letter left behind in General Kreipe's car:
TO THE GERMAN AUTHORITIES IN CRETE

23rd April 1944
Gentlemen,
Your Divisional-Commander Kreipe was captured a short time ago by a British Raiding Force under our command. By the time you read this he and we will be on our way to Cairo.

We would like to point out most emphatically that this operation has been carried out without the help of Cretans or Cretan partisans, and the only guides used were serving soldiers of His Hellenic Majesty's Forces in the Middle East, who came with us.

Your General is an honourable prisoner of war, and will be treated with all the consideration owing to his rank.

Any reprisals against the local population will be wholly unwarranted and unjust.
Auf baldiges Wiedersehen!
Patrick Leigh Fermor, Major, Commanding Raiding Force
Stanley Moss, Capt., Coldstream Guards
PS We are very sorry to leave this motor-car behind.[10]

Special operations in Italy were mired in politics. Major William White, OSS officer in Italy:
'The partisans I was working with were 20 per cent for liberation and 80 per cent for Russia. We soon found they were burying arms to save them for use after the war was over and the Americans had pulled out. What the Italians did after the war was their own business, but we were dropping weapons to the partisans for the purpose of saving American lives. I wanted our weapons used for this. As a result of my frequent protests, I discovered that the local communist political commissar was plotting to have me murdered.'

After the Allied landings at Anzio in January 1944, OSS concentrated on disrupting German communication and supply lines. On the night of 23 March 1944, two officers and thirteen enlisted men in an OSS operational group were put ashore from a Patrol Torpedo boat on the Ligurian coast of Italy. Their mission, code-named 'Ginny', was to blow up a railway tunnel on the line carrying German supplies from Genoa to Rome. All fifteen men were captured by the Germans and executed without trial on 26 March, despite being in full uniform. Captain Al Materazzi planned the mission:

'We left from Bastia at dusk on a PT boat with just one escort. There were supposed to be two, but the motors on the other one had conked out. We were going to go ashore at a place called Framura, near the rail station. My function was to see them safely ashore, stay in communication with them, make the necessary decisions as they reported to me and pick them up after the mission later that night.

'They went ashore in three rubber boats. It was a very dark night. The station at Framura had some lights and that was going to be their aiming point. Each of the three boats had walkie-talkies, as I did, and I know they rendezvoused because I heard Paul Traficante, the number two guy, say, "Vinny, I see you. Wait for me." Vinny Russo was the leader. As they started to paddle ashore, my PT boat started to move away. I immediately protested to the captain that if we moved I would lose communication with the raiding party, but he pointed to the south where there was a large German convoy well out to sea, moving north. They could not see us, but suddenly they fired their guns, which I later learned is a common practice with military vessels leaving port. Our escort boat was about a mile offshore and they had not been seen, but I was told they were in trouble.

'When we got to the escort boat we found it had lost its rudder. By the time the escort boat had got its rudder fixed, it was way too late to go back and pick up the guys. The contingency plan was for them to hide and set the charges the following night when we returned to pick them up. Unfortunately, there was a terrible storm on the second night and we couldn't get out of Bastia. On the third night I decided to go ashore myself and find them, but when we arrived off Framura, there was all kinds of activity. Lots of boats about, including a couple of E boats, and lights on the shore. There was no question of going ashore. We hung about a bit, hoping we might see a signal from them, but there was nothing.

'Next day we heard that an American unit which had landed on the Italian coast had been killed in combat. We knew it must be the Ginny mission. Only later did we discover that they had been executed. They had been lined up on the shore and shot and buried in a big pit. Then the grave was hidden with shrubbery. When the German officers responsible were brought to trial after the war, I asked if I could command the firing squad. That's how I felt about it. I had lived and trained with those guys for a year. Vinny Russo and I were like brothers. I had briefed them and had made sure none of them carried anything that would identify them as members of the OSS, so that the Germans would have no excuse to execute them if they were captured. What good did it do? I can never forgive the people who did that.'[11]

Statement by General Anton Dostler during investigation for war crimes, June 1945:

> I, the undersigned, General of Infantry, Dostler, Anton, hereby declare that in the early part of 1944 I was in command of the 75th Corps, which was detailed to the coastal defence of the Ventimiglia sector, south of Livorno . . . One day it was reported from the fortress brigade that soldiers from a unit composed of American sabotage troops which had the assignment of blowing up a railroad tunnel had been captured. There existed a very strict order from the Fuehrer, the number and date of which I can no longer remember, according to which it was forbidden to take enemy sabotage troops prisoner. They had to be killed in such a manner that no evidence would remain. I gave the required report to the AOK [*headquarters*] with the request for decision as to whether this order of the Fuehrer should be carried out in this instance. The AOK ordered that the saboteurs were to be shot . . . I gave Colonel Almers of the 135th Fortress Brigade the order to further carry out the command.[12]

Major John McCulloch, OSS officer in Italy shortly before VE day:
'One evening I found a great commotion in the square. A number of trucks had suddenly appeared with Italian partisans and they were about to batter down the doors of the German officers' building. A man who appeared to be in charge gave me to understand they intended to lynch a certain German lieutenant who, they assured me, had been guilty of various war crimes. Summoning up my best Italian, I told the partisan leader that, although the Germans were still technically in charge of the town, authority had passed to the British and Americans and that we couldn't permit a bloodbath. I sent one of our GIs, who happened to be in the neighborhood,

back to our headquarters to summon help, moral, if not physical, and arranged that an American tank, also there by chance, should circle the square with the Stars and Stripes prominently displayed. Within a few minutes an American officer arrived who was of Italian descent and who had worked closely with the partisans. He was able to persuade them that no good would come of an Italian–German confrontation and that justice would, in the end, be served.

'After this, VE day itself was something of an anti–climax. We celebrated it with champagne, which we had taken from the Germans, who had taken it from the French. In the midst of our party, a German major arrived, sat down casually at the piano and started playing Strauss waltzes. This was interrupted when an upper-class British officer gruffly declared that this was a "bad show" and "not at all the thing to do". It was left to me to explain to the German major that while we liked his music, this was neither the time nor the place for it.'[13]

OSS headquarters in Washington diligently kept in touch with families on behalf of agents in the field, who were often away for months on end. While Captain Edward Baranski was on the 'Dawes' mission to help organize resistance in Czechoslovakia, for example, his wife, Madeleine, received a letter once a week and his mother, Anna, a letter every two weeks:

September 15, 1944
Dear Mrs Baranski,

I have the pleasure of informing you that your husband is quite well in every respect. He has been away from this Headquarters and expects to be for some time yet. Special conditions under which he is performing his work make it difficult for him to send letters. This, however, should not be cause for worry.

We are in frequent communication with him and are able to assure you that he is rendering an outstanding service. We will gladly, from time to time, inform you of his well being as we hear from him. All of his mail and packages are being forwarded to him.

If there is ever in your mind any matter concerning your husband in which you think that we might be of help, please write us.

Very sincerely,
D.L. Connelly
Lt. (jg) USNR

Oct. 20, 1944
Dear Mrs Baranski,

I am writing to you again to reassure you that your son, Edward Baranski, is quite well, that we are hearing from him regularly, and that we are forwarding to him his mail and anything else that he is not likely to find locally.

Please write to me if there is anything you want us to do in this respect.

Sincerely yours,
D.L. Connelly
Lt. (jg) USNR

Less easy to write were letters explaining to parents, wives and loved ones what had happened to those men and women who did not come back. This one, dated 11 June 1945, was to Mr George Brown, of 3819 West Athington Street, Chicago, Illinois:

Dear Mr Brown,

Since General Donovan's letter to you of 5 April 1945 concerning your son, Cpl Robert R. Brown, we have received a report which gives us more information than we formerly had on the group of which your son was a member. I think you must be told that the report is not a hopeful one.

Your son landed in Czechoslovakia during the middle of September of last year to serve with a liaison group with the Czechoslovakian Forces of the Interior. One of the major functions of the group was to gather together fliers who had been forced to land in that region and to arrange for their evacuation. At the end of October the work of the unit was stopped as a result of capture by the Germans of the air strip that had been used as their means of physical contact with the outside world. From that time the group was kept on the move seeking to avoid capture until the second week in December when they found a hiding place in a log house in the mountains near Polomka. The capture occurred late in December at the cabin; all of the group but a few (who happened to be at another place) were captured.

Your son was in uniform when he landed, and the report indicates that he and his companions were in uniform at the time of capture. We have a further report that early in January the group (including your son) was taken to Mauthausen. Beyond that we have nothing on which we can base a definite statement concerning him.

We are, however, continuing our investigation and should we receive further information regarding your son, it will be sent to you promptly.

Sincerely yours,

Charles S. Cheston

Assistant Director

Six weeks later, on 7 August 1945, there was more, sad, news:

Dear Mr Brown,

By this time you will have received the official War Department notification concerning your son's death. He was executed in a German prison at Mauthausen, Czechoslovakia, late in January of this year.

I have been conscious over the months since we first received the news of your son's capture of the strain which uncertainty about his fate has placed upon you. I never abandoned hope, as I know you did not, that the final report would be favorable. It is for this reason that I waited for definite evidence before writing this letter.

Your son was a very brave man. He volunteered for one of the most dangerous assignments of the war to help American fliers get back safely and to aid the Czechoslovakian patriots who were engaged in a gallant fight to liberate their country. He showed great fortitude in escaping capture for almost two months in unfamiliar and difficult mountainous terrain after the presence of his unit had been discovered by the Germans.

Since the evidence still indicates that your son was in uniform at the time of his capture, he was entitled to be treated as a prisoner of war in accordance with the provisions of the Geneva Convention. Our people are already at work to bring to justice those responsible for his death.

With deepest sympathy and respect,

Yours sincerely,

Charles S. Cheston

Acting Director[14]

9

Politics, Chicanery and Mischief

BOTH OSS and SOE were willing to consider trying to alter the course of the war with a judicious assassination or two and both meddled in international politics, not always successfully. British intelligence cooperated with Soviet plans to kill Hitler by bombing his headquarters and SOE trained the two agents who assassinated Himmler's deputy, Reinhard Heydrich, in Czechoslovakia in 1942. Black propaganda and bribes were an integral component of the 'dirty war', as was a willingness to blithely switch allegiances with scant consideration for traditional virtues like loyalty and integrity. A secret plan for 'eliminating Hitler' had been drawn up as early as 1941, but no action was taken since the difficulties proved too formidable. However, 'freelance assassins' who offered their services were certainly not discouraged.

Captain Julian Amery, SOE officer stationed in Cairo:
'I had this little Bulgarian team in Cairo in 1941 and they produced a gentleman who had been quite an active member of one of the Macedonian terrorist groups and was a very good shot – he couldn't miss an empty bottle at a hundred yards with a revolver. He had ghastly scars where he had been tortured by the police and he said that he had cancer and had six months to live. He said he would like to end his life gloriously and if we would give him a posthumous decoration and look after his wife if we won the war, he would try and kill Hitler. This seemed to be a good idea and we got him to Lisbon with false Bulgarian papers alleging that he was a Bulgarian businessman. From Lisbon, he went to Switzerland where he waited a bit and then he got to Vienna.

'He had seen in the papers, or discovered somehow, that Hitler was likely to visit Vienna in the next few weeks. He struck up a friendship with the Bulgarian consul and expressed his undying admiration for the Führer and asked if he could be introduced to him. The consul said that would be very difficult, he didn't think that even he himself would have the chance of shaking hands with the Führer, but there was likely to be a procession and he would be very happy to have our friend in his box where he would have a very good view of Hitler going by. This seemed a golden opportunity but human nature is fickle. He reckoned that as he was going to kill Hitler the next day and he would certainly be killed himself, he might as well make a night of it the night before. So he went to a nightclub, boasted about his exploits – he didn't actually reveal what he was doing – drank people's health with some of the girls and a couple of pistols fell out of his jacket. The nightclub girls thought this was a bit fishy and called the police. So he was duly arrested. Nothing much happened to him, he was deported, went back to Bulgaria and sent us a message explaining how it had all failed!'

From its early days, the OSS was obsessed with the character and psycho-logical make-up of Hitler and was always looking for ways to undermine his position. Nothing was too bizarre to be considered. Lieutenant Steven Rusko, OSS:
'There were dozens of OSS committees operating in offices scattered across Washington and working on various hare-brained schemes to undermine the German war effort, but I don't think any of them were more hare-brained than the one to which I was assigned. A group of OSS psychologists had suggested that it might be possible to induce a nervous breakdown in Hitler if he could be exposed to vast quantities of hard-core pornography. My job was to find pornographic books, pictures and films, preferably in German. The plan was to drop all this stuff around Hitler's headquarters in the hope that he might step outside, pick it up and start foaming at the mouth. Nothing ever came of it, however. When the idea was put to the Army Air Corps, they swore that they would not risk the life of a single airman for such a nutty scheme. I didn't blame them.'

Memorandum from William Donovan to psychoanalyst Walter C. Langer, requesting a psychological and psychoanalytical evaluation of Hitler:

What we need is a realistic appraisal of the German situation. If Hitler is running the show, what kind of person is he? What are his ambitions? How does he appear to the German people? What is he like with his associates? What is his background?

And most of all, we want to know as much as possible about his psychological make-up – the things that make him tick. In addition, we ought to know what he might do if things begin to go against him.

Langer concluded, presciently, that Hitler was likely to commit suicide if the tide of battle turned against him:

Not only has he frequently threatened to commit suicide, but from what we know of his psychology it is the most likely possibility. It is probably true that he has an inordinate fear of death, but being an hysteric he could undoubtedly screw himself up into the superman character and perform the deed. In all probability, however, it would not be a simple suicide. He has too much of the dramatic for that and since immortality is one of his dominant motives we can imagine that he will stage the most dramatic and effective death scene he could possibly think of. He knows how to bind the people to him and if he cannot have the bond in life he will certainly do his utmost to achieve it in death. He might even engage some other fanatic to do the final killing at his orders.

Hitler has already envisaged a death of this kind, for he has said to Rauschning, 'Yes, in the house of supreme peril I must sacrifice myself for the people.' This would be extremely undesirable from our point of view because if it is cleverly done it would establish the Hitler legend so firmly in the minds of the German people that it might take generations to eradicate it.

Whatever else happens, we may be reasonably sure that as Germany suffers successive defeats, Hitler will become more and more neurotic. Each defeat will shake his confidence still further and limit his opportunities for proving his own greatness to himself. In consequence he will feel himself more and more vulnerable to attack from his associates and his rages will increase in frequency. He will probably try to compensate for his vulnerability on this side by continually stressing his brutality and ruthlessness.

His public appearances will become less and less, for, as we have seen, he is unable to face a critical audience. He will probably seek solace in his Eagle's Nest on the Kehlstein near Berchtesgaden. There among the ice-capped peaks he will wait for his 'inner voice' to guide him. Meanwhile, his nightmares will probably increase in frequency and intensity and drive him closer to a nervous collapse. It is not wholly improbable that in the end he might lock himself into this symbolic womb and defy the world to get to him.

In any case, his mental condition will continue to deteriorate. He will fight as long as he can with any weapon or technique that can be conjured up to meet the emergency. The course he will follow will almost certainly be the one which seems to him to be the surest road to immortality and at the same time, drag the world down in flames.[1]

The OSS office in Berne, Switzerland, headed by Alan Dulles, was a vital listening post on Hitler's doorstep. Dulles recruited more than a hundred paid informants reporting on what was happening in Nazi Germany, among them a high official in the German Foreign Ministry and members of internal opposition to Hitler. Dulles also had a lifelong interest in psychology and on 3 February 1943, dispatched a perceptive memo to Colonel David Bruce, head of the OSS office in London:

I have been in touch with the prominent psychologist, Professor C. G. Jung. His opinions of the reactions of German leaders, especially Hitler, in view of his psychopathic characteristics, should not be disregarded. It is Jung's belief that Hitler will [not] take recourse in any desperate measures up to the end, but he does not exclude the possibility of suicide in a desperate moment. Basing his statement on dependable information, Jung says that Hitler is living at East Prussia headquarters in underground quarters, and when even the highest officers wish to approach him, they must be disarmed and X-rayed before they are allowed to see him. When his staff eats with him, the Fuehrer does all the talking, the staff being forbidden to speak. The mental strain resulting from this association has broken several officers, according to Jung. Jung also thinks that the leaders of the Army are too disorganised and weakened to act against the Fuehrer.[2]

As the Allies consolidated the Normandy landings after D-Day, senior officers within SOE and OSS returned to the subject of mounting an operation to assassinate Hitler. Some held the view that killing the Führer would only turn him into a martyr and that his bungling war strategy made him more valuable to the Allied cause alive rather than dead. Others argued his death would immediately lead to the collapse of the German war effort and bring the conflict to an end sooner than anyone could hope.

In the latter part of 1944, Operation Foxley, a detailed blueprint for the assassination covering 122 pages, was drawn up:

OPERATION FOXLEY

INTRODUCTION

1. *Object:* The elimination of Hitler and any high-ranking Nazis or members of the Fuehrer's entourage who may be present at the attempt.

2. *Means:* Sniper's rifle, PIAT gun (with graze fuse) or Bazooka, H.E. and splinter grenades; derailment and destruction of the Fuehrerzug [*Hitler's train*] by explosives; clandestine means.

3. *Scene of operations:* The most recent information available on Hitler and his movements narrow down the field of endeavour to two loci of action, viz. the Berchtesgaden area and the Fuehrerzug.

4. *Operatives:* Austrian or Bavarian PoWs with an animus against the Nazis (and Hitler in particular); Poles or Czechs (in view of the large number of foreign workers of these nationalities in the Berchtesgaden – Salzburg district). Operatives might be trained in this country or abroad (e.g. Italy or Slovenia), and dropped over or infiltrated into enemy territory in the vicinity of Salzburg, where, if necessary, they could make contact with, and receive assistance, from anti-Nazi friends and relations (Austrians and Bavarians) or from foreign workers (Poles and Czechs).

5. *Planning:* Whereas it might be possible to plan and execute the operations described in Part 1 – Berchtesgaden area – from 'the book', a final check-up of conditions in the Salzburg area and/or on the Fuehrerzug's routes would be advised before drawing up the final plan of action. This, it is suggested, should be made on the spot by the operatives (or their leader) entrusted with the execution of the project.

Personalities in the Obersalzberg and their habits

1. *Hitler*
   (a) *Appearance* Photographs of Hitler, who is now 55, often show such changes in appearance that one is tempted to credit the popular belief that he has one or more doubles.

Thus the air of good health, calm and collected bearing mentioned by officers visiting FHQ in 1943 contrasts with the description of officers actually serving there at the time, that the Fuehrer was looking 10 years older. The photograph showing the Fuehrer in his train was taken in 1943 and bears out the report at first-hand of Hitler looking grey and bent in May 1944; yet the photographs of Hitler after the attentat of July 20th, 1944, indicate the very reverse. How much these changes in appearance are to be ascribed to the frequent injections given the Fuehrer, who is in general well-known to enjoy poor health, or to the employment of a double, it is impossible to say, evidence on the latter point being particularly conflicting. Hitler's dress varies from the greenish-khaki jacket and breeches, such as he usually wears out-of-doors on formal occasions, to the brown or grey double-breasted jacket and black trousers that he normally affects indoors and at the Berghof. Apart from the Iron Cross Hitler wears no military decorations.

(b) *Hitler's doubles* Evidence is conflicting about the truth of this popular rumour. The only confirmation comes second-hand from a Gestapo official, who describes in some detail his surprise at seeing the Fuehrer pass him twice (in the same direction) within a few minutes at the Reichskanzlei in Berlin and first-hand from a number of the Wachkompanie of the SS Leibstandarte Adolf Hitler. In the latter instance, the double is described as a Ministerialgehilfe employed at the Reichskanzlei, Berlin, who wore the prescribed uniform of brown jacket and black trousers and was so much the exact double of Hitler as frequently to be mistaken for him and saluted by the SS guards. On the other hand the evidence of another SS Leibstandarte man who was one of Hitler's three body servants from 1936–40 refutes the above report of one or more doubles.

(c) *Routine at the Berghof* Hitler is a late riser, never getting up before 0900 or 1000 hours. He is first seen by his barber, after which he either goes for his morning walk to the Mooslaner Kopf, or attends a conference. He always walks alone to the Mooslaner Kopf, strolling in a fairly leisurely manner. The walk takes 15 or 20 minutes at normal pace. There is an SS guard at each end and an SS patrol (one man) patrolling the route. Hitler cannot bear to feel himself watched, and if he sees an SS man following him about, he shouts at him, 'If you are frightened, go and guard yourself.' In consequence, guards have been instructed to keep him in sight but to remain unobserved themselves. This order has, however, been countermanded and reinforced several times. When Hitler is on this early morning walk, an RSD official patrols the area with a dog.

When Hitler arrives at the Teehaus on the Mooslaner Kopf the tea-room is opened for him and he takes breakfast. Hitler *never* walks back, but drives with his Kolonne [*entourage*] past the piquet Gutshof 1 along the Fuehrerstrasse past piquet 3 into the Berghof.

Otherwise Hitler breakfasts 1100 and 1130 hrs. Breakfast normally consists of milk and toast (Keks).

In the afternoon, Hitler receives visitors: bearers of the Knight's Cross, artists and other personalities, the arrival of whom must be previously notified. Dr. Morell, his physician, sometimes sees him in the morning.

If he has official visits, he leaves by road for Schloss Klessheim at 1200 hrs. The cars are mostly Mercedes-Nuerburg 6-seaters. Hitler himself has two or more cars, which are armour-plated, with windscreen and side-screens two inches thick. Colour: dark blue. Flies Fuehrer's pennant on the right mudguard.

1600 hrs – lunch. Vegetables only. Hitler would sometimes invite Goering or Bormann's family to lunch.

After lunch Hitler works until 2200 hrs usually with Eva Braun, who is fetched by telephone from the Gaestehaus, or with a clerk.

2200 hrs – conference on the military situation. The generals etc. used to arrive by car, entering the Berghof at piquet post 3, where they were all checked.

0100–0130 Hitler has supper. As for lunch.

0300–0400 or later he goes to bed.

When arriving at or departing from Obersalzberg, Hitler always travels by his special train, which has a quadruple 2cm AA gun at each end. He usually drives down to Schloss Klessheim and leaves from there; sometimes, however, from Berchtesgaden via Reichenhall. There are three other special trains – Ribbentrop's, Keitel's (which is stationed at Bischofswiesen, where there is supposed to be a magnificent chancellery), and the guest train which fetches guests from Salzburg or from the aerodrome at Ainring to Berchtesgaden.

Hitler used to go up the Kehlstein at one time but seems to have dropped this practice of late.[3]

Barely had Operation Foxley been drawn up, than Foxley II was being planned – to eliminate Hitler's likely successor, Himmler. In a particularly ludicrous flight of fancy, one SOE officer seriously suggested that Rudolf Hess, who had flown to Britain in 1941 in an ill-starred attempt to negotiate peace, could be hypnotised to carry out the deed. Unsurprisingly, neither plan was put into effect. Hitler left Berchtesgaden on 14 July 1944 and never returned. By April 1945, Foxley II was overtaken by events: SOE turned its attention to destabilising the Reich with black propaganda rather than dispatching its leaders.

Meanwhile, OSS had been instructed to investigate the possibility of negotiating separate peace treaties with Axis partners in the hope of bringing the war in Europe to an end more rapidly.

Colonel Florimund Duke, OSS, was the luckless officer chosen to lead an ambitious, and ultimately disastrous, mission into Hungary:
'The plan was that three American officers would jump by parachute into Hungary during the moon period, between 10 and 15 March 1944. These men would then turn themselves over to the Hungarian military authorities and thereby immediately become prisoners of war of the Hungarian Army. All soldiers and officers of the Hungarian Army would naturally consider us as regular prisoners of war, and we would be passed along until we finally reached General Stephen Ujszaszi, then the Chief of Intelligence of the Hungarian Army, who had agreed to act as the go-between for us and the Cabinet members.

'Major Alfred M. Suarez, an engineer officer and radio technician, was already in Algiers. Lieutenant Guy T. Nunn, a radio operator with language qualifications (German and French), was also in Algiers. They were asked if they would volunteer for such a mission and agreed. I was in Washington when asked if I would volunteer for the mission. I agreed and arrived in Algiers on March 6, 1944.

'After a week of preparation, we left Algiers on March 12, 1944, spent that night in Naples, then went to Brindisi, where we spent the nights of the 13 and 14. On the night of the 15, we left Brindisi in a

British bomber, a Halifax, and flew first over northern Croatia, where we threw out several bundles, then we flew near Vienna, where two Austrian boys jumped and their radio was thrown after them. Then we flew back to our pinpoint near the junction of the Mura and Drava rivers, just over the border in Hungary from northern Croatia.

'I jumped first, followed by Suarez and Nunn, and then the radios. We landed perfectly at two thirty in the morning in a plowed field, signaled the plane as it made a circle to come over us and drop the three containers from the bomb racks packed with our extra clothing, food and other supplies.

'We first located the radios, buried them in the woods, then buried our jumpsuits and the seven parachutes and three large containers. This took until daybreak – about six in the morning. Having completed this job, we walked to the nearest village we could see about a mile and a half away. Very few people were to be seen in the village at such an early hour, but we finally ran into one man who spoke French, who had been a waiter in Paris. He took us to the town hall, and in a short time the entire small village turned out and crowded around the outside of the building. These Hungarians said we would be treated kindly by the Hungarian authorities. They brought us breakfast and appeared most friendly in every way.

'We insisted, however, that we talk to the "military". Having no telephone in the small peasant village, they sent a boy on a bicycle to the next town about ten kilometers away, to a large Hungarian military barracks. About nine o'clock, the first military appeared. Thereafter, about each half-hour, a higher military rank would appear and they started questioning and examining us. We told them that we were part of a crew of a large bomber which had been hit by anti-aircraft, and in order to lighten the load so that the plane could return to its base, the three of us had jumped.

'However, the Hungarian military authorities became alarmed and put out searching parties to look for more parachutes, since they feared that there were many more of us. In this search of the countryside, they discovered our containers and some of the parachutes, but did not find our radios, which we had taken particular care to conceal.

'There were about a dozen Hungarian military around us by that time, and around about eleven o'clock one of these men in civilian dress took me aside and said that he had been waiting for us for two or three days. I then realized that he was the representative of General Ujszaszi. He spoke English, was a major in the Hungarian Air Force, named Kirali. He said we would have to go through the

213

theater of being examined, et cetera, but when they had finished he would take us and our equipment along with him.

'It was about noon when we went with him and our equipment to a town next to this large Hungarian military barracks. There we had lunch at the officers' mess, spent the night in a small room under heavy guard. The next morning, Major Kirali took the three of us and our equipment to Budapest, arriving there about seven o'clock in the evening.

'We went to the headquarters of the Internal Security Police in Budapest and were put in jail in the basement of this large building. The guards were quite friendly, left our cell door open during the daytime and brought us good food from the restaurant around the corner. That evening, March 17, about nine o'clock, the major brought us upstairs to the office of General Ujszaszi, who was most cordial and pleasant, welcoming us to Hungary, asking what proposition we had. He spoke in French and was a very smooth diplomatic sort of person. I replied that we had no proposition, we came with none other than our regular terms of unconditional surrender, but that we were there to help and would be interested in learning of their plans or ideas. He then explained that the two members of the Cabinet we wanted to see were out of town for the weekend and would return on Monday at which time he would arrange an appointment. He expressed his apologies for the necessity of our being held as "prisoners". After about twenty minutes or half an hour with him, we returned to our cell.

'On Sunday morning, March 19, at five o'clock, we were awakened with the request that General Ujszaszi wanted to see us immediately. We dressed hurriedly, went upstairs and found him in a very nervous state. He had not slept all night – practically had tears in his eyes and was as white as a sheet – and informed us that three German Panzer Divisions had crossed the border from Austria into Hungary and were occupying the country and surrounding Budapest. He asked if we could send a message, but we informed him we could not until about eleven o'clock because it would take us that long to set up our equipment. Actually, we could not send a message before that time because eleven o'clock was our call time. The general then said that eleven or twelve o'clock would be too late. We asked him if he had an airplane hidden on some large estate outside Budapest that we could all get on and get out of there. He said that he had not made any such preparations. We then told him that if we worked fast, he could get us down to the Yugoslav border and we would then make our way through Yugoslavia to join the partisan resistance forces and in that way make our escape. He replied that it would be impossible because the German troops were already practically surrounding Budapest. In other words, the Hungarians offered no resistance whatsoever to German occupation and they did nothing to help us get away.

'Later on that morning, at General Ujszaszi's request, we entrusted our two radio transmitters and code pads to his care. He offered to conceal the transmitters in a safe place to keep them from falling into the hands of the Germans, so that we could still make use of them if successful in returning to Hungarian jurisdiction. It should be noted that the "one-time" code pads mentioned above could not be of any use to either the Hungarians or the Germans.

'That was the last we saw of Colonel Ujszaszi, but his assistant, Major Kirali, visited us occasionally in our cell to tell us of developments of the occupation and what was going on in the city and the surrounding country.

'Germany had an agreement with Hungary that they would have the right to interview all Allied prisoners of war who landed in Hungary, but after this interview these prisoners would become prisoners of the Hungarians. At that time, when we were there, there were about eighteen United States Army airmen who had landed in Hungary and who were being held as prisoners of war by the Hungarians. According to our plan, after the German authorities had had their interview with us, we would have been taken outside of Budapest and allowed to set up our intelligence operations.

'But under the circumstances, with the German Army in occupation of Hungary, Major Kirali told us all Allied prisoners of war now held by the Hungarian authorities would automatically become prisoners of the Germans, and that would be our fate. Therefore, we sat in this Hungarian cell for the remainder of the week, and on Saturday, March 25, we were turned over to the German authorities.

'Because, as far as they knew up to this point, we were simply airmen who had jumped into Hungary, the Germans took us to Pancova, the headquarters of the *Luftwaffe* intelligence for all of the Balkans, just across the river from Belgrade. Here we were questioned and we told the story (in order to protect the Hungarians), that we had agreed to tell with Major Kirali, namely that we had intended to join the Yugoslav partisans in northern Croatia, but had gone too far and landed in Hungary by mistake.

'We were apparently getting away with this story so well that we were actually in a bus to be moved to Frankfurt, Germany, which is the intelligence centre for all of the *Luftwaffe*, when a Gestapo official arrived and asked the three of us to come out, leaving the other eight or ten British, American and Canadian airmen on the bus to proceed to Frankfurt. This official then took us back across the river to Belgrade where we found ourselves in the hands of the Gestapo, and were thrown into single cells on April 1. The three of us were kept absolutely apart and were questioned on numerous occasions. We were still holding to our "partisan" story and they were particularly anxious to learn if we had a radio since rumors had come back from Budapest that we were connected with a mission to Hungary. In fact, they were questioning me one day as to whether or not we had a radio when they produced one of our code books and said, "What is this?" I then replied we did have a radio.

'After about a week, they asked me why I did not tell them the truth because the German authorities had under arrest in Budapest three high-ranking officers of the Hungarian Army who had said that we were directly connected with a mission into Hungary. I still insisted that I knew nothing about this and asked them to bring the three men to Belgrade and have them admit their statement to me, since I wanted to see whom they had under arrest. This they did not do, but on the night of April 11, we left Belgrade by train for Berlin. We spent two nights on the train and arrived in Berlin on the morning of April 14, where again we were put into solitary confinement with no cigarettes, no reading material and very little food until April 26. All during this time in Berlin absolutely nothing happened – no one came to see us, there were no questions asked, no interviews, no communications with the outside world, no Red Cross parcels, no exercise – just waiting all day in a small cell.

'On the morning of April 26, they told us to get ready to leave. This time we were handcuffed with our hands behind our backs. On all future moves, we had been handcuffed, the three of us, together. They took us then in the usual "Black Maria" to an airport, with a guard for each one of us for the trip by airplane back to Budapest. Arriving in Budapest, we were again put into solitary confinement in a large civilian jail in which the Gestapo had already taken over two of the six floors. When we left, they occupied four floors.

'The next morning, the Gestapo representative took me, again handcuffed, to the Gestapo headquarters. Here were the "big shot" interrogators, as the questioning in Belgrade by the Gestapo had been rather second-rate. These men in Budapest were clever, smooth operators, well dressed in expensive civilian materials. On my first interview, I still held to the story that we were to join the partisans and after sparring around for about ten minutes, my questioner looked at me and said, "You look like an intelligent guy – there is no use kidding each other and beating about the bush – here is the story." With that he tossed over to me twenty type-written pages, a signed statement by General Ujszaszi telling the entire story. I looked at this dossier and then told him enough to confirm what Ujszaszi had already told me, but was very vague as to where we had come from – that is, what organization. I said we were air corps intelligence and that I had volunteered for a special mission for the Joint Chiefs of Staff and State Department. On returning to the jail I had an opportunity to tell Major Suarez and Lt Nunn that the story had come out on the part of the Hungarian general so that in their interviews the following day they could confirm the story. After about a week, when we had told our individual stories, they moved the three of us together into one cell in the jail. We were told about the middle of May that the Gestapo was finished with us and that we would be transferred to an officers' prison camp.'[4]

By this time Duke was convinced that he was the victim of a set-up and that General Ujszaszi, who was soon released from prison, had been secretly cooperating with the Germans throughout. He believed his mission was used as justification for the German occupation of Hungary, since it seemed to indicate that certain members of the Hungarian Cabinet were planning to double-cross Germany by negotiating a separate peace. Duke and his companions ended up in Colditz castle, the notorious prisoner-of-war camp for persistent escapers, from where they were liberated by the US Army on 16 April 1945.

A few days after General de Gaulle's triumphant entry into Paris on 25 August 1944, Lieutenant Colonel H. Nason, OSS, arrived in the city, ostensibly to protect the general's interests. In fact, his orders were to spy on the French; the French, in turn, spied on him:

'My mission was to report on political conditions within France, with particular attention to any personality that might be put forward by the Resistance in opposition to General de Gaulle. I was also to observe and report on political trends or activities that might hamper the operations of the Allied armed forces. My "cover" was to be liaison officer between French Section SI and the French Special Services, later called the Direction des Études et Recherches (DGER).

'I reported as liaison officer to Lieutenant Colonel Roulier, acting chief of the French Special Services, at 0900, August 28. He had an office in the Hotel Majestic and received me with cordiality, assigning me an office beside his. Paris was under the complete control of the Resistance, which was itself controlled by the mob, and only the local town halls seemed to be in any state of organization, as they were all controlled by the Communist Party. Neither Roulier nor the French Paris command seemed to have any idea of receiving American troops, or even that any were expected to stay in Paris. Organized looting was going on unchecked, under the name of "requisitioning".

'On August 30, the Hotel Majestic was requisitioned by the American forces and Roulier was given twenty-four hours to evacuate it. He reported to me that he would fight first and so I notified OSS Paris. It must be remembered that everyone involved was tired by the long campaign and that nerves were taut, and that both nationalities had rubbed the other's fur the wrong way for a long time. Roulier finally agreed to move, after a session of hysteria which would have done credit to Napoleon, but only after he had been allowed a week to find another place to install his services. He told me afterward he was resigning his command and returning to England, and reproached not only me, but OSS, with extreme bitterness for not having prevented the ousting of the DGER from the Hotel Majestic.

'My routine duties with DGER would take up most of the day. My political mission had to be carried on either after hours, or by slipping in a meeting during the day at odd hours when I might be free. As the winter came on and the deadly cold and snow hampered communications, I was forced to meet my contacts in public places for the little warmth there was in them. This was extremely dangerous, but I always took precautions in case anyone was watching my contacts – or me – and I am certain the French had no suspicion of any special interest on my part in their household affairs. I am led to this belief by the fact that early in my detail, a jovial officer, on the one hand, and a very attractive lady, on the other, were given the mission of finding out what they could about me, my purposes and intentions. As their mission was quite obvious, they got nowhere, the lady putting in a laudatory report that I was a perfect gentleman, occupied only with my mission as a liaison officer.

'However, shortly before Christmas, the DGER aimed another woman at me, a rather glittering blonde and a professional agent. I had crossed this woman's trail in North Africa and knew that she was a professional agent and a highly capable one, although I had never had any dealing with her. Moreover, although I had never spoken to her, I had seen her in Paris for months, often at the DGER where she never gave any sign that she was even aware that I existed. Suddenly, shortly before Christmas, I find this woman beside me at a dinner given by a French officer, and practically in my lap. Her interest in me rapidly became embarrassing. The night before I left Paris, she called me at midnight and said she must see me at once on an important and extremely urgent matter, but at once! I made an appointment for the following afternoon, at which time I hoped to be in Le Havre.'[5]

As the tide of war turned in favour of the Allies, increasing efforts were put into devising ways of undermining the morale of the German troops. When, on 20 July 1944, a cadre of German army officers led by Colonel Claus von Stauffenberg mounted a brave attempt to assassinate Hitler, planting a bomb in his headquarters in East Prussia, OSS was quick to exploit the incident for its own ends. It was decided to recruit German prisoners of war willing to go back behind German lines and distribute black propaganda. The operation was given the code name 'Sauerkraut'. Private Barbara Podoski played a vital role:

'We were always figuring out how we could undermine the morale of the front-line soldiers. When we learned about the attack on Hitler we immediately fell to discussing how we could take advantage of it. I can't remember whose idea it was that we should use German dissident PoWs to be our agents – it was strictly against the Geneva Convention – but I was assigned to do the interviewing to identify suitable candidates. I was taken to a PoW camp near Naples, where the CO gave me a little Beretta to wear under my jacket and pointed out the potential dissidents. I interviewed about twenty, from whom fourteen were selected. We took them back to Rome, changed their identities and prepared them for their mission.

'In the meantime, we had to dream up the material they were to distribute. While I was interviewing the Germans, I asked one of them what bothered him most when he got letters from home. I thought he would say something about the shortage of food or the air raids, but he thought for a while and then said that what would bother him most was if he learned his wife was messing around with another man. This gave us a wonderful idea. We created a completely fictitious "League of Lonely War Women" with branches all over Germany and a little badge of intertwined hearts. Mothers, wives, sweethearts, daughters, everyone joined. The idea was that they would make themselves available to soldiers returning home on leave and at the same time bolster Germany's birth rate.

'We wrote a little prospectus describing the members' duties:

"When a soldier comes home on leave all he has to do is show us his intertwined-hearts badge and one of us will immediately take care of him, take him home, feed him, house him, sleep with him, love him. We not only want him to feel good, we also want to get pregnant again and have babies in case our own men don't come home."

'We had leaflets printed and badges made. A badge was pinned to each leaflet before they were distributed. The whole thing was apparently so convincing that in October 1944, the *Washington Post* reported the existence of the league under a headline "Free Love Offered to Nazis on Furlough". The source was said to be a "captured circular from the Eighth Army front". At the time, no one had any clue that it had all been dreamed up by OSS.

'Another hare-brained idea we had was to create a fictitious order signed by Field Marshal Kesselring indicating that only units issued with green cards would be allowed to retreat. It was completely meaningless, of course. But as there were no green cards we hoped it would not take long for German soldiers to discover their unit didn't have one and to start fretting about the implications of not being allowed to retreat.

'It was a very hazardous operation for the sixteen dissidents sent across the lines to distribute this material and I was amazed they all came back. We rewarded them for a job well done by procuring prostitutes to entertain them one afternoon in an apartment in Rome. I had to sit outside in a jeep with a driver and pay the girls when they came down. I used to wonder about how the expenditure was going to be explained to American taxpayers.'[6]

Letter from the 'League of Lonely War Women':

Dear front soldier,

When will you come back on leave? We are waiting for you, whom the war has robbed of his home, for you who stands alone in a world without wife or fiancée.

Take this badge and display it visibly. Soon a member of our League of Lonely War Women will take charge of you and your front-line dreams and longings will find fulfillment. It is you we want, not your money.

There are members everywhere, since we German women understand our duties towards the defenders of our country. Naturally, we aren't selfish. Naturally, we long to have a real German boy to press to our bosom.

Don't be shy. Your wife, sister and sweetheart is one of us. We think of you, but we also think of the future of Germany.

Report by Lieutenant Colonel K.D. Mann, Morale Operations Branch, to director William Donovan:

The new technique of infiltrating POW agents back into enemy lines as demonstrated by 'Sauerkraut' Missions I-II-III has proved successful in spite of skepticism on the part of some OSS and Army officials and British opposition to employing the same agent more than once on a fixed front.

'Over a period of three months in which some 14 POW agents were infiltrated three different times into the lines:
1. No instance of their acting as double agents occurred.
2. Their security was never blown.
3. Instead of 'dumping' their MO propaganda material, it was definitely proved that the POW agents took it deep into the lines in some sections and planted it in proper places as evidenced by its appearance on regular POWs and deserters.

At present, the POW agents are being held in a villa, where MO Rome is using them to check the exactness and accuracy of details to be employed in writing MO material. The familiarity of the POWs with the current homely expressions used by the German troops and the home front, is being exploited.[7]

SOE also used German prisoners of war for its own ends. In October 1944, a special directorate was set up under Major General Gerald Templar to recruit PoWs as agents to spread black propaganda aimed at creating panic and confusion behind German lines. Among its wilder dirty tricks was an extraordinary plan to drop an agent into Germany, but to make sure his parachute did not open.

Leo Marks, SOE codebreaker:
'Operation Periwig was the most surprising operation of the entire code war. I was sent for by Colin Gubbins [*by then, Executive Director of SOE*] and there was somebody standing at the back of the room who was a complete stranger to me, who turned out to be Templar. He was very anxious to give the Germans the impression there was an active SOE resistance movement in Germany where

none at all existed. He'd heard I could devise a few codes and asked me if I could devise a code that would persuade the Germans that there was a resistance movement in Germany. I, of course, agreed.

'He used to come in regularly wanting to know why it was taking so long, and after five weeks I was able to show him a code book that could be printed in German. Opposite every German phrase there was a four-figure group, and if this code were found in Germany, it would look as if we were sending instructions to a resistance movement in Germany who were ordered not to answer, to stay silent until operations began. He looked at the code in great detail and smiled for the first time since I'd met him. I then pointed out a little something that had escaped his attention, which was that the four-figure groups were so constructed that if you added together the first two figures they would always come to the sum of the last two figures, so that if there was Morse mutilation which affected one of the figures you could work out what the code group should have been. I did this to show the Germans how thorough we were and that delighted Templar, though he didn't fully understand how it worked.

'The only problem was, how was the book going to be found in Germany? He then disclosed that there was a German prisoner of war in this country whose name was Schiller, who was a double agent. He'd worked for the British and he'd worked for the Germans and he'd cost the lives of agents on both sides. Schiller now wanted to return to Germany to work for the British and Templar intended that he should, but not quite in the way he thought. He was going to be dropped over Germany, but his parachute would fail to open and when he was found on the ground the code would be with him.

'Templar then broke the news that I would have to go down and brief Schiller. I would have to be very, very careful because he had to be convinced that his mission was genuine and that he was really going in to do a job for the British. We arrived at a prisoner-of-war camp not far from Basingstoke and I was escorted up some stairs to meet the German I was to brief before we virtually murdered him. He was very intelligent, very courteous and I briefed him carefully in every single detail of this code. I urged him he must use his security check with great care in case he were caught and I warned him that if he lost his silk codes he must fall back on a poem. I briefed him as thoroughly and conscientiously as I could and then returned to London.

'About two weeks later I was informed by Templar that my friend Schiller had met with a fatal "accident" and I was told to start broadcasting dummy traffic immediately. We broadcast tens of thousands of dummy messages in four-figure groups round the clock to convince the Germans we were broadcasting to people in Germany.'[8]

Leo Marks was convinced that Schiller was deliberately and callously sacrificed to aid the Allied cause. Other SOE veterans, while agreeing that the plan existed, claim that it was never put into effect.

Douglas Everett, scientist at SOE 'dirty tricks' department, Station IX:
'Either the end of '44 or in January '45, I was called to see Gerry Templar and someone else from the German section and he said it was important to try and stir up trouble in the German high command and proposed faking documents implicating the high command in a major uprising. For this to be believed, it had to be delivered in such a form that it was not obviously being planted and the proposal was that a prisoner of war would be sent out carrying these documents, that he would be parachuted in but his parachute would fail, and he would be found dead with the documents on him. I was asked if there was a technical possibility of so organising a parachute which would be 100 per cent certain of failing and that there would be no incriminating circumstances that might suggest that it was a plant.

'I went up to Ringway, where the parachute school was. I had to give them a cover story, which was that one or two of our agents had had parachute failures and could there be anyone in our organisation who was deliberately mishandling parachutes? We had two or three days' discussion and made a few tests and we decided that as far as we could see there was no means of doing this without it being found out. One reason was that all agents either packed their own parachutes, or supervised the packing of their parachutes, and no agent would be foolish enough deliberately to interfere with his packing.

'It might have been possible if you could discover a way of substituting a faulty parachute, but then the agent would have to know that something curious was going on. And the only other way would be to implicate the air crew by requiring the dispatcher to detach the ripcord before the jump, or for the pilot to be told to come in at 150 feet instead of 250 feet, so there was no chance of it opening. So there were ways in which it could be done, but it either involved highly unlikely circumstances or would incriminate quite definitely the air crew and I was not sure whether one would be able to brief an air crew in this way.

'So I came back five or six days later, went to see Templar and began to tell him this story. He said, "Don't bother, old boy, it's cancelled. The prisoner-of-war section of the War Office have condemned it as being against the Geneva Convention and it will never happen."'

The problem of infiltrating Germany and the Nazi Party to prepare the way for the advancing Allies remained intractable but nevertheless high on the agendas of both SOE and OSS. Memorandum from Colonel V. Lada-Mocarski to Director of OSS, on the difficulties of infiltrating agents into Nazi Germany, January 1945:

Generally speaking SI penetration of the Nazi-occupied 'periphery states' such as France, Italy, the Balkan countries, etc. has been reasonably successful. It is true that the resulting intelligence was mostly limited to military and economic data, to the exclusion of high-level political intelligence, but it had a definite practical value to our own Armed Forces and to those of our Allies. On the other hand, the penetration of Germany proper has so far been barren of results. The only exception will be found in intelligence received from Switzerland. If our Swiss outpost is eliminated, one is forced to admit that the efforts made from all other bases, such as Turkey, Mediterranean and European theaters, have produced precious little.

Reasons for failure to penetrate Germany

These are many – some are entirely beyond our control, while others are definitely of our own making. To the first category belong difficulties we have experienced with the British agencies which had the final say regarding most of the steps we had to take in this connection. Still in the same category are various difficulties inherent in the penetration of 'Festung Deutschland', such as safe addresses, proper documents, etc. However, we cannot cite all these difficulties as a complete alibi for our inability to establish a network of undercover agents in Germany. At least some of the fault can squarely be laid at our own door.

Our shortcomings fall into two broad categories. The first can be summed up by our failure to plan ahead. Had we had a general plan prepared in advance, it would have been possible to arrange for several of our agents operating on the Continent, including the Balkans, to follow – or even to precede – the German armies in their retreat into Germany proper. The mass movement into Germany of various nationals, at the time of the Nazi evacuation of France, the Balkans and other countries, afforded unusual opportunities for such an action. Even today it may be possible to take advantage of any temporary setbacks such as we are now experiencing in Belgium and Luxembourg to leave behind intelligence teams to be overrun by the Germany army.

The other fundamental shortcoming on our part was the failure to realize the vast difference in conditions underlying the penetration of Germany compared with that of any Nazi-occupied country, and to adjust our action accordingly.

Conditions which existed in Nazi-occupied countries

The most important feature of SI work in these countries was the ready support given us by a majority of the population. This made it possible to use, as agent personnel, a relatively simple and at times even ignorant class of people. The majority of our informants in Yugoslavia and Greece came from the rank and file of the armed forces of these countries. Practically anyone who hated the Invader and had the patriotic 'fire in his eyes' was able to do the job.

Difficulties of German Penetration

These are numerous and must be taken into account in recruiting and training the prospective personnel. The total mobilization of manpower in Germany creates a special problem regarding the use of young, able-bodied men. Therefore, an increasing emphasis should be laid on the use of women. A special effort should be made to recruit from among French, Belgian and Dutch women those who have consorted with the Germans during the occupation and who have formed interesting connections in the higher strata of the German authorities. A short experience of our recruiting in Paris reveals the feasibility of such a plan.

As regards the use of German nationals for undercover work in German, a striking feature is the almost complete absence of rabid anti-Nazis. Once in a while such a German is discovered among the prisoners of war or the deserters, but they are rare and far between and are often disqualified by the lack of other necessary attributes. Over ten years of

Nazi high-pressure propaganda either won over the German population or intimidated it to such an extent that a German with anti-Nazi 'fire in his eyes' is rarely found. Therefore, we must look to other 'incentives' for undertaking this hazardous work. Such other incentives from time immemorial formed the basis for espionage work. If modified by due allowances for present-day conditions, they will be found as effective as in the past. Feminine charm has not lost its savor; the desire to whitewash themselves with the Allies, or to create a position for post-war intelligence work, as means of sure livelihood, will also produce sufficient recruits for our work. Even 'double agents' can reasonably safely be employed at this stage of the war when the downfall of Nazism is generally accepted to be merely a question of time. People among the Germans who came over to the Allies, even if their German background does not make them eligible to be a Methodist minister, can still be profitably used. This category would include German officials, military or civilian, who have a record of Black Market operations, petty blackmail, etc. but it need not include real 'criminals of war'.

Conclusion

While the use of French escaped prisoners of war, or French forced labourers will undoubtedly produce some military and economic intelligence, the penetration of the Nazi Party and higher placed Nazi officials will not be achieved in this way. It is by the use of agent personnel such as described above, including women, that the most profitable work is likely to be done.[9]

Briefing for Operation Felspar, an SOE plan to infiltrate agents into Germany ahead of the advancing Allies, dated 18 April 1945:

1. General Ideas

You will proceed to Hamburg where you will contact an organiser who has been working in this town for several months. Your communications will normally be sent to Denmark where they will either be transmitted by W/T to London, or sent by courier to Sweden. You may at a later date, should the progress of the Allies be temporarily slowed down, receive instructions from us to work as a courier between Hamburg, Kiel and Flensburg. You have already met and arranged rendezvous with leaders of the organisations in these latter towns.

2. Method

You will leave Stockholm for Gothenburg on the evening of April 19th and will report to a place indicated to you. You will be accompanied on your journey by a man to whom you have already been introduced. You may decide with him whether you travel together or separately. Your Danish papers will be supplied to you in Gothenburg, but you should provide photographs for these documents. You will also be given Danish ration cards in Gothenburg. You may have to remain in this town for several days; you should therefore discuss with our contact where it is safest for you to stay.

On your arrival in Denmark you will proceed to the following safe house – the man who is accompanying you has a password and other means of recognition:

Johs, Skriver Petersen,

Dalhavegaard, Taps Station.

You will remain at this safe house until arrangements are made to infiltrate you into Germany. You will proceed immediately to Hamburg. Your main tasks on arrival in Hamburg will be as follows:

a) To contact our organiser in this town to whom you will explain your mission and ask him to assist you to the maximum of his ability. You will contact this organiser at:

  Grosse Bergstrasse 48,
  Frau Frieda Voigt,
  Altona, Hamburg.

You can prove your bona fides in the following way:

i)   You can refer to training which this man received on the second floor of Styrmansgatan 16, in a rather dark room with a bed and a fireplace.

ii)   To appendix A of this brief is attached a micro-film typewritten copy letter received by this agent about 6 weeks ago. It was written in his Playfair code but contained many mistakes which rendered it indecipherable.

iii) During his briefing he met a gentleman who had a florid complexion and was extremely broadly built.

b) You will explain to this agent the substance of the general directive given at Appendix B. (Measures to promote panic and disunity in German cities.)

c) You will attempt by any means to liquidate the maximum number of senior Nazi officials. For this purpose you have been provided with anti-personnel tablets, a fighting knife and a .25 revolver.

d) You, yourself, will recruit with the utmost caution a small team of men and women who can assist you in the execution of your mission. To these you will agree to pay their out of pocket expenses whilst they are working for you, and to any really valuable agent whom you may recruit, you can promise on our behalf that a sum of money not exceeding £100 will be credited to an account which will be opened for the agent in London.

3. Information

Before you leave on your mission you must ensure that you have read the Danish and German files which are available to you.

4. Security

Before you contact our organiser in Germany you will endeavour to find out whether it is safe for you to make yourself known to him. No communication has been received from this organiser for the last six weeks, and as has already been stated, it was then not possible to decipher the message he was sending us.

You will establish at least two *boites aux lettres* addresses which you will immediately communicate to us. You will also arrange for safe houses, either in Hamburg or just outside, which can be used in an emergency.

5. *Action on arrival of Allies*

When the Allies enter Hamburg you will report to the nearest Intelligence Officer in the following terms:

'I am . . . (correct name), I should like to give a message to Major Rokeby of Special Force Headquarters.' You will then explain the work that you have been doing and produce your "H" badge as a means of establishing your bona fides. You will then be instructed what to do next.

Should you for any reason consider that you can no longer remain in Hamburg, owing to danger of arrest, or should you discover on arrival in Denmark that the route into Germany is not functioning, you will immediately go into hiding at some safe house. At your own discretion you may make your way back to Sweden if you are unable to obtain specific instructions from us as to the route you are to take. If an opportunity occurs before the Allied occupation of Hamburg to prevent the enemy from destroying some installation which could be of value to the Allies after the occupation of the city, every effort should be made to do this . . .

APPENDIX B: MEASURES TO PROMOTE PANIC AND DISUNITY IN GERMAN CITIES

The purpose of this operation is to create the maximum of panic and to destroy the enemy's will to resist by taking advantage of every opportunity of dividing him and of spreading mistrust between various classes and sections of the population. The best means of doing this, particularly in cities closely threatened by invading forces, is through the spreading of rumours which fall upon increasingly fruitful soil as the danger to the city in question grows.

Rumours are most easily spread by a small group or groups

working to a directive and under central leadership. The most favourable opportunities for rumour spreading are provided by queues outside shops in public places, such as restaurants, trains, railways stations, air raid shelters, etc. If possible the aid, conscious or unconscious, of people whose business it is to go about among the population should be enlisted. Such people are postmen, ARP wardens, messengers of all kinds, doctors, nurses, police, workers in large factories, small shopkeepers, clergy, etc.

Provided the rumour is sufficiently attractive, detailed and plausible (remember that most people are very much simpler than you are and that what may seem quite improbable to you may be fully plausible to them), people will not be able to resist passing it on, and in this connection as much detail as possible should be added – that is purely a matter for the imagination.

While the Allies are still some distance from your town, it should be emphasized that comparatively good conditions exist in the area of Germany under Allied Occupation. People from specific towns have arrived in your city and have reported that a British or American division has with it a specific number of lorries containing food for the civilian population (see sample story attached). The ration for the civilian population per person per day is, for instance, 2 kilos of white bread, sausage, dehydrated food from Army rations and tinned milk for the children. As many of these stories can be circulated as time and the imagination permit.

Simultaneously [suggest] Allied troops have landed in Denmark in strength of 25 divisions including 5 parachute divisions. As it is not desired that refugees from the South should move into Denmark this story in all kinds of varied forms can be plugged continuously . . . people have seen troops, have escaped from them, have been murdered by them – or anything you like . . . the King of England is in Denmark with King Christian – he was seen by X and Y, who have just come from Denmark, wearing full naval uniform.

To create panic upon imminent invasion [suggest] the 25th Australian Army has suddenly appeared on the Hamburg front. This is a particularly tough formation which gives no quarter.

Leaflets may now be discreetly scattered and after a lapse

of 24 hours which people will spend in wondering what they are about, the rumour may circulate that 150 pounds will be paid to any civilian or soldier who produces a member of the SS or Nazi party, dead or alive.

At this point also the Incendiary Cigarettes should be used on any inflammable material into which they can be conveniently thrown. These small fires will be attributed to an invisible incendiary powder which has been dropped from aircraft over the city.

Circumstantial eye-witness accounts of the fate of other cities which have allowed themselves to be completely destroyed by refusing to capitulate [can be circulated]. Stories of Nazi bosses using women and children as shields always go well at this stage, but they must be circumstantial. Ascertain the position and name of the local lunatic asylums. Say that the guards have fled because the asylum has been hit and that some of the lunatics are armed and wearing Volkssturm arm-bands.

[Rumours about] water supply: Frau X was surprised to see a decomposed portion of a baby's finger come out of the tap, and other people have found their water pipes blocked with matted human hair, etc. Build up the idea that bodies have been found in the reservoir, that the water is polluted and that the Allies have plenty of the necessary disinfectants which the German authorities lack.

The next phase is to stop panic evacuation and to recruit as many workers as possible to assist the Allies in putting the town, and particularly the harbour, into good order again. When military events reach a stage when it appears that the town cannot hold out more than two or three days, rumours should be circulated that the entire population will mass in the largest square in their town and demonstrate their unwillingness to continue the fight any further. The Allies are expecting this meeting and if they see from the air a really large body of people all waving white clothes, they will realize that the civil population wish to give up and will treat the civilians accordingly when they enter the town. They will also cease bombing.

Well, anyhow, it looks as if the people down south have a better time with the Americans than we do here. I've got an aunt – just arrived here from Frankfurt – terrible journey she had, too, but she had to come here to look after her little boy. She came on foot most of the way, but the Tommies gave her a lift once all the way from Kassel to Hanover. They gave her some chocolate for the boy, too – lovely stuff – I ate some last night. It felt quite like peace for a moment until I remembered where we were. Well, my aunt says that when the Yankees came into Frankfurt they had hundreds of lorries – somebody told her every regiment had twenty-five of them – great big lorries there were with a special green star on the cover and 'Food for Liberated Germany' painted on each lorry in big letters. Well, of course, Auntie thought it was just a propaganda trick until they actually started issuing the rations – a kilo of white bread a day – white, mind you – and 250gm sausage, dried fruit and vegetables, 2kg of potatoes every day. Well, of course Auntie thought this was still a trick just to make a good impression, but next day more loaded lorries came into the town and the empty ones went back to load up again. Auntie says she hates the Yankees, but all the same she would never have believed it if she hadn't seen it with her own eyes. She brought some of the sausage and vegetables with her – they're the same as the Yankee soldiers eat. We had a proper feast last night. And Auntie says the Tommies who gave her a lift had lorries with them, just the same thing and at every village one of these lorries stopped and an officer with a special blue arm-band, so Auntie says, got out and fetched the mayor and unloaded enough food for the people for some days. It seems the Tommies know just how many people there still are in every town. Only their food was a bit different from the Yankees, no sausage because the Tommies said the English don't like sausage, but tinned beef and dried vegetables and flour – white flour – instead of baked bread. And it seems they have field kitchens which they set up in heavily bombed towns. Et cetera, et cetera.[10]

10

Jungle Fighting

O SS AND SOE both established a presence throughout Asia early in the war. After the fall of Singapore in February 1942, a number of SOE agents commanded 'left behind' parties to organise guerrilla warfare in Malaya, while SOE set up its own organisation, known as Force 136, with headquarters in India and Ceylon.

OSS supplied liaison officers to both the Nationalist and Communist armies in China, but its most active theatre of operations was Burma, where the now legendary Detachment 101 created havoc behind Japanese lines. Detachment 101, the predecessor of the Green Berets and the first unit in US military history to be set up specifically for the purpose of conducting warfare behind enemy lines, was the brainchild of General 'Vinegar Joe' Stilwell, who was convinced that one of the reasons the Japanese had given the Allies a 'hell of a beating' in Burma was the efficiency of their 'fifth column' operations. Stilwell chose an officer called Carl Eifler to command Detachment 101 and under Eifler's inspired leadership the unit perfected the art of guerrilla warfare in some of the worst combat conditions of the war – impenetrable jungle, monsoon rains and leeches; malaria was unavoidable and cholera, plague and typhus a constant threat. Enlisting the support of the native Kachin and Karen people, Detachment 101 formed a guerrilla army 10,000 strong that fought a savage jungle battle against determined Japanese troops, harassing the enemy with strike and evasion tactics, baiting them into retaliation against native population and inflaming the smouldering embers of local resentment towards occupying forces..

Report by Lt Col. F.S. Chapman, SOE, in charge of a three-man 'left behind' party to harass Japanese forces in Malaya in February 1942:

Our routine was to leave the hideout at about 5 pm, with our faces and hands darkened and wearing camouflage battledress;

we were each armed with a Tommy-gun and carried our gear in Army packs. We reached the rubber by nightfall when it was quite safe to walk along the roads and railways as the Japs seemed very reluctant to go abroad at night and in any case, as I found time and time again, their night sight is unbelievably poor and they add to their blindness by using torches.

We made a point of walking at least half a mile up running water as the Japs brought two large dogs to T. Malim to track us. When we found a safe place we would have a meal, sleep for a few hours, then take down the three Tommy-guns we always carried with us and pack them, as well as our packs, battledress and any demolition gear left over, in gunny bags. We would then make up our faces, arms and legs with a brew of lamp-black, potassium permanganate, coffee and iodine (this was not very satisfactory as it frequently had to be renewed) and put on Tamil clothes so that we could safely return through the rubber and estate roads in broad daylight, keeping our .32 automatics and a grenade hidden in our dhotis in case of emergency. On our return trips we tried to include a recce of future targets.

When we started operations, convoys were moving south at all hours of the night, but to attack them with only three men armed with Tommy-guns and grenades needed considerable low cunning and most careful planning. Our technique was to choose a lonely stretch of road bordered by jungle or rubber, and find a place where the speed of the convoy and the distance between vehicles would be decreased. It was also essential to find a good position for covering fire and with a safe getaway such as a ditch or the crest of a cutting. To stop the leading vehicle (nearly all convoys consisted of civilian lorries with occasional 12 or 20 cwt trucks, presumably left behind by our forces) we placed a bomb of 5lbs of blasting gelignite inside a length of bamboo and initiated it with a pull switch or length of instantaneous fuse. We sometimes put several other bits of bamboo in the road so that the driver could assure himself that they were quite harmless.

As a rule the leading lorry was destroyed, the second, and once the third also, crashed into it. At that moment, spread over a 30 yard front and only far enough back to be safe from the bomb explosion, we would each empty a 20 round magazine into the trucks, then sling as many grenades as we had been able to carry (or bombs made with a ½ lb explosive and stones from the railway line enclosed in a tin, or a section of bamboo). While the bombs were bursting we took cover and put in another magazine, fired that, threw some more bombs and then ran like hell. The whole action took about 20–30 seconds and to make the Japs think we were much stronger than we were, we shouted all the time as loud as we could . . .

Our only near shaves were once when the leading lorry exploded (we were using a 10lb mine on that occasion), being filled with either petrol or explosive, and we were so shaken that we retired without firing a shot. On another occasion a grenade bounced back off the side of the truck and exploded within a few feet of where one of my team lay behind a low bank, stunning him and covering him with earth. When we retired he failed to appear to my usual rallying cry. We had already given him up for dead when he joined us having had to wait until the Japs ceased fire before crawling back. He reported that on this occasion the Japs were firing into the rubber on both sides of the road; he also saw at least 30 casualties.

Chapman eventually stumbled into a Japanese patrol, was captured, but quickly escaped:

All day I had been looking out for *sakai* [native Malays] and at last I saw two bathing in the river. I approached them cautiously and when I was within 20 yards I explained in Malay that I was not a Jap but a friendly Englishman. Immediately a hubbub broke out and I found myself surrounded by Japanese and Sikhs with Tommy-guns and rifles. I was dead weary and unarmed, having travelled for 12 hours over frightful country with a heavy rucksack, and was easily taken prisoner. One Jap hit me over the head with the butt of his rifle – which fortunately broke – and another made a pass at my wristwatch, but the officer in charge soon stopped this and, after assuring himself that I was alone and unarmed, started to question me. He spoke a little English and one of his NCOs spoke Malay. After friendly relations had been established he said, 'You are English gentleman and officer; you must not speak lie.' I had to explain away maps of the whole area marked 'Printed in India 1942' including – idiot that I was – my route marked in pencil, a diary since leaving the Kuala Busok camp which unfortunately contained the names of *sakai* who had helped us and my Singapore identity card as 'Major Chapman'.

I told them I had lived with the guerillas in Pahang some years ago but as they were communists I had quarrelled with them and travelled north. I had met some Chinese robbers at Larek and they had taken my weapons but had let me go. The OC listened carefully then started asking questions. Did I know of any Englishmen living in the jungle near the Cameron Highlands? No, I had heard rumours of them and had searched for them, but had heard they had gone over to Pahang. Did I know a Colonel Chapman who was the leader of all the guerillas? Yes, he was my elder brother, had they any news of him?

I said I had lived with the *sakai* for the last year, hated the Chinese communist guerillas, about whom I would be only too pleased to give any information tomorrow, and how happy I was to be among civilised people again! I only wanted a good meal and night's rest and would then tell them anything they wanted to know. All this went down very well and they gave me some excellent food, only apologising for the absence of any whisky . . .

There were about a hundred Japs and two hundred Sikhs in this party. Most of the men slept in lean-to shelters of banana leaves and ataps but the headquarters shelter, in which I was accommodated, together with 20 Japs including the OC and his NCOs, was of canvas.

Fortunately, by a little judicious juggling, I was able to burn my telltale diary in the brilliant bamboo fire that they kept burning all night. There were three sentries, one an NCO apparently unarmed and two Japs with fixed bayonets. I was placed between two officers in the middle of the canvas lean-to. We were so closely packed that several times during the night I had to push the Japanese away from me. However, they slept so soundly – a typical Japanese characteristic – that they did not wake up. About 0100 hours, after a good sleep, I put on my shoes and, collecting the gear of the OC – a haversack, a tin hat and a dispatch case which unfortunately I was unable to open – I pushed them into the bottom of my sleeping bag so that it appeared to be full of my legs, while I doubled myself up and squeezed further and further back into the corner where the canvas was pegged into the ground. I had, during the last few hours, eased it a little to make a big enough space through which I hoped to be able to slip out. At 0200 hours one sentry was on his beat, the other was making up the fire and the NCO happened to look away for an instant. I slipped out. There was a sudden gasp from the NCO as I was half way out, but otherwise no move.

In brilliant moonlight I crashed through a bamboo thicket, raced along a fallen tree, slipped into a stream and after slithering down for a short distance, stopped to listen. There was not a sound, no shots, babel of voices or even the snapping of a twig.[1]

Diary of Captain Jack Bernard, Detachment 101, recording a nightmarish trek through the jungle with nine other men to cross the Irrawaddy River after a sabotage attack on a railway bridge in Burma, February 1943:

February 25: We left Point No 3 on the map at dusk, and taking every precaution to obliterate our traces, plodded on through the jungle from dusk to dawn, stopping periodically to rest or explore the route ahead. We had to bury a lot more of our stuff as our loads were still a lot too heavy. This kit was buried at the foot of a single tall tree amongst the grass and cane at the side of an overgrown cart track.

February 26: We reached the hills and climbed to the top of Loi Hpa. From here, we gazed down into the Irrawaddy Valley and looking at the eastern horizon, saw the unshapen mass of peaks which formed the China–Burma frontier. After collecting some yams and chillies found growing in an old hill plantation, we left at dusk. We went about a mile before striking a main track which, a little further on, went to a Kachin village. In the dark, a recce showed no way of skirting the village and, as there were several lights showing through the walls and open doors, we decided to retrace our steps. We slept that night in the jungle.

February 27: Early this morning we found the source of a stream which we followed through some of the thickest untrodden jungle imaginable. At last we struck an open clearing where we spotted a small hut. Creeping with the greatest of care to avoid any noise, we crossed the clearing and a few seconds later, there was a shout from the hut and someone blew on a horn. We had been seen, at least we thought so, but it turned out to be Kachins shouting and blowing the horn to frighten off any tigers or elephants in the vicinity. After trying to penetrate thick cane jungle, we found a second path. Following this, we ran into a second hut from which came laughter and talking. We could not locate ourselves on the map and, so, to be quite sure of not getting lost, returned to our previous camp.

February 28: This morning we found another path which

we followed. It went east but up a hill which, according to our calculations, was wrong. Only when we got to the top of the ridge were we able to place ourselves. We had followed the wrong stream from Loi Hpa and consequently returned to the Kaukkwe drainage, from where we had come. On paper it may look foolish but it is very easy to lose yourself in the jungle and to follow a wrong track, as so many of them look identical. From the top of the ridge, we continued due north to a large path going in the right direction. We went down the hill and camped near a stream and started to cook. No sooner had a fire been lighted than we heard singing and shouting. A minute or so later, two Kachins, one with a rifle, passed by a few yards from us. This was not the first time we had been surprised and we found that no matter how thick the jungle is and how far off a path you are, you got there and so can someone else.

March 1: At 0230 hours we ate a meal cooked the previous night and by 0300 we were off along the path. It followed the stream and all went well until, passing near a clump of bamboos, we came out into a village. A dog growled, muffled voices and groans came from the nearby hut and we withdrew to work out the problem. To skirt by the village at night would take us into more trouble and so we decided to walk through as quickly and as quietly as possible. A few more growls and mumbles were all that we heard and so, when we passed the last hut, we hurried on. The path dwindled away and so we decided to sleep until dawn before pushing on. This was fortunate because when we lay down to sleep, we did not know we were on the verge of a great swamp.

March 2 & 3: Two hours this morning were spent dodging the thick black mud and cane and trying to get clear of the bog. A slip and the mud squelched up to your knees and sucked you further down while you struggled under the heavy load on your back. At last, in an exhausted state, we got on to dry land and stopped to review the situation. Not bad – not good. We were going in the right direction, but we could find no path through the very thick jungle. After climbing a tree and taking a compass bearing, we decided to cut through the jungle. The first thing we encountered was a herd of wild elephants in the long grass. At our smell – by then, pretty high – they crashed off into the denser undergrowth and left us alone. We plodded on for two days which marked the climax of physical discomfort. To begin with, it rained, secondly, our food was almost exhausted and thirdly, the W/T batteries all but ceased to function. We found a small trickle of water which we followed into another black swamp buzzing with mosquitoes, smelling of elephant dung, and alive with leeches. We sank up to the knees but went on. Cane tore the flesh of one's arms and faces and almost ripped the shirts off our backs. Our shoes came off and sunk into the mud while our loads got caught in the mass of creepers which entwined every tree like great snails hanging down in loops to stop the intruder. Most of them had thorns like steel spikes. After going one mile, we had to stop. Normally we could have gone on but, owing to the strained conditions under which we were living and the lack of proper food, we were different persons. During the night it rained heavily and the shelter made of bamboo and waterproof sheets collapsed and we had to sleep in a heap under a dripping roof. During this period we ate chocolate made into a drink, cane roots and Oxo cubes. We had reached the stage where food held no interest for us. The leeches fed on us during the night without any objection on our part, we were that tired. There were thousands of ticks and they were definitely painful as they showed poor discretion in the spots selected to feed. Between the toes was a favorite spot. The only clothes that we had during this period were what we wore, which were chosen by us to fit in with our cover story in case we met anyone. Oscar [*Captain Oscar Milton, another member of the party*] was dressed as a French missionary and we were his disciples accompanying him to the China border.

March 4: This morning our one thought was to get out of the hilly country and so, with this in mind, we went down the stream. Half a mile further on was more cane and reeds and when we were in the center of the clump, we heard voices. Lying low like animals, we waited till the people had passed and then crept out into the open. We found a cart track which seemed too good to be true, and, on the other side, we stopped for a rest.

March 5 & 6: Previously we had asked for supplies to be dropped on the 7th and so we had two complete days to rest. We found a good dropping ground. Our two days' rest was more than welcome. Owing to the increase of Japs in the area we had to pass through, we decided to cross the Irrawaddy and go toward the China border where we would rest.

March 7: Our food is completely exhausted, so all of us went to the drop point and waited with ears strained for the sound of a plane. At 1500 hours it arrived very silently. A number of sacks and chutes were pushed out and the plane left. A word of praise must be said for the prompt arrival of the plane and the care with which supplies were packed so as to avoid breakages, and the consideration given when choosing the various articles. Food was checked and loads distributed amongst the ten of us. Before leaving, we burned and buried all tell-tale articles. Our plan was to steal a boat and then cross the river, hiding on the other bank a few miles inland. We staggered to Tahona in the darkest of nights with an average weight of 60lbs on our backs – not easy going by any means. Leaving the village on the south, we climbed down the bank and waited on the water's edge for a five minute rest. Twenty minutes elapsed before we embarked on our crossing. With five stolen boats tied together to form a raft, we floated downstream. It was still early and visibility was poor. We tried to avoid sandbanks but got stranded on one for five minutes. The sky became lighter and we still remained far from the opposite bank. We managed to get off and went on drifting. Suddenly we heard splashing and we concluded that someone was chasing us. We listened again, but all was quiet. A few seconds later, we heard the sound again and thought it might be a whirlpool, which are very common. All of our guesses proved incorrect when we went into a herd of some seven elephants having an early morning bath. Although we paddled as hard as possible, we went closer and closer. They must have been as surprised as we were because with trumpetings and roars they plunged off into deeper water in the opposite direction. We took fully one and a half hours to cross the river and once on the other side, the boats were unloaded. Another sandbank had delayed us and as the time was about 0500 hours, we were later than anticipated. We had to skirt Nyaugnbintha village before we found the road. Just near the houses, someone tripped and someone else slipped on the bank and fell backwards into a buffalo wallow. Someone would be sure to hear and come out but no one came. We tried two or three paths but failed to find the correct one. So we pushed into a thick patch of cane and decided to move on again after dusk. In the afternoon, two or three people came from the village and started chopping wood. They came closer and closer and just when we felt certain that they had seen us, the noise stopped. We waited for a crowd of people to return but no one ever came back. As we moved on, we all expressed a sigh of relief at having crossed the river safely.[2]

Communications with Force 136 were controlled from a headquarters near Colombo, Ceylon. Rosemary Drury, aged twenty-two, an SOE decoder:
'We were billeted in a hut with roofs made of palm tree leaves. We slept about twenty in a long room; at the end was an ablution thing with showers. We worked watches and we were all on different watches so that when we came off at midnight, we couldn't put the lights on to get to our beds. There were no doors on these rooms, they were just open to the garden and so every insect under the sun came in at night. We were much troubled by the insects. We used to sit on cane chairs which were full of bugs and we used to be bitten raw across the backs of our legs, so we used to get up and poke them out with matchsticks and tread on them. There were dreadful huge insects that we would cover up with our coffee mugs but they were so huge they would push the mugs across the floor.

'We worked in a building just on the outskirts of Colombo; it was specially built and very closely guarded. The material I was dealing with was radio intercept material. When it arrived on my desk, it just looked like a foolscap sheet of paper with about five columns of figures with six numbers, all different combinations of numbers and you had to try dividing them by different combinations of numbers and if you could find the number that would divide into all of them, then you had it. Mostly it would turn out to be one number, often quite low. You might work the whole of your shift on one number and hand it on to the next person but usually we got through four or five in a four-hour watch or discover we couldn't get anywhere with it and take it back and start on another one. We did it all by long division, no log tables, no slide rules. There were no machines, everything was done in your head and with pencil and paper. If you got something that you thought might be it, you would take it through to a naval officer or one of the civilians working out there and they would take it further and then, when they had finally got it out, they would turn it into Japanese and then into English.

'We were under a lot of pressure, to be quick, to be terribly accurate and not make mistakes and we knew how important it was. We knew if we were quick and could get the message up quickly we could save a lot of lives. We were all very, very wholehearted about it, we tried very hard. I got to know a lot of the Force 136 men and I should think we helped them quite a bit with information about where Jap submarines were lurking, but we weren't told very much about it. They told us just enough to keep us interested.'[3]

Sergeant Eric John Grinham, aged twenty-seven, wireless operator with Force 136:
'We were supposed to have three months' jungle training in Ceylon but it never materialised. The first I saw of the jungle was when I dropped into it. I don't know why it happened like this. They wanted an operator and I was available and I was used. We had had lectures on jungle warfare and how to look after oneself in the jungle, but that was all. The lectures were about how the Japs operated and how to avoid ambushes, how to set up ambushes and how to look after oneself, tropical hygiene, personal hygiene – not eating fruit with broken skins, how to make certain that you didn't get infected cuts, to treat them straight away, how to treat dysentery, what medicines to take with you. The main things were malaria and dysentery. They hammered home the personal care of yourself as regards malaria, rolling down sleeves, wearing long trousers to stop the mosquitoes getting to you. We had to start taking Mepacrine which was a suppressant, not a cure, but it did keep the malaria away. We also had sizeable issues of chlorine to purify the water in our water bottles.'[4]

Fighting alongside the Chinese added to the environmental difficulties. Report by Major R.N. Broome, SOE liaison officer with the Chinese Anti-Japanese Union Force (AJUF) in Malaya:

Much of the time I was extremely ill and without medicine. I had malaria when I first went into the jungle and was unconscious for 17 days, then, after a year's complete immunity from fever, I fell ill again and for the last 18 months had a relapse practically every fortnight. I also had blackwater, suffered much from various forms of dysentery and was immobilised for months at a time with septic leg ulcers; also my wounds, though they healed quickly with the application of herbs, kept on breaking out when diet was low. My teeth also gave me considerable trouble.

For over a year I did not see another European except for one week and practically every European I did meet seemed to die while I was with him, which was most depressing. Books were very hard to come by and intelligent conversation – except on politics, which I barred – was above most of the AJUF, quite apart from the language difficulty. The jungle itself has a subconsciously depressing effect – no sky or sunlight, no vista of more than 50 yards and above all, no colour. I had no reliable news of the war, I saw only Jap and AJUF papers; the former although I knew they were pure propaganda, had an incredibly depressing psychological effect – Ceylon had been bombed out of existence, Burma had fallen without resistance and the Japs were about to conquer India, where British influence was non-existent. The AJUF news sheets, on the other hand, were equally fantastic but in the opposite direction.

For a European, life in an AJUF hut is sheer bedlam. Twenty or thirty men will be arguing at the tops of their voices, yelling with laughter, learning to sing half a dozen different songs, hammering at some weapon etc. all at the same time. They ignore anybody else's feelings and expect the same treatment themselves; for instance, if you are sick, they blow bugles and stamp across the sleeping bench. In an AJUF hut there is no peace and no privacy.

As the Chinese in the camps are of all dialects, in the early days many of them could not understand each other and had to converse in Malay. Mandarin is now the regulation lingua franca, and is taught in all camps. On entering the jungle I could not speak a word of Mandarin or Malay, though I took in the necessary books with the intention of learning both. Unfortunately, we soon lost our books and I found it unbelievably difficult to pick up more than the elements of either language. Chinese, even without mastering the characters, is an exceedingly difficult language to learn without a teacher or books.

Ninety-five per cent of the personnel are rural coolie types – tin miners, rubber tappers, vegetable gardeners, squatters, timber workers, 'boys', etc. The other five per cent are masters from small Chinese schools (the worst type, educated far beyond their intelligence; short-sighted, knock-kneed, and purblind communists), coolie foremen, mechanics, tailors, small contractors, barbers, shopkeepers and occasionally a towkay's son or daughter who has swung 'left' to communism. There are no artisans, skilled workmen or other urban types. The best jungle men were gelutong (rubber) tappers and dulangers (illicit tin washers).

I was driven to distraction by the equivocation, shilly-shallying, evasion and direct lying of the H.Q. man with whom I had to deal. The Chinese sense of politeness also precludes them from giving you any information which they think you will not like. Had I realised earlier how hopeless things were I would assuredly have left them and tried to get out of the country alone, but my orders were to help the AJUF and either get back to India with information or stay with them till the liberation.[5]

OSS officers experienced similar problems. Report by Major Arden W. Dow, Detachment 101, on his frustrating attempts to train Chinese troops in Hunan province, March 1943:

Having lived and worked quite intimately with the Chinese officers and soldiers of General Tai's organization for the past seven months, I have come to the following conclusions:

1. General Tai and the men of his organization are interested in just one thing – getting all the arms and equipment they possibly can. I believe the training by us Americans is merely a cover to get more equipment and make us think we are doing so much for them by giving advice and assistance. It was made quite evident to me that all training, advice and assistance we gave them was neither taken seriously nor followed.

2. This organization does not want us to know what is actually going on in occupied territory. They refused to give us any intelligence data and would not allow us to see for ourselves. They tell you only what they want you to know and let you see only what they want you to see.

3. They try to impress and deceive us about the 'fighting' front and all the action that is taking place there. This seems to be just another one of their tricks not to let us know the truth. I didn't see any 'front' and I didn't hear of any fighting other than the two projects we assisted in.

4. No officer under General Tai can act without his orders or approval. Consequently, any sabotage or guerrilla activity by the men we are training must be according to General Tai's orders. Because of this, constant and progressive sabotage seems impossible. As the General told us, the camps cannot operate a unit; therefore, we have no control of the men or the supplies after the training is finished. The students we trained all belonged to different Army or Special Service commanders. Upon graduation, they return to their immediate commanders

who have full control of them. An arrangement of this type gives us no authority to operate the men after we train them.

5. It seems that they are afraid to actively employ sabotage against the enemy because of reprisals that the Japanese will take. As I stated earlier in my report, they don't want to blow rails because the Japanese will kill the farmer guarding the rail.

6. They tell you anything and make all kinds of promises but very seldom produce. They take their own sweet time to do anything and always do it when and how they want it done. It seems to me they let you suggest things just to be polite.

7. My association with this organization and the men in it has brought me to the point where I both disbelieve and distrust any of them, regardless of rank or position. I've been put off and promised too many things that never came through to have any faith in them from now on.[6]

China was a hotbed of spies and OSS personnel entered enthusiastically into the spying business. OSS files from the China Theater are stuffed with mysterious reports from agents identified only by codes.

Report by Agent BN-012, 1 October 1944:

In Liuchow, most of the prostitutes originally operated in Kweilin. As these girls evacuate from certain areas, they follow the American soldiers to Army installations. Many are presently seeking transportation out of Liuchow since the Chinese government has ordered the civilians to evacuate. It was quite a habit for these prostitutes to ask the American soldiers where they are moving their camp. However, the majority are asking the American soldiers for transportation to Kweiyang and Kunming.

Most of them live in Chinese hotels in pairs and take their customers there. They frequent the places mentioned in the report 'Survey of cafés, restaurants and places of entertainment', since American personnel can be found there. They can usually be found in these places after 1500 hours. Their prices range from 1000CN to 3000CN for merchandise and services rendered. All of them speak a little English but have difficulty in conversing with the soldiers.

In some cafés, such as the Allied Forces Social Club, the Four Musketeers Café and the OK Café, there are hostesses who are also prostitutes. This offers them (1) a good place to obtain customers and (2) a cover in case of a crackdown by the local police. In the Allied Forces Social Club, they said that they do not receive any salary from the café owner as a hostess but receive a percentage of the cost to the café's customers to have a hostess sit at your table. They are more or less dependent on their prostitution for an income.

While no evidence was developed which would indicate that any of these girls had pro-Jap sentiments or were actually aiding the enemy by collecting information etc., there is certainly little doubt but that Japanese intelligence has attempted at times to utilize prostitutes as information gatherers and spies.

Individually, the prostitutes in Liuchow are very low grade and unless they are operating under close and competent supervision, there is little possibility that they are accomplishing much.

Report by Agent BH-202, X2 Branch, OSS, Chungking, 5 June 1945:

Information concerning Chang Hisu, aka Mary Chang

Writer had dinner with subject and another girl by the name of Lulu Che. Subject claims to be a movie star – having made one picture in the past two years. As far as the writer can ascertain the name of this picture is *Chang Hi Su* from which she took her present name.

During the course of dinner this writer was subjected to quite a bit of questioning, ie, Where do you live? What is your rank? Where is your office? What kind of work do you do? What is your full name? Where do you live in the States? The two girls also wanted to know the name etc., of another OSS employee that the writer is frequently seen with. During the course of the dinner the writer asked subject what the other girl did, in regards to work. The answer was that she, also, was a movie star. Later in the evening the writer asked the same question, in a different manner, and was told that she was not a movie actress.

Subject and writer later went to her uncle's apartment, on Chung Erh Lu. Subject went in first and then came out and escorted the writer into the apartment. About two minutes after entering the apartment another Chinese man came in – said about two words, in Chinese, then sat and listened for approximately ten minutes before leaving. While in the apartment the same questioning, as before, went on. This time the writer went a little further in regards to his work and said that he was doing security work. The writer was then subjected to a lot of questions about what security meant and what did I do along these lines.

At the beginning of the evening, subject suggested going to a party – then after a brief discussion, in Chinese, with the other girl, she changed her mind and said, first, that she really hadn't been invited – then that she had been invited by so many Chinese boys and had refused them. She also complained of a, rather sudden, sore throat. She was seen, later, by BH-011 at this party – alone. Subject is frequently seen at these parties, given by the Moving Picture crowd, and at nearly all the dances attended by American personnel. Sometimes she is in the company of Americans, officers or enlisted men, and sometimes with Chinese.

Subject is not a professional prostitute – but is known to give her talents quite freely to a certain few. When the writer asked for another date subject said she was going to the country on Friday afternoon, to visit her mother and wouldn't return until Monday evening; subject was seen in town on Saturday night and Sunday afternoon.

Subject claims to be Szechuanese, living in Chungking for the past eight years. Subject is approximately 4′11″ tall – has a figure that would even be considered voluptuous for a western girl – round face not pretty, but cute – has nice even white teeth, light complexion – dresses very well – has black hair (well kept). Dresses in Chinese style clothes. Is approximately 20 years old, understands English but speaks it poorly. Is a very good dancer.

Undeveloped lead: This case is being carried on a closed status. If any important information regarding subject's activities is learned the case will be re-opened.

Report on the use of female agents by Detachment 101:

Plans to recruit several women agents were first discussed in Kyaukpyu in late January 1945. Mr E.M. Law Yone and Dr Lucien M. Hanks, Jr., were strong advocates for their use, and it was their feeling that an intelligent woman agent would be able to get more information than a well-trained man agent. In early February contacts were made with Ma Mya Khin, daughter of the postmaster of Gonchwein Village. She seemed to possess all the attributes of a perfect female agent – intelligent, spoke good English and Burmese, some Japanese, and she was extremely pretty. Furthermore, during Jap occupation of Ramree Island, she had known several Jap officers and she seemed to feel that she could get information for us from these contacts. It was decided to recruit her and to start her training when the SI unit moved to Ramree Town.

That was the start of the so-called Female Academy located in a two-storey wooden house beside the chaung which cuts through the village. Mr Law Yone and Dr Hanks were duly installed as custodians of the inmates, and visits from outsiders were frowned upon. Originally there were two women – Ma Mya Khin and an amazing character named Ma So Ma from Pyade Village, who was not unlike the Wife of Bath in her attitude toward life and who served in the same capacity as the nurse did to Juliet. Ma Mya Khin was given the name of Frieda, and her training began at once. She did map work and, in general, was briefed on types of intelligence. Her period of training lasted over one and a half months because it was difficult to arrange suitable transport for her to the mainland.

However, before she departed, two other women were recruited. The first was a mistress to a Jap officer. She was living on Myochaung Island, and an agent (her brother-in-law) was sent out by country boat to get her. His journey was one hazard from beginning to end, for his boat was swamped by the rough sea going over, and, judging from the appearance of the female he brought back, the return journey was just as wet. We had hoped for the prostitute type in this woman because we wanted her to contact the Japanese personally, but she turned out to be exactly the opposite – demure, modest, shy, and definitely not the daring sort. She spoke of her lover in fond terms and it seemed that he spent most of the time singing 'The Red River Valley' to her. This shot in the dark was a flop, and the woman returned to her home in Kyaukpyu.

The other recruit was one named Ni Ni who lived near Ma So Ma. She, too, spoke English and some Japanese and she was intelligent. She took up her training with Frieda and continued on after the latter departed.

Frieda's departure was finally arranged for the 21st of March. She was taken down the Arakan coast together with her cousin Ba Hla. They were to pose as an eloping couple, and their mission was to cover the Gwa and Bassein areas. Transport was on one of our P-Boats. Apparently it was a rough trip – Frieda was sea-sick all the way down and her escorting officer, Mr Law Yone, could barely raise his head. However, she and her cousin were successfully put ashore.

Two weeks later a report reached us from one of our informants that Frieda and Ba Hla had been seen walking down the street of Gwa with a Kempei Tai [*Japanese secret police*] officer. That was all we knew, but we decided then and there that she was compromised. Many attempts were made to learn about her fate through the local grapevine, but none were successful.[7]

OSS went to extraordinary lengths to undermine Japanese morale. Lieutenant Elizabeth McIntosh, MO [Morale Operations] Branch, OSS, New Delhi:
'We had a problem in Burma trying to get the Japanese troops to surrender. They were trained to believe that if they surrendered they would lose their birthright and bring dishonor to their families and to the Emperor. Soldiers who surrendered were declared legally dead and were denied entry into the sacred shrine, the *Yasukuni*, where all souls went. If they were recaptured after surrendering they were severely punished, banished from Japan or even sentenced to death. So it was no surprise that they were fighting to the end. It was tough going.

'I was working on an MO project with a very talented Japan scholar, an Italian-American called Bill Magistretti, a lieutenant in the OSS who had gone to school in Japan, to try to break this resolve down. Since the Japanese government was changing around that time, I thought it was conceivable there might be a change in the rule about surrendering, a more lenient policy, that under certain conditions, if they were surrounded, wounded, with no food or ammunition, surrender might be possible.

'Our idea was to try to forge and distribute such an order, but we knew we would have to get it done by a Japanese prisoner, preferably one with headquarters experience. There were Japanese prisoners all over the Red Fort in Delhi, where the British had their compound, but to date none of them had been willing to work with us. Then Magistretti heard one day that there was a prisoner who was pretty bright and had been on the General Staff in Rangoon. He wouldn't talk to anyone, he was just so desolate at being captured, but we decided to try it anyway.

'Bill Magistretti and I took this jeep and went over to Old Delhi and went up to see him. He was in a very small room, sitting on a stool looking out the window in his yellow prison uniform. He wouldn't turn round and look at us, he just continued to stare out the window. Then Bill said something to him in Japanese and all of a sudden he turned around, looked intently at Bill and broke into a huge smile. He pushed me to one side, held out his hand and said, "*Biru-Biru, Magistretti. Otomodachi!*" [Friend!] It turned out that they had been roommates at Waseda University in Japan.

'They talked for quite a while. Bill warned him that Japan was going to lose the war and told him he could help the young people who were going to have to rebuild the country. Eventually Bill convinced him that by joining us he would ultimately be helping Japan. From that point on, he was with us and helped us forge the fake order that was to be issued to convince the Japanese soldiers that surrender was possible. He knew how to do it because he had been on the General Staff in Burma and we had all the materials – the proper ink and rice paper and chops, the official seals – because they had captured a lot of such stuff in Burma. We ended up with an official-looking order coming from the new government in Japan. It was a really beautiful job – we tried it on some of the Japanese-Americans we were working with and they were completely convinced that it was genuine.

'The next problem was to get it to the front lines. An officer from Detachment 101 happened to be in town at the time and he came up with a plan. He knew a Kachin working for OSS who made a specialty of ambushing and killing Japanese couriers who traveled alone in Burma carrying the official mail. This man was told to plant the forged order in the pouch of the next courier he killed.

'It is very hard to measure the success of operations of this kind, but we heard later that many Japanese units accepted the new surrender order as a valid document and Detachment 101 certainly reported that toward the end of the Burma campaign Japanese troops were no longer fighting with the same fanaticism they had displayed earlier and that PoW compounds were packed with Japanese troops who had surrendered. So as far as I am concerned, it worked.'[8]

Despite the best efforts of OSS black propaganda, the Japanese remained tenacious fighters. Personal Field Report by Lieutenant Philip S. Weld, Detachment 101:

On October 15, 1944 I left base by light plane and landed

at Hpungkan-Tingsa, 60 miles south of Myitkyina, the headquarters of Area II. I was assigned to command the Chingpaw
[*ethnic*] troop designated as 'A' company. Shortly before my
arrival, reports had come in of reprisal raids on Chingpaw
villages to the southeast. Early in the month a 60-man Jap
patrol had gone up into the hills from their base at Myazedi
and had wantonly slaughtered some 75 Kachin women, children
and old men and had then burned and looted the village.

The agent reports said there were 300 Japs in Myazedi and
it was decided that my first mission with 'A' company would be
to join up with Lt Archer's company at a point west of Myazedi
from where we would harass the Japs and if possible drive them
back across the river to Bhamo. After a week's march 'A' and
'E' company had joined at Nantan and on November 11 we
moved in to attack. It was to be a daybreak operation in which
we were relying on surprise to overcome what we suspected
would be the lack of tactical control we would have over
our troops. Unfortunately one soldier's accidental shot a few
moments before jump-off time gave the Jap outpost sufficient
time to hit their foxholes. When we moved in, with two 'A'
company platoons leading, the Jap was already in his hole with
LMGs ready to open up. In the first minutes' heavy exchange
of fire, one Chingpaw sergeant was hit. The Japs were well
dug in, with mutually supporting positions, and before many
minutes our men were pretty well confused. One platoon was
seen drifting to the rear through the morning mist. When asked
by 'Puncha', my interpreter and the only '101' man with me,
where they were going, they replied that 'Going forward didn't
seem like a good idea'.

Being new to the outfit and quite ignorant of the language,
I had taken on faith the doctrine: 'Leave direction of the troops
to the Subhadar, just give him your general plan.' This I had
done, only to observe that every time the Japs opened up with
mortar or machine-gun fire, the Sub. would hit the dirt, put his
hands over his ears and explain 'I all mix up'. So were we all,
for the soldiers from the withdrawing platoon had gone so far
to the rear that it was impossible to check promptly how many
men might have held their ground and whether it was safe to
use our mortars.

After inconsequential exchanges of fire for about two hours,
Lt Archer and I decided that a strategic withdrawal was the wisest
course. We later learned that the Japs had simultaneously decided

the same and pulled out a few minutes after we did with their wounded, leaving behind a dozen packs and full equipment.

On December 27 we moved both companies to Lwewein atop a ridge just north of the Shweli river. We figured we had an ideal location from which to harass the Jap garrison of some 200 troops outposting the ridge to the east at Mawnhawm and also the larger Jap garrison in the Molo area. From that day until we were finally driven off the ridge on January 6, we were in almost continuous contact with the Japs. For several days we had things pretty much our own way, killing four Japs in a riverside ambush one day, surprising a party of 60 on the trail west of Lwewein another, and generally causing the Molo commander distress. But on January 3 it began to rain hard, with a heavy fog settling over the ridge, which made it impossible for the drop planes to reach us with the extra ammo requested. That afternoon a large Jap force hit 'E' company's block to the west of town but withdrew before dark.

They did not attack again until 0700 Jan 6. But this time it was evident they were in earnest, for they laid heavy mortar fire, and we knew only a sizeable Jap force would be armed with heavy mortars. 'E' company soldiers fought damned well for almost four hours but when their ammo began running low, they lost confidence. Some Japs with a Nambu had infiltrated into the village behind the block, visibility was about ten yards, ammo was getting shorter. So Lt Archer and I decided to pull back east on the ridge. This we did in orderly fashion getting out all important supplies. But the Japs did not take long in following up. Within half-an-hour, they had followed us and hit the two 'A' company platoons left to cover the withdrawal. These platoons folded like a paper bag, came rushing down the trail shouting, 'Japon, Japon.' Panic seized virtually all but the Americans and it was with difficulty that we got some 'A' company men into position to meet the next attack.

Archer and I decided we could take our drop at Yemu and remain on the ridge if the weather cleared so that we could get more ammo. But when a drop plane circled, unable to find us, and drew heavy ground fire at each pass over the ridge, we decided that even if we could hold, the risk to drop planes would be too great and we decided to withdraw. The withdrawal problem was complicated by the fact that we had 24 elephants, two stretcher cases, and almost 75 refugees from all the villages on our ridge who had sought shelter inside our perimeter during the preceding week.[9]

Report by Captain W.R. Mansfield, OSS, attached to the 3rd Main Guerrilla Group in China, February 1945:

I arrived in the Tiento area on 9 February, after walking miles through rain, mud and snow to find Colonel Chao, the commander of the group, at his HQ about 10 miles west of Paikwoshih. He is a man of medium stature about 40 years old, somewhat of a dandy (always dressed in a natty uniform quite unlike his troops), rather talkative with constant toothy smile, energetic, with all the appearance of a little warlord in his own area. He put us up in part of his own fairly comfortable quarters. After cordial greetings back and forth and the usual diplomatic diddling and dinners, I got from him in several long talks the picture of his area, most of which I have radioed, including Japanese disposition and size and location of his own troops as well as targets.

I went over our supplies with him, and he was pleased with all of them. Meanwhile I pressed for action, suggesting several targets and stating that I would like to see his men pull off a few good jobs, warranting our presence and more supplies. We finally worked out a plan for a major ambush on a Jap convoy on the Hengyang–Siangtan road, to be combined with blowing a 30-meter bridge. His intelligence reports showed large convoys of from 30 to 100 trucks passing down the road at night, protected by tanks and truck-borne soldiers, despite the heavy snow. We worked out a plan for the attack together.

We started out in heavy snow – the first here in 20 years – with a group of about 500 men, including 100 coolies. The Colonel brought along his sedan chair on these trips and often hopped in for a spell, but we walked. When we got about 12 miles east we promptly ran into about 200 Japs. Both sides started firing (the Japs using a little mortar fire) and we withdrew, leaving the Second in Command in charge. He came back to report 27 Japs killed, 1 Sino killed and 4 wounded.

I sent all my party back to a safer spot while I holed up with Colonel Chao and some men in a dirty little hideout for 2 days. Here I began to learn a great deal more about Colonel Chao and his intelligence system, which consists of hot and cold running soldiers and civilians who are constantly appearing at his CP as if it were Grand Hotel, with all kinds of conflicting messages on little scraps of paper. At one time we had 900 Japs bearing down on us in a three-pronged drive and must evacuate back to original headquarters and make a stand. Then as if by magic, the figure goes down to 300 going in an entirely different direction. Then nothing more is said about retiring. Then we must go back in an hour. We end up by finally going to our original destination. During all this, Colonel Chao dispatches one group to attack a house in which 20 Japs are living, but the attack is abandoned when the Japs are fortified. A little later Chao gets mad at a Lieutenant who failed to carry out some minor order and beats him personally with his cane over back and face.

At this point, to my astonishment, a report comes in that no convoys are running on the road because of the snow. When I learned that the bridge we were to blow was probably unguarded during the snow, I proposed that we blow it, to which Chao agreed. The plan was that I would go with them to a point about a mile away, but stay back because they would disguise themselves as civilians to avoid Jap patrols. They went down and blew it about 2100hrs (you could hear the boom for miles) and we got away. Everyone reported there was nothing left of the bridge and both stone abutments fell in, but I did not, repeat not, see it.

About the 6th of March we left Tiento with Colonel Chao and about 400 men and marched southward through rice paddies and mountains to a point several miles southwest of Nanyo. The men were well armed, since we had both the four bazookas and all the Tommy guns and hand grenades. The plan was to attack a Jap garrison of 300 soldiers near Tinminshin on the main road below Nanyo and also make a night ambush on a Jap convoy. I went over the plans in detail with Col Chao and it bid fair to be a decent sized job. We camped for the night at a point on the west side of the mountains about 10 miles from the road. The following day we waited there while civilian soldiers went out to reconnoitre the target area. It was the first good weather we had had in a long while.

As usual, Chao kept stalling and I kept pressing to get on with the job, so we moved up into the mountains to a point about 4 miles from the Japs. When we got less than 2 miles from the target, Chao called it off, saying that he just received word from agents that the Japs had concentrated large numbers in the vicinity, possibly in anticipation of our attack. If this was true, I attribute it to his foolishly giving away our presence by the smaller ambush.

We then made a long withdrawal, back up over the mountains in rain and mud for 25 miles, and waited. Chao said he was waiting for reports showing the target area was safer before going back to attack again. We started back for the target area with Chao's 2nd in Command, Tiao, and 250 men, after Chao said at the last minute that he had to return at once to his HQ at Tiento on pressing business. Once more we stopped a couple of days in transit for reconnaissance. Again we went up to the mountain hide-out and waited. Again we got reports there were too many Japs and that large numbers were moving up the road north. We were getting completely fed up. I pointed out there were 300 Japs encamped that night in houses about 4 miles away and proposed we get up at 3 a.m., even though it was raining cats and dogs (it always is out here), go down in the dark and ambush them.

The next morning we went down to the roadside and took up positions under cover on two hills directly above the road, waiting for Jap trucks (it was a cloudy, wet, cold day) or troops. The chief difficulty was that Tiao would not put the men (particularly those with bazookas and Tommy guns) close enough to the road to give them a fair chance of hitting Japs and trucks. This was absolutely necessary under the circumstances, especially since the Chinese are such poor shots. The men were placed at least 200–300 yards away. It was all I could do to persuade Tiao to let two trucks and then a third one pass because it was not big enough game. Finally I first spied through binoculars what looked like a Jap column, about 90 men, moving south towards us about one mile away, marching in formation.

As they approached, I had to argue with Tiao to change the position of our men and put one group directly by the roadside on a small hillock and another across the road in a house so that we could get an enfilade fire. As usual he was too slow and I had to force the issue by going out myself to the little hill with two or three men, whereupon he got about 50 more out there. The Japs were now 500 yds off and I agreed that the signal 'Fire' would be given when they got to a point about 100 yards off. Now it became pretty exciting. We all waited with beads drawn on them as they marched down in close order drill formation. Following them were three cannon and three caissons drawn by horses.

At the signal 'Fire!' (given by bugle and whistle) we let them have it and all hell broke loose for about 10 minutes. On the first burst we got about 10 or so, dropping some on the road. The rest quickly jumped, as if by magic, for cover in a ditch by the road, where the machine guns across the road began peppering them. Two of our men were killed bringing this machine gun over to the other side. After another 10 minutes I could hear some Japs in the ditch (only 50 yards away) yelling and Tiao said they were asking to surrender. He ordered 'Cease fire!' (blowing both bugle and whistle) but his troops would not obey. Just as all were almost quiet, someone would see a Jap, fire and start everyone off again. I also found the Sinos were going hog wild on automatic fire. Even when we could sight no Japs (who were ducking behind the bank) long bursts of machine gun and Tommy gun fire continued all over the place, way off the target. Bazookas were foolishly being fired at no target at all, despite exhaustive training of the men and an order sent up from our position that the bazookas were not to be used. By just calmly waiting for a Jap to raise his shoulders to take aim, I was easily able to pick him off, then another.

Next we tried to order a general charge, but while some Sinos started, the rest balked, with the result that the few Chinese who started out were picked off by the 20 or so Japs left. Finally some of our men got down the hill in the ditch on our side of the road opposite the Nips, who started to worm north behind it in order to try to get away. About seven hid under a very small bridge but our men got them by tossing grenades under it. The rest escaped after a running hand grenade battle. Our men then destroyed the three 75mm guns and caissons with hand grenades, and took off about 20 rifles, 2 MG's, and other equipment from the dead Japs lying around. We left about 38 dead Japs and another 20 or so wounded, lying in the ditch and paddies by the road.[10]

Report by First Sergeant Donald S. Spears, wireless operator with Operation Gorilla, a five-man OSS mission which jumped blind into Indo-China on 24 April 1945 with orders to gather intelligence on Japanese activities and sabotage enemy installations:

On the morning of April 28, 1945 at 10.00am we were attacked by a patrol of approximately 65 Japanese soldiers. We were caught completely by surprise, and completely disorganized, as far as any resistance to the enemy was concerned. At the time of the attack, Major Summers was in the stream bathing. Captain Guillot had just finished bathing and had on only his underwear and shoes. Captain Gennerich and Captain Trumps were fully dressed and attending to various duties around camp. I was busy setting up the radio preparatory to working an 11 o'clock sked with Kunming.

Captain Trumps noticed the enemy first, at the end of a clearing about 150 yards distance. At first he didn't believe them to be Japanese, but they immediately deployed from the trail and opened fire. My Tommy-gun was several yards away, between me and the Japs, so I didn't try to get it, but headed for the nearest cover. To reach this, I had to cross a small clearing and wade the river. On the opposite bank was some tall elephant grass, very difficult to crawl through but under the circumstances I made good progress. It was then I noticed Captain Trumps behind me. After crawling several yards we ran across Captain Guillot and a French Legionnaire who had camped the previous night with us. Our arms then consisted of a Tommy-gun, a carbine and a .32 pistol. The Tommy-gun had jammed and Captain Guillot gave it to me to see if I could clear it. I couldn't clear it, so we threw it away. Captain Trumps lost the clip to his carbine, and threw that away leaving us with just a .32 pistol. Our only hope was to escape, if possible. We continued crawling through the grass until we reached a bend in the stream. We crossed the stream and tried to climb the bank to get back onto the trail, but it was too steep and we couldn't make it. We waded upstream until we could scale the bank, crossed a clearing about 100 yards long, and very luckily hit the trail. During all this we drew fire a few times, but none of us were hit. While crossing the stream, Captain Guillot lost his shoes so I gave him mine as his feet were cut by the grass and stubble.

We walked at a very fast pace for about two hours, then overtook six French soldiers who had passed us the day before. We decided to travel with them, heading for the Chinese border. We walked until 10pm over some very rough trails then decided to rest by a stream until morning. My feet were pretty sore and we were all very tired, hungry and thirsty.

We started out at 7.00am April 29, walked two hours, and while resting by a stream were overtaken by Lieutenant Ettinger and a party of French who had stayed in a neighbouring village the night before. One of the French Captains gave me a horse to ride, as by that time my feet were in pretty bad shape. They went on ahead and said they would wait for us in the next village. We walked for another two hours and came to a small village where we managed to get a meal of eggs and rice. After resting there a while, we continued on our way and at 5.00pm reached the village of Kang-Tung. Lieutenant Ettinger and about one hundred French soldiers were camped there, and we at once made contact with a Chinese colonel who spoke French very well and a general who spoke a little English. They treated us very well, gave us a good meal, a place to sleep and the next day we felt much better.

During this time we had heard nothing of Major Summers or Captain Gennerich and supposed they had either been killed or were lost in the jungle.

Monday, May 30 we decided to look for a suitable landing strip for an L-5. The one we found required but a little work, and the next morning the Colonel had 100 coolies getting it into shape. That night we sent a message by means of the Chinese radio to OSS Kunming telling them that we had a landing strip ready and asked for a plane as soon as possible.

Wednesday morning, May 2, Captain Gennerich showed up, but knew nothing of Major Summers. That afternoon at 2.00pm an L-5 landed on our strip with Captain Patti and the pilot, Lt Sullivan. We decided to stay in Keng-Tung until we got some news of Major Summers, and to send Captain Guillot out to get medical attention and supplies for us. The plane intended to come back that afternoon for Captain Guillot but apparently it was too late. The next day it rained hard and was definitely not flying weather.

Friday May 4 the weather was still bad so all we could do was wait. That afternoon Major Summers arrived with a small party of French. He was in pretty bad shape but still very much alive.

Report by Major John W. Summers, OSS, leader of operation Gorilla:

On the morning of April 28, we were camped near a stream. Captain Trumps was on guard and I went down to the river to bathe. I took a .32 automatic with me. While I was in the middle of the stream Captain Trumps yelled a warning to me but I didn't hear it. My first warning was rifle bullets cracking around my ears and splashing in the water. I grabbed my .32, ran up the bank of the stream and saw Japs charge down on me from the right. The other men took cover and continued the fight while I tried to make it to camp to get some clothes and weapons. Three Japs were very near to me on the right. I emptied my .32 at them, saw one fall, and the other two stopped. I threw the empty gun away and made it to camp. I grabbed a pistol belt and a pair of pants, looked around and estimated 15 Japs were within 50 yards, yelling 'Banzai' and firing erratically as they ran. Bullets were cracking all around, one hit at my feet and grazed my left foot, and I decided that it was time to take cover myself.

By that time the other men had moved around to the flank and I was unable to contact them in the thick underbush and elephant grass. I was without maps, shoes or food, and the situation didn't look very good by myself and my feet already injured and cut. I observed the Japs around our camp and estimated about 50 yelling over our equipment. They brought up about 15 packhorses and I then decided to get some distance between us before they started following. I took a little-used animal path and the first night I slept in the brush near the trail. The second day I circled back trying to find a trail going NW as I only knew that was the general direction of Szemao.

About dusk I hit a better trail that I figured was about 10 miles NW of where we were attacked. I stayed in the brush near the trail that night and twice observed Japs go back and forth. The next day, April 30, I took another little-used animal path, avoiding the main trail and all natives. By May 1, I had forgotten the Japs and was concerned with just getting out of the jungle. My feet were getting infected, so I wrapped them in leaves, got some rice from a native and was making headway NW.

May 2, I hit a well-used trail going the right direction and my hopes picked up. That night I hit my first occupied village, found some French who had a map and they said I was at Bon Noi at the China border. Two more days and I made it to Keng-Tung where I found the other men of my team, received food and medical attention. They had built an L-5 strip and on May 10, I was picked up and flown to Szemao, and from there to Kunming, on May 11.[11]

Vital to Japan's control of the Chinese interior was the mile-long bridge across the Hwang-Ho (Yellow) River that connected the Japanese armies in the north and south of China. On 9 August 1945, a band of Chinese guerrillas under the command of Lieutenant Colonel Frank Mills and Major Paul Cyr of OSS Detachment 202 mounted an attack on the bridge and blew away two large spans of the bridge just as a Japanese troop train was crossing. The entire train, carrying some 2,000 soldiers, plunged into the river.

Lieutenant Colonel Frank Mills:

'I had five teams operating against the Japanese railway system along the Yellow River in eastern China. The Japanese were moving their troops from north to south along the railway from Peking to Hang'chou and it was essential that we destroy the bridge if we were to stop or delay Japanese troop movements for any length of time. The air force had been attacking the bridge for a long time from an airfield about a mile from our headquarters at Siang, but the bridge was very heavily defended and every time the bombers went over they got shot at, so they didn't really like that method very much.

'I sent in a team under Paul Cyr to plan an attack on the bridge after they had become oriented with the Chinese guerrillas they were training. They built a small wooden boat which they loaded with explosives and floated down the river to the bridge under cover of darkness. Then they climbed up on to the bridge, placed the charges under two spans and blew them as a train was crossing. Paul Cyr and his team made their way back to headquarters and the Chinese guerrillas just melted away.

'Immediately after destroying the bridge, Paul reported the success of the mission in a short radio message to me. All he said was: "It's a lovely day." I was never sure if he was referring to his own mission, or to the fact that almost at the same time as the bridge was blown we dropped the second atomic bomb, on Nagasaki, which ended the war.'[12]

Recommendation for Award of the Distinguished Service Medal to Colonel Carl F. Eifler, commander of Detachment 101:

On 20 March 1942, Colonel Carl F. Eifler, then a captain, reported to the office of the Co-ordinator of Information, and was given the task of organizing a small group of officers and men for the purpose of espionage and sabotage activities behind enemy lines in the Far East. A group of twenty-one officers and enlisted men were personally selected by Colonel Eifler in the United States, and were trained in British and American schools on secret operations. On 28 May 1942, this group left the United States for the Far East. The unit was known as Detachment 101, or Task Force 5405-A.

On 12 June 1942, Major Eifler reported to General Stilwell's headquarters in the CBVI theater. In September 1942, General Stilwell directed that operations begin in Burma by establishing radio bases in enemy-occupied territory. It was the general's desire to make friends with the natives, prepare to sabotage the railway in Northern Burma, and establish an intelligence unit which was to operate in support of his command. Headquarters were established in Northern Assam in October 1942, and a training program was immediately put into operation. Twenty-six separate schools were established for the purpose of teaching espionage and sabotage, and agents were recruited from among natives of the areas occupied by the Japanese.

Agents were taught modern radio communications, demolition, use of small arms, and to maintain communication with Allied headquarters, sending and receiving messages in English without being able to read English, despite the fact that they coded and decoded all messages. Natives were also taught to jump by parachute into areas occupied by the Japanese.

On 26 December 1942, Major Eifler led the original operational group to return to Burma, consisting of two American officers, seven British officers, and five native agents, to establish a radio station in Northern Burma. This base station was established 10 January 1943, to handle all radio communications from sub-stations in the field.

On 7 February 1943, the initial agent radio station was established in Japanese occupied territory. This original station was approximately 250 miles south of the foremost Japanese outpost. Agents mined the railway in Northern Burma, and in the first weeks of February, cut this railway line in twenty-one places.

Four air strips for light planes were completed while the Japs controlled the territory where they were located. These airports were camouflaged, and were not discovered by the Japanese troops. All of these strips were later used by military forces during the battle of Northern Burma; some for evacuating wounded by light plane, and some as headquarters for advancing troops. The use of these permitted the generals commanding the troops to have easy access between their troops and the commanding general's headquarters.

On 1 October 1943, the first plane controlled by 101, with Colonel Eifler as a passenger, landed in Japanese occupied territory. Colonel Eifler was able to make contact with the agents in a matter of hours, which previously had taken about six weeks. In November 1943, the second field was completed approximately twenty miles from the Japanese headquarters in Northern Burma. This field was afterwards used by General Merrill as his headquarters, and allowed him to communicate with General Stilwell's headquarters in a matter of minutes.

Also, in November the third field was completed, thirty miles north of Myitkyina. This field was later used to evacuate wounded to base hospitals.

The first Japanese Pilot officer to be captured in this theater was kidnapped in November 1943, in occupied territory, and was flown from Burma to India by Colonel Eifler in a small single-seater civilian plane. The Japanese officer had landed two miles from the Japanese strongpoint of Nsopzup believing he was landing in his own or friendly territory. The natives who had been organized into an agent chain under Colonel Eifler's direction led him instead to the spot where Colonel Eifler took him into custody. This whole remarkable episode was made possible only by the superior planning and execution of Colonel Eifler's program for that area. Further, as a result of the capture of the officer, information was obtained definitely locating the position of Japanese airfields from which the enemy operated in their molestations of Allied cargo and passenger planes flying over routes, commonly known as the Hump, between China and India. This, of course, afforded the Allied Air Forces an opportunity to attack the areas of the fields thereby greatly diminishing the effectiveness of enemy air opposition.

Toward the latter part of 1943, 101 had grown to where 84,086lbs of equipment, food, ammunition, radio supplies, etc were introduced into enemy occupied territory in a period of thirty days. This was doubled in the early months of 1944. Also, during this period of thirty days, a total of thirty-five agents, officers and enlisted men assigned to 101, were introduced into Japanese territory. A total of twenty-six air-corps men who had been shot down by Japanese aircraft were rescued or assisted by agents of 101 during this thirty-day period.

By May 1944, hundreds of agents were operating under the direction of Detachment 101, in addition to a native population of approximately 15,000 directly influenced by this organization.

Colonel Eifler's personal indomitable courage, fortitude and bravery along with his amazing stamina further enhanced and inspired the agents who assisted him in operations he introduced and directed.

Signed: M. Preston Goodfellow, Colonel GSC, Deputy Director, OSS

Postscript

BY THE autumn of 1944, with the end of the war in sight, senior officers in both SOE and OSS began to think about the future, about whether the agencies could survive and continue in peacetime in some intelligence-gathering or national security role. At the request of President Roosevelt, General Donovan prepared a secret paper outlining the creation of a permanent American intelligence service. 'When our enemies are defeated,' he wrote, 'the demand will be equally pressing for information that will aid us in solving the problems of peace.' He suggested prompt action to transform OSS into a 'central intelligence service' that would report directly to the president, noting that OSS had the trained and specialised personnel needed for the task and this talent should not be dispersed.

The memorandum became the focus of a political storm after J. Edgar Hoover, the powerful director of the FBI, leaked the details to the *Chicago Tribune*, which published a series of articles denouncing the idea as a 'super spy system' that would 'pry into the lives of citizens at home'. Hoover was determined to ensure the eclipse of OSS, which he perceived to be a rival of his own organisation and thus a threat to his influence. For the time being, the White House backed down.

SOE had similarly powerful enemies. Aware that plans were being made in Washington for OSS to survive the war, General Colin Gubbins submitted a strongly-worded memorandum to Downing Street suggesting that the nucleus of SOE should also endure, but the Secret Intelligence Service, which had always resented the existence of SOE, had no intention of allowing their territory to be usurped by an interloper and the Foreign Office argued strongly against it. After the Labour Party won the general election in 1945, the new prime minister, Clement Attlee, decided that SOE-type operations would be hard to justify in peacetime and announced that SOE would be dissolved, or 'amalgamated', with the SIS, which effectively amounted to the same thing.

In Washington, meanwhile, hopes of preserving OSS intact were dashed after the death of President Roosevelt. On 20 September 1945, his successor, Harry Truman, signed an executive order formally disbanding OSS and dispersing the remnants around other government agencies.

In a letter to General Donovan dated 1 October 1945, the President explained his decision:

My Dear General Donovan,

I appreciate very much the work which you and your staff undertook, beginning prior to the Japanese surrender, to liquidate those wartime activities of the Office of Strategic Services which will not be needed in time of peace.

Timely steps should also be taken to conserve those resources and skills developed within your organization which are vital to our peacetime purposes. Accordingly, I have today directed, by executive order, that the activities of the research and analysis branch and the presentation branch of the Office of Strategic Services be transferred to the State Department. This transfer, which is effective as of Oct. 1, 1945, represents the beginning of the development of a co-ordinated system of foreign intelligence within the permanent framework of the government.

Consistent with the foregoing, the executive order provides for the transfer of the remaining activities of the Office of Strategic Services to the War Department; for the abolition of the Office of Strategic Services; and for the continued orderly liquidation of the office without interrupting other services of a military nature the need for which will continue for some time.

I want to take this occasion to thank you for the capable leadership you have brought to a vital wartime activity in your capacity as Director of Strategic Services. You may well find satisfaction in the achievements of the office and take pride in your contribution to them. These are in themselves great rewards. Great additional reward for your efforts should lie in the knowledge that the peacetime intelligence services of the government are being erected on the foundation of the facilities and resources mobilized through the Office of Strategic Services during the war.

Sincerely yours,

Harry S. Truman

Shortly afterwards, an emotional Donovan addressed some 2,000 men and women on Potomac Flats, below the OSS headquarters. 'We have come to the end of an experiment,' he said. 'This experiment was to determine whether a group of Americans constituting a cross-section of racial origins, of abilities, of temperaments and talents could meet and risk an encounter with a long-established and well-trained enemy. This could not have been done if you had not been willing to fuse yourselves into a team – a team that was made up not only of scholars and research experts and active units in operations and intelligence who engaged the enemy in direct encounter, but also of the great numbers of our organization who drove our motor vehicles, carried our mail, kept our records and documents and performed those innumerable duties of administrative services without which no organization can succeed. You have made a beginning in showing the people of America that only by making decisions based upon accurate information can we have the chance of a peace that will endure.'

But the increasing hostility of the Soviet Union, and the outbreak of what Churchill had memorably dubbed the 'Cold War', soon made it clear that there was a pressing, and continued, need for an organisation exactly like that which had so recently been disbanded. On 18 September 1947, after a heated debate, Congress passed the National Security Act, setting up an information gathering organisation to be known as the Central Intelligence Agency and largely made up of ex-OSS staffers. Two years later, the CIA dropped its first agent behind the Iron Curtain.

In Britain, the demise of SOE was appropriately murky. In February 1946, just a month after SOE had merged with SIS, a mysterious fire broke out in a stationery store, on the top floor of the Baker Street headquarters. Thousands of files, some 85 per cent of the headquarters' records, were destroyed. Many of these papers documented dirty tricks that would undoubtedly have caused acute embarrassment, both to individuals and to the government, had they ever seen the light of day. The cause of the fire has never been satisfactorily explained.

Over the years since the end of the war, many historians and military experts have attempted to analyse the operational effectiveness of special operations. None have succeeded, largely because of the impossibility of measuring the impact of what in essence was warfare conducted in the shadows with the intention of undermining enemy morale as much as making quantifiable gains in territory or supremacy. In the early years of the war, agents parachuting into occupied Europe probably achieved little apart from providing clandestine communication with countries under the heel of the jackboot and helping to organise and arm embryonic resistance movements. Sabotage operations were more valuable in occupying combat soldiers on guard duties than in the actual damage caused.

But as SOE and OSS agents became more experienced in their ungentlemanly duties, there is little doubt that special operations began to play an ever more increasing role, both operational and psychological, in the war. By stepping up undercover operations, although many were still no more than needlepricks in the night, they helped create a hostile environment which played havoc with the enemy soldiers' nerves, kept them constantly looking over their shoulders and sapped their will to continue the fight. To lonely and homesick German troops on sentry duty, it must have seemed at times that nowhere was safe from saboteurs and assassins. Repairing a bridge or a railway line for the umpteenth time, only to have it blown up again the following day, similarly did nothing for morale.

Special operations also stiffened the will of local people to resist, to join in the shadow war, to organise. The arrival of parachutists in the night and the ability of a radio operator to miraculously arrange drops of arms and ammunition created resistance cells everywhere. Young men and women, who previously felt impotent in the face of the mighty German war machine, suddenly realised there was much they could do to help win the war.

D-Day was perhaps the moment that special operations came of age. The resistance movement, with the invaluable help of the Jedburgh teams, enabled the Allies to establish a bridgehead in Normandy by preventing German reinforcements being moved to the front. All the main telephone cables were put out of action, effectively destroying communications; in the space of three weeks, 3,000 sabotage attacks were carried out on railway lines; and every unit moving along the roads towards Normandy was delayed by ambushes and booby traps.

'I consider,' General Dwight D. Eisenhower, the Supreme Allied Commander in Europe, noted at the end of the war, 'that the disruption of enemy rail communications, the harassing of German road moves and the continual and increasing strain placed on the German war economy and internal security services throughout occupied Europe by the organized forces of resistance, played a very considerable part in our complete and final victory.'

After D-Day, those sceptics who had loudly voiced doubts about the efficacy of special operations in Europe were silenced. But in the Balkans and the Far East, OSS and SOE operations were severely hampered by terrible reprisals carried out against the civilian populations. While in the Balkans special operations tied down several German and Italian divisions, the cost in innocent lives was high. Local resistance leaders were often understandably unwilling to assist OSS or SOE if it meant that subsequently twenty or thirty of their friends and neighbours would be dragged out of their homes and shot.

The same situation applied in the Far East, where the Japanese would not hesitate to massacre an entire village in reprisal for the killing of a single Japanese soldier. Nevertheless, during the first eight months of 1945, OSS units numbering fewer than 2,000 men killed no less than 12,348 Japanese soldiers, destroyed a vast quantity of enemy supplies, mounted a devastating sabotage campaign against Japanese lines of communication and provided a constant stream of intelligence to HQ, US Forces, China Theater.

General Albert Wedemeyer, the China Theater commander, said the achievements of OSS constituted a 'chapter beyond parallel' in the successful prosecution of the war.

In the final analysis, perhaps the fact that there is no analytical balance sheet for special operations does not matter. The men and women who joined OSS and SOE were essentially loners. They know what they did.

Notes

1 SET EUROPE ABLAZE!

1 Interview courtesy Darlow Smithson, producers of BBC2 television series, *Secret Agent*.
2 Imperial War Museum Sound Archive, accession no. 9851.
3 Ibid., accession no. 12423.
4 Ibid., accession no. 13930.
5 Darlow Smithson.
6 Author's interview.
7 Darlow Smithson.
8 IWM Sound Archive, accession no. 9332.
9 Hawes, Stephen, and White, Ralph, *Resistance in Europe, 1939–45*.
10 Manderstam, Major L.H., with Heron, Roy, *From the Red Army to SOE*.
11 Darlow Smithson.
12 Ibid.
13 Ibid.
14 Ibid.
15 IWM Sound Archive, accession no. 9925.
16 Langelaan, George, *Knights of the Floating Silk*.

2 FIRST FORAYS

1 Courtesy Channel 4 (*Churchill's Secret War*).
2 Darlow Smithson.
3 Ibid.
4 Ruby, Marcel, *F Section, SOE: The Buckmaster Networks*.
5 Darlow Smithson.
6 Ibid.
7 Author's interview.
8 Darlow Smithson.
9 IWM Sound Archive, accession no. 12423.

10 Author's interview.
11 Author's interview.
12 Author's interview.
13 Public Record Office, HS4/39.

3 WASHINGTON WEIGHS IN

1 National Archives, Washington DC, record group 226.7.
2 Lankford, N.D. (ed.), *OSS Against the Reich: The Wartime Diaries of Colonel David K.E. Bruce.*
3 Public Record Office, HS1/165.
4 Ibid., HS7/283.
5 National Archives, record group 226.
6 Author's interview.
7 Author's interview.
8 Lindsay, Franklin, *Beacons in the Night: With the OSS and Tito's Partisans in Wartime Yugoslavia.*
9 Bank, Aaron, *From OSS to Green Berets.*
10 Author's interview.
11 'An Allied Team with the French Resistance', MS posted on Internet, www.odci.gov/csi/studies.
12 Author's interview.
13 Paper delivered at The Secrets War conference, Washington DC, July 1991.
14 Author's interview.
15 Casey, William, *The Secret War Against Hitler.*
16 Author's interview.
17 National Archives, record group 226.

4 LA VIE CLANDESTINE

1 IWM Document Archive.
2 Public Record Office, HS6/568.
3 Author's interview.
4 Darlow Smithson.
5 Ibid.
6 Ibid.
7 IWM Sound Archive, accession no. 12423.
8 Jones, Liane, *A Quiet Courage.*
9 Ruby, Marcel, *F Section SOE.*
10 Author's interview.
11 IWM Sound Archive, accession no. 9851.
12 Author's interview.
13 Marie-Claire Diary report, Public Record Office.

14 Author's interview.
15 Darlow Smithson.
16 Public Record Office, HS6/567.
17 Excerpt from a privately printed manuscript loaned to the author.
18 IWM Sound Archive, accession no. 11717.
19 Dormer, Hugh, *War Diary*.
20 Darlow Smithson.
21 Author's interview.
22 Public Record Office, HS1/332.

5 THE HEAVY-WATER RAID

1 Author's interview.
2 Author's interview.
3 Public Record Office, HS7/181.
4 Author's interview.
5 Public Record Office, HS7/181.
6 Public Record Office, HS2/118.

6 BOFFINS AND BACK-ROOM BOYS

1 Interview from *Churchill's Secret Army*, courtesy Channel 4.
2 Darlow Smithson.
3 IWM Sound Archive, accession no. 15482.
4 Darlow Smithson.
5 IWM Document Archive.
6 McIntosh, Elizabeth, *Sisterhood of Spies*.
7 Darlow Smithson.
8 Author's interview.
9 Darlow Smithson.
10 Ibid.
11 Public Record Office.
12 National Archives, record group 226.

7 D-DAY.

1 Darlow Smithson.
2 Cave-Brown, Anthony, *Bodyguard of Lies*.
3 IWM Documents Archive.
4 Taken from a speech by Ambassador Bruce to the annual dinner of OSS veterans, Washington DC, 26 May 1971.
5 IWM Sound Archive, accession no. 12521.
6 Author's interview.
7 National Archives, group 226.

8 IWM Sound Archive, accession no. 12612.

9 Ibid., accession no. 8744.

10 Ibid., accession no. 13172.

11 Ibid., accession no. 12354.

12 National Archives, record group 226.

13 Ibid.

14 Author's interview.

15 From a paper delivered to The Secrets War conference, Washington DC.

16 NA 22 – National Archives.

8 STIRRING THE BALKANS CAULDRON

1 Public Record Office, HS5/634.

2 IWM Sound Archive, accession no. 8980.

3 Author's interview.

4 IWM Sound Archives, accession no. 5378.

5 Darlow Smithson.

6 National Archives.

7 Ibid.

8 National Archives.

9 Public Record Office, HS4/52.

10 Ibid., HS5/728.

11 Author's interview.

12 National Archives.

13 Ibid.

14 Ibid.

9 POLITICS, CHICANERY AND MISCHIEF

1 National Archives, record group 226.

2 Heideking, Juergen, and Mauch, Christof (eds), *American Intelligence and the German Resistance to Hitler*.

3 Public Record Office, HS6/624.

4 National Archives.

5 Ibid.

6 Author's interview.

7 National Archives.

8 Author's interview.

9 National Archives.

10 Public Record Office, HS2/73.

10 JUNGLE FIGHTING

1 Public Record Office, HS1/109.

2 National Archives.
3 IWM Sound Archive, accession no. 11295.
4 Ibid., accession no. 8744.
5 Public Record Office, HS1/109.
6 National Archives.
7 Ibid.
8 Author's interview.
9 National Archives.
10 Ibid.
11 Ibid.
12 Author's interview.

Select Bibliography

Alcorn, Robert, *No Bugles for Spies: Tales of the OSS* (Jarrolds, London, 1963).

Aldrich, Richard J., *Intelligence and the War Against Japan* (Cambridge University Press, 2000).

Atherton, Louise, 'SOE Operations in Africa and the Middle East' (Public Record Office, London).

    'SOE Operations in the Balkans' (PRO).

    'SOE Operations in Eastern Europe' (PRO).

    'SOE Operations in the Far East' (PRO).

    'SOE Operations in Scandinavia' (PRO).

    'SOE Operations in Western Europe' (PRO).

Bank, Aaron, *From OSS to the Green Berets: The Birth of the Special Forces* (Presidio, Novato, CA, 1986).

Bowman, Martin W., *The Bedford Triangle: US undercover operations from England in WW2* (Thorsons, London, 1988).

Butler, Ewan, *Amateur Agent* (Harrap, London, 1963).

Casey, William, *The Secret War Against Hitler* (Simon & Schuster, London, 1989).

Cave-Brown, Anthony, *Bodyguard of Lies* (Harper & Row, New York, 1975).

Corvo, Max, *OSS in Italy, 1942–1945: A personal memoir* (Praeger, New York, 1990).

Courvoisier, André, *Le Réseau Heckler* (France-Empire, Paris, 1984).

Cunningham, Cyril, *Beaulieu – The Finishing School for Secret Agents, 1941-45* (Leo Cooper, London, 1998).

Davidson, Basil, *Special Operations Europe* (Gollancz, London, 1980).

Dear, Ian, *Sabotage and Subversion: Stories from the files of the SOE and OSS* (Arms & Armour, 1996).

Dodds-Parker, Douglas, *Setting Europe Ablaze* (Springwood Books, Surrey, 1983).

Dormer, Hugh, *War Diary* (Jonathan Cape, London, 1947).

Dunlop, Richard, *Behind Japanese lines. With the OSS in Burma* (Rand McNally, Chicago, 1979).

Escott, Beryl E., *Mission improbable, a salute to air women of the SOE in wartime France* (Patrick Stephens, Yeovil, 1991).

Foot, M.R.D., 'SOE in France' (HMSO, London, 1966).

Hawes, Stephen, and White, Ralph, *Resistance in Europe, 1939–45* (Allen Lane, London, 1975).

Heideking, Juergen and Mauch, Christof (eds) *American Intelligence and the German Resistance to Hitler* (Westview Press, CO, 1996).

Hilsman, Roger, *American Guerilla* (Brassey's, London, 1990).

Howarth, Patrick, *Undercover, the Men and Women of the SOE* (Routledge, Kegan Paul, London, 1980).

Jacobs, J.J., *Spies and Saboteurs* (Macmillan, London, 1999).

Jones, Liane, *A Quiet Courage* (Bantam Press, London, 1990).

Kellas, Arthur, *Down To Earth* (Pentland Press, 1990).

Langelaan, George, *Knights of the Floating Silk* (Hutchinson, London, 1959).

Lankford, Nelson Douglas (ed.) *OSS Against the Reich: The Wartime Diaries of Colonel David K.E. Bruce,* (Kent State University Press, OH, 1991).

Lees, Michael, *The Rape of Serbia* (Harcourt Brace Jovanich, New York, 1990).
Special Operations Executed in Serbia and Italy (William Kimber, London, 1986).

Lindsay, Franklin, *Beacons in the Night: With the OSS and Tito's Partisans in Wartime Yugoslavia* (Stanford University Press, CA, 1993).

Mackenzie, William, *The Secret History of SOE* (St Ermin's Press, London, 2000).

Manderstam, L.H., *From the Red Army to SOE* (William Kimber, London, 1985).

McIntosh, Elizabeth, *Sisterhood of Spies: The Women of the OSS* (Dell Books, Random House, New York, 1998).

Marks, Leo, *Between Silk and Cyanide: A Codemaker's Story, 1941–1945,* (HarperCollins, London, 1999).

Moon, Tom, *This Grim and Savage Game: OSS and the Beginning of US Covert Operations in WW2* (Da Capo Press, 2000).
'Operation Foxley; The British Plan to Kill Hitler' (Public Record Office, London, 1998).

Poirier, Jacques, *The Giraffe Has A Long Neck* (Leo Cooper, London).

Ruby, Marcel, *F Section SOE: The Buckmaster Networks* (Leo Cooper, London, 1988).

Seaman, Mark, *Bravest of the Brave* (O'Mara Books, London, 1997).

Simpson, John, *The Quiet Operator, Special Forces Signaller Extraordinary: The Story of Major R.D. Willmott* (Leo Cooper, London, 1993).

Smith, Richard Harris, *OSS: the Secret History of America's first central intelligence agency* (University of California Press, 1972).

'SOE Syllabus; Lessons in Ungentlemanly Warfare' (Public Record Office, London, 2001).

Stafford, David, *Secret Agent: The True Story of SOE* (BBC Worldwide, London, 2000).

Verity, Hugh, *We Landed By Moonlight* (Ian Allen, London, 1978).

Index